THE MAKING OF
A CHINESE CITY

"An original and brilliantly conceived work which uncovers the history and historiography of the modern Chinese city in particularly illuminating fashion. This collection of Harbin local histories (covering a wide range of events, groups, and institutions) is edited and explained in such a way as to help the reader understand both the complexities of urban life and the multilayered nature of history writing in China."

—*David Strand, Dickinson College*

"In a multilayered approach to modern Chinese history, this eminently readable study artfully moves between the authors' own narrative of Harbin's tumultuous history and the narratives of recent Chinese historians. Through this, the book not only provides insights into the history of an important corner of China. It also brings to life the interplay between objective history writing and local image making in the city that Russian railway officials founded, that Japan conquered, and that the People's Republic of China built into a center of socialist heavy industry."

—*Jonathan Unger, Australian National University*

Studies on Modern China

Studies on Modern China

THE MAKING OF
A CHINESE CITY

HISTORY AND
HISTORIOGRAPHY
IN HARBIN

SØREN CLAUSEN AND STIG THØGERSEN

An East Gate Book

M.E. Sharpe

Armonk, New York
London, England

An East Gate Book

Library of Congress Cataloging-in-Publication Data

Clausen, Søren.
The making of a Chinese city : history and historiography in Harbin /
Søren Clausen and Stig Thøgersen
p.   cm.
"East gate book."
Includes bibliographical references and index.
ISBN 1-56324-475-6.—ISBN 1-56324-476-4 (pbk.)
1. Harbin (china)—history.
I. Thøgersen, Stig.
II. Title.
DS796.H4C57   1995
951'.84—dc20
94-30519
CIP

Printed in the United States of America

The paper used in this publication meets the minimum requirements of
American National Standard for Information Sciences—
Permanence of Paper for Printed Library Materials,
ANSI Z 39.48-1984.

BM (c)   10   9   8   7   6   5   4   3   2   1
BM (p)   10   9   8   7   6   5   4   3   2   1

Contents

Preface

We first became aware of Harbin's peculiar history after a sister city arrangement between Harbin and Aarhus, Denmark, had brought us into sporadic contact with people from the city in the mid-1980s. Before then we had thought of Harbin only as a smog-shrouded station on the Trans-Siberian railway line, but we soon realized that there was more to the place than just heavy industry. During visits in 1986 and 1987 we were struck by the prominent Russian architecture of the city's downtown areas, and meetings with Danes who had grown up in Harbin during the 1920s and 1930s further sharpened our interest in the city's complicated and cosmopolitan past. Evaluations ranged from "the Paris of the Far East" to "a city of sin" to "a total dump." In 1987 an interview with historians responsible for compiling the new Harbin gazetteer, a mammoth work of several thousand pages, convinced us that this writing process was as interesting as the history itself. We therefore returned in the spring of 1989 to interview researchers and cadres from all corners of the local history community and to collect as many of their writings as we could put our hands on. While the Harbin students were demonstrating in the streets, we tried to divide our attention between the history created outside our windows and the one that had already been reconstructed and put in print.

Our meeting with Harbin's local history community revealed to us the immense amount of work and energy invested in writing and rewriting history at the local level in post-Mao China. We were able to gain access to most of the materials we wanted to see, although there were restrictions on what we were allowed to copy. Still, we returned with what we see as a good and representative selection of contemporary Chinese writings on the history of Harbin. As no historical survey of the city existed in any Western language, we decided to combine such an overview with commentaries on and examples of Chinese treatments of selected historical issues.[1] We have had no ambition of writing an exhaustive city history, a task that would demand a close examination of vast amounts of Chinese, Russian, and Japanese sources, but we hope that the reader will get an impression of the uniqueness of the city's history and of the work of its historians.

Pinyin has been used to transcribe Chinese names and terms, except where other forms are in general use, like in the cases of Peking (Beijing) and Harbin (Haerbin). We have tried our best to identify Russian and Japanese names from the Chinese characters, but have had to guess in some cases and give up in others.

We are grateful for financial support from the Danish Social Science Research Council and the Aarhus University Research Fund. David Tugwell did a fine job with the basic translations of the Chinese texts, although the responsibility for any mistakes remains ours. We also want to thank the Harbin city government and particularly those Chinese colleagues who devoted their time to explain to us the ins and outs of their work. We have benefited much from the advice of David Strand, Susanne Weigelin-Schwiedrzik, and Graham Young, who have commented on this or earlier versions of the manuscript, as well as the help of Glen Dudbridge, Susanne Juhl, Inge M. Larsen, Roy Starrs, and Henrik H. Sørensen.

Note

1. This does not mean, of course, that nothing has been written on Harbin in English before. Of particular value for our work has been R. K. I. Quested's study of the city's Russian community (Quested 1982), and other references to Harbin can be found in the works cited in the notes. A forthcoming book by David Wolff will deal with the first phases of the city's history.

Introduction

Harbin, capital of Heilongjiang Province, is the northernmost metropolis of China. It is situated on the banks of the Songhuajiang (Sungari River), which cuts across the northern part of Manchuria, and its climate is affected by the proximity to Siberia: winters are long, dry, and extremely cold, and summers short and hot. The strangely non-Chinese name gives the first hint of an atypical Chinese city. To the visitor, this feeling is reinforced by the Western-style buildings along the cobble-stoned Central Avenue and the silhouettes of onion-shaped Russian church cupolas in the central urban areas. Yet Harbin also strikes the contemporary visitor as a fairly "traditional" Chinese city in the sense that it appears less influenced by the internationalization and "opening up" of the 1980s than the metropolitan centers on the coast.

These contradictory features are rooted in the extraordinary history of the city. In the short course of a hundred years, Harbin has been ruled by Russia, by an international coalition of Allied powers, by Chinese warlords, by Japan, by the Soviet Union, and finally by the Chinese Communists, who established their control of the city in 1946. Probably no other Chinese city has experienced such dramatic shifts and such a rapid succession of widely different regimes. Harbin is a product of the century-old rivalry between China, Russia, and Japan for control of Manchuria, as well as a major point of contention in this struggle. In a larger perspective, Harbin has experienced all the stresses and strains associated with China's modern transformation, but to an exceptional degree. The early twentieth-century Western penetration of China was more pervasive in the case of Harbin than in most other cities, the Japanese occupation lasted twice as long as in intramural China, and the effects of "socialist transformation" were more striking. In this way the modern history of China is written all over Harbin, but with such brutal strokes that the city also stands out as a very special case.

It is the task of Chinese local historians to integrate local experience with the overall national pattern of historical development. In the case of Harbin this challenge is daunting. The many hidden shoals that have contributed to making modern Chinese history writing a generally frustrating and sometimes dangerous business are particularly abundant in the history of Harbin, where local historians are confronted with a whole range of painful questions:

• How is the early history of the Harbin region as a breeding ground for non-Han "barbarian" tribes and dynasties of conquest to be integrated into a macro history set to a Chinese tune?
• How should one look at "economic imperialism" when foreign inputs have contributed so evidently to the construction and development of the city?
• Where lies the dividing line between Soviet "legitimate interests" in the area and pernicious imperialism?
• What is the proper evaluation of early Chinese capitalists in the city, forced as they were to collaborate with foreign masters?
• How should one deal with the serious political mistakes committed by the Chinese Communists during the Japanese occupation as well as later on?
• In what ways should the reforms of the 1980s and the changing international environment lead to a re-evaluation of the city's history?

Issues like these, often taboo but always significant and active, make the job of history writing in Harbin an unusually difficult task. To complicate matters, the local history of Harbin is really *four* histories. The Russian chapter is actually a separate history in itself, since a large Russian community survived in the city for several decades after the period of Russian rule, complete with its distinct culture and its own memories. The Western-dominated international community, whose businessmen and missionaries put their mark on Harbin from the "internationalization" of the city in 1907 and well into the 1930s, have another story to tell. And obviously there is a Japanese version with detailed surveys and statistics, but also with dark memories of harsh rule and misdeeds.

The object of this study is the fourth history of Harbin, the Chinese version, which is in many ways the most troublesome of them all, because the establishment of the "Chineseness" of Harbin has been such a protracted and hard-won battle. Contemporary historiography in Harbin is by necessity a *rewriting* with the purpose of writing China and the Chinese back into the history and establishing a proper and dignified role for them in this City of Many Masters. The feeling of *hurt* that unites all modern Chinese historiography, across political changes and historiographical disputes, is even more concentrated in the case of Harbin: it is the agony—and outright fury —of having been exploited, mistreated, and ignored, not only by the city's non-Chinese citizens, but also by foreign historians. This passionate drive is important to bear in mind when one looks at the way Harbin historians maneuver in the minefield of modern history writing. There are plenty of dark corners and forbidden zones, but there is also, behind the historians' work, a sense of mission and a strong emotional energy. The sinification of Harbin's history is more than just the routine implementation of a national standard model. It is also an attempt to rehabilitate a corner of China that Chinese south of the Great Wall have invariably considered wild and un-civilized.

The way local history is being written in Harbin can, therefore, tell us more about how national and local identities are being constructed in China, in a situation where patriotism is becoming an ever more important legiti-mizing factor for the Chinese Communist Party (CCP). Many of the trans-lated texts clearly illustrate that local historians are freely "using the past to serve the present." This comes as no surprise, since ideological legitimation is normally identified by Western scholars as the central, and sometimes sole, function of Chinese history writing.[1] But besides being sources of knowledge on present-day ideological constructs, the writings of Chinese local-level historians at the same time provide Western students of modern Chinese history with unique materials that are indispensable for our under-standing of Chinese local history. The historians are also, one could say, "preserving the past for future use" by meticulously going through piles of archival materials, interviewing thousands of people, and presenting their findings in voluminous publications.

The writings of the Harbin historians serve a similar double function in this book: On the one hand, we use them, together with works by non-Chinese scholars, as sources of knowledge about Harbin's history. On the other hand, we look at them as ideological constructs reflecting the bureau-cratic, academic, and mental structures inside which they have been pro-duced. In doing so we have no wish to set ourselves up as judges of the validity of present history writing in Harbin. Instead, we want to present the work of our Harbin colleagues on a background that makes the interaction of external political and ideological constraints, bureaucratic and academic structures, and personal judgments and beliefs stand out more clearly.

Each of the first four chapters deals with a major phase in the history of Harbin: the period before the construction of the Chinese Eastern Railway, the era of Russian dominance, the Japanese occupation, and the years since the Communist takeover in 1946. Each chapter gives a historical outline of the period focusing on those issues that have been subjects of local research, and a discussion of local historical writings. The last part of each chapter is followed by translations of articles by Chinese historians. Our first criterion for selecting a text for translation has been its intrinsic interest. Only when we found that a text was worth reading did we start to consider to what extent it represented a genre or a viewpoint characteristic of local history writing. Still, the text collection contains samples from most of the major periodicals and institutions of the local history community, as well as treatments of all major phases of the city's history. A few of the translated texts do not completely match the chronological divisions; in those cases where a text spans the main historical periods, we have chosen to incorporate the entire text under the period where its prime relevance lies rather than cutting it up into fragments. We hope that this approach involves comparatively less inconvenience to the reader.

Chapter 5 discusses the historiographical framework for local history writing and presents the producers, infrastructure, raw materials, and products of the Harbin history enterprise. The structure and institutions of local historical research in Harbin are similar to those found in comparable cities all over the country, and even, though in a reduced version, in rural counties. In this way the local history writing of Harbin, despite the unique features of the city, is also a window to a general view of local historiography in contemporary China.

Note

1. For recent examples, see the contributions to Unger 1993.

Map 1. **Old Harbln.** From Hansine Schmidt and Chr. Madsen, *Harbin. Den store, nye By i det fjerne Østen og Missionsarbejdets Begyndelse dér* [Harbin, the new big city in the Far East and the starting-up of missionary work there] (Copenhagen: DMS, 1939), p. 5.

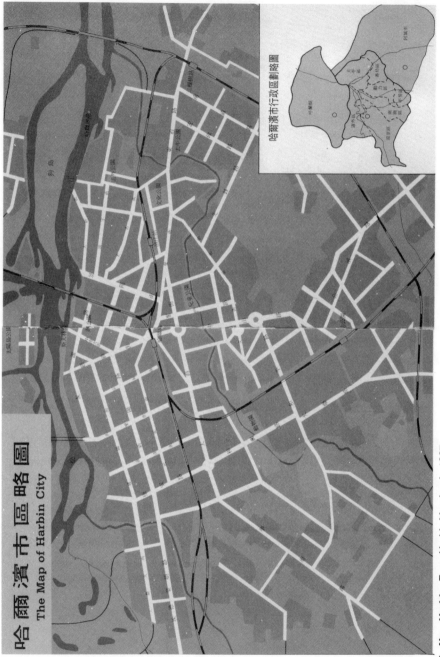

Map 2. New Harbin. From Harbin Yearbook, 1987.

THE MAKING OF A CHINESE CITY

1

Genesis: Pre-1898 History

Origins of the City

The year 1898 is crucial in the history of Harbin. That year Russia designated the place where Harbin lies today as the headquarters of its Trans-Manchurian railway construction project, and before long a city of sizable dimensions sprang up. For this reason 1898 has traditionally been considered Harbin's year of birth, not only by Westerners, but even by most Chinese. As this genesis rather unmistakably depicts Harbin as a Russian creation, it constitutes a major obstacle to the writing of the history of Harbin as a Chinese city, and the local historians therefore work hard to unearth Harbin's pre-1898 Chinese heritage.

The general trend is to dig very deep for Chinese roots. Based on a survey of recent archeological finds in the Harbin area, with the 22,370-year-old remains of a "Harbin man" being the most ancient, Text 1A actually claims a historical continuity all the way back to the Old Stone Age. This account of the various cultural layers demonstrated by archeological discoveries includes astonishing statements such as "Around three thousand years ago our city (*wo shi*) gradually evolved from the Stone Age to the Bronze Age, almost keeping in step with developments in the cradle of the Chinese nation in the Yellow River basin . . . ," and "Our city was already advancing at this time [the Bronze Age] from primitive to class society . . . ." On closer examination the text nowhere claims the existence of an actual city in those early times; it simply superimposes the present administrative boundaries of Harbin upon the archeological material, suggesting a continuity that is retrospective only. The real significance of this viewpoint is, perhaps, its claim of "equal birth rights" for Manchuria in the Chinese cultural genesis. Archeological evidence is used to suggest a pattern of cultural and social evolution that has been on parallel tracks with the Chinese core areas throughout history.

As an alternative to 1898 some contemporary local historians have pointed to 1097 as the birth year of the city. Evidence for this claim has been presented by veteran local historian Guan Chenghe, who, based on linguistic research, has tried to show that the name of Harbin can be traced back to a place name Alejin in the Nüzhen language, later influenced by Qidan (Khitan) pronunciation, and with the original meaning of glory, honor, or prestige (Guan Chenghe 1985, passim). The phonetic argument is then connected to the fact that the *History of the Jin Dynasty* records a village by the name of "Alejin" for the year 1097. This establishes a connection between Harbin and the Tungusic Nüzhen (Jurchen or Jurched) people, who defeated the Qidan Liao dynasty as well as the Northern Song and ruled North China under the dynastic name of Jin from 1115 to 1230. The Nüzhen are considered ancestors of the Manchus, who ruled China under the dynastic name of Qing from 1644 to 1911. This line of thinking can be found in Text 1B.

In any case, there seems to be solid evidence that the area around present-day Harbin was important in the evolution of Nüzhen society. The Jin dynasty "upper capital" of Huiningfu, one of the six capitals of the Jin, was located some forty kilometers from the heart of contemporary Harbin, which makes it possible to establish a continuity between an important political center of a thousand years ago and the contemporary metropolis in the area. The local historians make much of the Jin dynasty connection, and they have suggested that Harbin should be the national center for Jin research (Wang Yulang 1986, pp. 35–37).

The Harbin Area in Qing Times

While much emphasis is put on the area's glorious past in Jin times, the local historians have almost nothing to say about the following centuries. Apparently, the Nüzhen were still the dominant ethnic group in the area in the sixteenth century, but there was also a considerable presence of Korchin Mongol nomads. Some of the tribes inhabiting the area of confluence between the rivers Songhua (Sungari) and Nenjiang (Nonni) were incorporated in the Manchu banner system as "Old Mongols" by Nurhachi (1559–1626), founding father of the Qing dynasty (Lee 1970, p. 34). During early Qing, two towns, which are now centers of the two counties under Harbin administration, began to develop. Alchuka, now called Acheng and located to the southeast of the city proper, was established as a Manchu garrison town under Jilin administration during the reign of the Kangxi emperor (r. 1662–1722). On the northern bank of the Songhua River, Hulan became a garrison town under Heilongjiang in 1734. A government ferry post between these two towns was located at the present-day Harbin river-front.

With its abundantly fertile land, Hulan had been chosen for the establishment of government farms already under the Kangxi emperor, before becoming a garrison town. There were forty such farms, worked by 510 former Chinese bondservants, and the farms were rather successful, at least in the beginning (Lee 1970, p. 38). Alchuka appears to have had less farming than Hulan in those early days, but a larger share of Manchu officialdom, being the seat of a Jilin deputy military governor and home to a school since 1727. The social structure in these Manchu outposts was hierarchical, with a military elite of banner officers of which Manchus from Peking held the highest offices, and a second layer of tribal chiefs, whose official titles were not always matched by actual prestige, however. Below these ruling groups were the ordinary bannermen, merchants, craftsmen, and exiled Chinese officials, and at the bottom of society were the slaves, servants, and criminal convicts (Lee 1970, p. 114). Outside this established society were the hunters, ginseng diggers, and other illegal immigrants.

Hulan and Alchuka can be seen as the early seeds of *Chinese* Harbin, but in a larger perspective they were for a long time only tiny outposts surrounded by a vast sea of potentially fertile virgin lands. Until the last decades of the dynasty, the policy of the Qing was to keep this situation unchanged. Having established themselves as masters of China in 1644, the Manchu elite had two main objectives in relation to their original power base in the Northeast. One was to maintain it as a reservoir of undiluted Manchu cultural values, and the other was to prevent the emergence of new tribal alliances in the region that might challenge Manchu supremacy. The banner system secured a measure of control over most of the region's ethnic groups, and with the Sino-Russian Treaty of Nerchinsk (1689), which determined the border between tsarist Russia's possessions in Siberia and the Manchurian regions of the Qing empire, the conflicts arising from the Russian eastward push in Siberia were settled and a potential Russian menace to Manchuria was removed. The policy of isolation, including from 1668 the prohibition of Han immigration, was the logical outcome of these conditions, since Han immigration might disturb the delicate balance of power in the region. After the system of political control in Manchuria, which granted local tribes a high level of autonomy, had been firmly established under Kangxi and Yongzheng (r. 1722–35), the region entered a quiet, uneventful period of more than a century.

Isolation was never airtight, however. Even during the periods of strictly enforced prohibition against Han migration there was an influx of Han Chinese, brought in by the government as political and criminal exiles. In

1676, for example, several thousand families were sent to Jilin (Lee 1970, p. 79). These involuntary immigrants were soon joined by unauthorized ones: ginseng diggers, illegal peasant settlers, and, in the second half of the nineteenth century, goldminers.

A tightening-up was attempted with an imperial decree of 1740 that ordered all illegal residents in Manchuria to be expelled within ten years, with the exception of merchants, craftsmen, and servants, who were indispensable to the Manchu and Mongol bannermen (Lee 1970, p. 102). At the same time idle bannermen from the Peking region were resettled in Manchuria, with Alchuka as one of the main centers. Both policies failed, however. It was impossible to enforce the expulsion order against the Han immigrants, while the Manchu bannermen from Peking, softened by decades of easy life on government grants, were unable to cope with the hard work of frontier farming. In the end most of them leased or sold their land allotments to the Chinese immigrants (Sun 1969, pp. 7–10). After 1850 the Qing policy toward Manchuria was jolted out of its complacent course by two major shocks. One was the Taiping Rebellion (1850–64) and other large uprisings in mid-nineteenth-century China, which drained the dynasty of those financial resources that should have supported the administration in Jilin and Heilongjiang and forced it to use the greater part of its military forces in the region to fight rebel armies in intramural China. The other blow was the loss of huge territories north of the Amur River (Heilongjiang) and east of the Ussuri to Russia in the 1858–60 Aigun and Peking treaties.

The immediate effect of the acute financial crisis in northern Manchuria was that the military governors had to look for new sources of income. In 1860 the governor of Heilongjiang memorialized the throne for the opening of Hulan to Chinese settlers (Lee 1970, p. 128), thus providing government revenue through the sale of land and through enlargement of the tax base. By this time Hulan already had approximately 2,500 Chinese peasants, who had obtained their land from bannermen in more or less illegal fashion. From 1860 to 1868 more than 200,000 shang[1] of land was sold in Hulan (Lee 1970, p. 128). This policy worked hand in glove with the new slogan of "strengthening the border by moving people in" (yi min shi bian) to bolster the Northeast against further territorial losses and encroachments. Ironically, the Manchu Qing dynasty in this way accelerated a gradual Han Chinese takeover of its ancestral land.

The new villages in northern Manchuria were dominated by immigrants from Shandong and Zhili in North China, areas that were particularly vulnerable to man-made or natural disasters because of the extremely high population pressure. New dangers awaited the settlers in the unaccustomed environment of the Northeast, and the rather weak administrative super-structure necessitated self-protection strategies. The generally scattered pattern of settlement, where most peasants preferred to build their homes on their individual parcels of land rather than in closely knit communities, added to the problem of security. Banditry was on the rise, and in 1875 villages around Hulan were sacked by goldminers from Sanxing, who had risen in rebellion (Lee 1970, p. 93). Villagers responded with self-organized militias (*lianhui*), and in 1898 the Peking government followed suit with a call for the formation of village battalions (*xiangtuan*).

The opening of more and more places in Jilin and Heilongjiang to Chinese settlers was accompanied by an effort to introduce regular, civil administration in the region. In the early days of the Qing dynasty, all the territories in the Northeast were ruled by a military governor in Shengjing (later Mukden, now Shenyang). In 1653 Jilin became an independent administrative unit, and in 1683 Heilongjiang was separated from Jilin. From this time the three districts of Fengtian (roughly equivalent to present-day Liaoning), Jilin, and Heilongjiang became known as the "Three Eastern Provinces" (*San dong sheng*), although in fact Jilin and Heilongjiang did not function as provinces in the full sense of the word until 1907–8. Administration remained very simple, with military governors and few subdivisions, until the late nineteenth century. In Heilongjiang, the first civil government institution was the Hulan subprefecture established in 1875. Jilin had only three subprefectures before this time. After 1875 several new government institutions, from prefectures down to districts, were set up, village militias were organized, and schools established. Administrative reform was piecemeal, however, always lagging behind the increasing complexity of tasks and the rapidly changing situation in the Northeast.

The Harbin historians have remarkably little to say about the early Manchu period, except for pointing out the "broad similarities" of social evolution among the "various peoples of China." The Marxist notion of stages of development is quite impractical in those cases, such as the Qing dynasty, where non-Han people of a clearly "lower" cultural level took control of the Chinese empire.[2] Even less is said, however, about the latter part of the Qing dynasty and the decaying Manchu power in the Northeast itself. Obviously the feeble Manchu administration of the Northeast in the second half of the nineteenth century made it easier for the Russians to penetrate the area, and the local Manchu elite came to play an inglorious role as a parasitical stratum and a conservative force in society until its final phaseout in 1907–8. On this aspect of the story, the Harbin historians are silent, maybe because source materials are scarce, but possibly also because of the ethnic overtones a critique of the Manchu elite would have.

Conflicting Views on Harbin around 1898

The Harbin historians generally claim, in the words of Text 1B, that "[t]here is a great amount of material proving that before the building of the Chinese Eastern Railway there were already many villages in all districts of Harbin, and these could be said to thickly cover the whole region like stars on the sky." An official description of pre-1898 Harbin follows the same line of argument: "There were more than a hundred villages which formed a community, with handicraft and commerce as the main body of the town, and a population of more than 50,000. This was about the size of a modern town" (Zou 1985, p. 76).

As shown above, increasing numbers of settlers and migrant workers had actually moved into the area during the preceding decades, and new villages had been formed. There are indications of growing marketization, and one may reasonably believe that this development would, in the course of time, have led to some measure of urbanization even without the Russian presence, but certainly not with the breakneck speed that characterized the early stage of city-building in Harbin.

The present-day Chinese descriptions contradict early Russian accounts of what the Harbin area looked like in 1898. When Russian surveyors and railway engineers arrived at the spot on the banks of the Songhua River where the main railway bridge was going to be constructed, they were quite disappointed to find the place so desolate. Several eyewitness accounts have been pieced together by the Russian historian G. Melikhov, himself an old Harbin hand:

> If there had been a cine-camera on the spot where the Railway Assembly building stands today, it would have filmed a group of horsemen with engineer Shidlovsky at their head, surrounded by a mounted guard, making their way through a field of green bristle grass and *kaoliang*. . . . None of the horsemen knew at the time that the terrain they were riding across would in a few years become a busy quarter of a busy and densely populated town. (Melikhov 1990a, p. 163)

The area was not uninhabited, but there was no trace of urban development:

> The fishermen's and farmers' huts that were scattered at fairly large distances from each other amid marshes and lakes in the future zone of alienation that would become Harbin, could in no way be considered a village, much less a town. The huts were not connected with each other, comprising just a few separate points on the map of the modern-day city. (Melikhov 1990a, p. 163)

There is, however, in one of these early Russian accounts a record of a Qing fortress on the river bank:

... we halted in dismay: at a considerable distance lay the river, on whose bank, upon a relatively narrow elevation we glimpsed a small *yimpan* (fortress) where the Sungari Flour Mill stands today. On the site of what is now the Gorodskoy *sad* (town garden) was a little village of two or three huts, with a similar village some way off in the middle of what is now the town of Fujiadian. (Melikhov 1990a, p. 163)

The fortress mentioned in this source turned out to be a customs station staffed by one hundred custom officers. One cannot help wondering why such a large number of custom officers was concentrated in an otherwise desolate environment, and the Russians may be marred by a culturally determined blindness to Chinese activities in what they wanted to see as virgin land, but still there is an authentic ring to these eyewitness accounts.

Why the large discrepancy from the Chinese version? Clearly, in the sovereignty dispute between tsarist Russia and Qing China, which erupted soon after the railway project had been initiated, it was important for the Russians to be able to point to the previously uninhabited status of the Harbin area, and equally important for the Chinese side to prove the opposite. Present-day Harbin historians are in fact faithfully defending a Chinese position that was formed very early in the process. Both views may, however, be "correct," but while the Russian version focuses on the exact location of their first headquarters, the Chinese side is talking about a much larger area, that is, contemporary Harbin, including the two counties of Acheng and Hulan, which by all accounts were in a process of rapid settlement already before the arrival of the Russians.

Even in China the Harbin historians' claim of budding urbanization before 1898 is not generally accepted. In an authoritative national level publication like the encyclopedia *Cihai*, Harbin is simply referred to as a fishing village before the building of the Chinese Eastern Railway (*Cihai* 1989, p. 836). The bitter comments of Text 1B are therefore directed not only at the "imperialist distortions" of Harbin's early history but at fellow Chinese historians from other regions, who, according to a senior Harbin historian, disrespectfully claim that "the Northeast has no history, and Harbin has even less."

In order to establish Harbin's roots as a Chinese city, present-day local historians can be said to fight a two-front struggle. On the one hand they are up against an interpretation that says Harbin was created in the middle of nowhere by Russian railway engineers. To this they respond first of all by extrapolating backward in history from the present: since Manchu and Mongols and others are today incorporated in "the Chinese people" (*Zhonghua minzu*), the area can be said to have been inhabited by Chinese for a very long time. Secondly, they claim that even admitting that the Han

Chinese entered the scene rather late, they were there well before the arrival of the Russians. On the other front, they are facing Chinese historians who tend to ignore the history of non-Han ethnic groups, and therefore feel that the Northeast generally "lacks history." Their answer is that for many periods the tribes of Manchuria were, in fact, not much behind the development in the Chinese heartland and that the Jin dynasty, for example, represented a refined culture which could match that of its intramural contemporaries. In this way the historians carve out a place for Harbin in Chinese history that can help strengthen local identity and pride without offending national level interpretations of history and ethnic relations.

Notes

1. One *shang* equals 0.737 hectares.
2. An authoritative exposition of this intricate problem is Fan Wenlan's 1962 article "Problems of Conflict and Fusion of Nationalities in Chinese History." The core of Fan's argument, based on an analogy with a family dispute, is as follows: "It is a good thing that a little brother toppled his rotten and cruel elder brother and took over the management of household affairs. It is another matter whether he ran the house well or not" (Fan 1980, p. 78).

Texts

Harbin before the Russians

The two texts on the pre-Russian period of Harbin's history both set out to document the Chinese roots of the city in a quite polemical tone.

Archeological evidence naturally plays a major role in the argument, because written sources on the history of the Northeast are scarce. In Text 1A Sun Zhengjia sums up some of the local finds, of which the Jin dynasty "Upper Capital" Huiningfu near present-day Acheng is the most important. Descriptions of this site have even made their way into national magazines such as Cultural Relics *(Wenwu). The fact that Huiningfu is presented as part of Harbin's glorious past shows two important assumptions behind local history writing in Harbin: (1) The city is defined as the area presently under its administration, thus making it possible to include the former Jin capital forty kilometers from the urban center; and (2) if an area has been inhabited by a people now living inside the borders of the People's Republic, or, as in the case of the Nüzhen, by the forefathers of such a people, the area is considered historically Chinese. Sun's article further demonstrates one of the weaknesses of the Chinese roots argument: the gap of almost seven hundred years between the blossoming of the Jin and settlements in late Qing.*

Text 1B turns to the more recent origins of Harbin. Published in the inaugural issue of Harbin History and Gazetteer, *this article can be read as the manifesto of the whole local history enterprise. It confronts head-on anyone inside or outside China who has questioned the Chinese roots of Harbin. The article is characteristic in its general aim, but unusual in the sharpness of its tone.*

1A. Looking at the Glorious Historical Culture of Harbin through its Cultural Relics (Excerpts)

Sun Zhengjia

Many people have previously been of the impression that the historical culture of our city was almost a total blank. The vigorous growth of archeological work and research into the history of the Northeast, however, has forced them to re-examine and revise these conceptions. This article will give a parade of the exotic jewels in the cultural treasure chest of our city (including the cities of Acheng and Hulan), revealing once more the flower of our history and enabling people to make a fair judgment on the historical culture of Harbin.

The history of our city must be considered to be of very great antiquity. In 1982, archeologists working in the city's western suburb of Yanjiagang found a fragment from a human skull, which according to Carbon-14 dating was 22,370 years old (+/–300 years) and belonged to the period of the Old Stone Age. These later *Homo sapiens*, known as "Harbin Man," are the earliest known forefathers of the people now living in our province and city. After almost four years of excavations, there have been a total of over 3,000 finds of stone implements, bone implements, and animal fossils, as well as two camping grounds for hunters, these being among the first found in the entire country. The discovery of "Harbin Man" and other relics has not only stretched the history of human activity in our region much further into the past, but has also provided the most recent material evidence to support the theory that the ancient Indians originated in the northern part of our country and traveled through the Northeast and now-Soviet Eastern Siberia before crossing the Bering Strait and arriving in North America.

Two of our city's most typical archeological sites belonging to the later period of the Old Stone Age are to be found at Guxiangtun and Huangshan, both of them covering the period from 40,000–50,000 to 10,000 years ago. Chipped stone tools, bone implements, and various types of ancient animal fossils have been excavated at both of these sites, although there have been no finds of ancient human fossils. The stone implements found at Guxiangtun have been very varied and include stone flakes, stone cores, and rounded

Sun Zhengjia, "Cong wenhua guji kan Haerbin de canlan lishi wenhua," *Haerbin yanjiu* [Harbin Research], no. 4 (1986), pp. 53–56.

scrapers. From an examination of the prehistoric tools and the fossils of animals from the Quaternary Period, which have been found, such as mammoth and woolly rhinoceros, there can be no doubt that they belong to the culture of the later period of the Old Stone Age.

The banks of the Hulan River were home to an early culture characterized by the manufacture of fine stone implements. These include chipped flint scrapers, chipped fan-shaped scrapers, and needles made from obsidian stone, as well as pointed stone shards made from quartz. Their bone implements include some of ivory, as well as pointed implements made from hollow bones and horns. Especially worthy of mention is the discovery of shard-shaped and small pellet-shaped pieces of charcoal at this site, which after analysis have proved to be evidence of the human use of fire.[1] The uncovering of this archeological site has provided us with another vital link to fit into the chain of our city's prehistoric culture.

Around three thousand years ago our city gradually evolved from the Stone Age to the Bronze Age, almost keeping in step with developments in the cradle of the Chinese nation in the Yellow River basin, and presenting us with a picture of an early cultural blossoming. The archeological sites at Yaolingzitun and Chengjiagang in the city suburbs have produced several pottery vessels and pottery pieces belonging to the "Baijinbao-Wanghaitun culture," among them pottery spinning wheels, pottery rings, hollow legs of the *li4* cauldron, and bridge-shaped handles. Most of these were made from reddish-brown clay; some of the surfaces were burnished and applied with line decorations, chief among them the comb decoration. These were the characteristic pottery utensils of our country in ancient times. The cooking utensils with the lower section composed of three hollow pouch-shaped legs were both aesthetically pleasing and practical, and are evidence of the genius of our forefathers. The *li4* cauldron had its origins over four thousand years ago in the Longshan culture, but it gradually spread in all directions because of its practicality. Our city was one of the sites the *li4* cauldron came to, illustrating the fact that our city had relatively close cultural links with the central plains region at a very early date. Although no bronze implements have so far been discovered at the two sites mentioned above, the "Baijinbao-Wanghaitun culture" as a whole did develop many kinds of bronze implements and the two archeological sites at Yaolingzitun and Chengjiagang, which belong to the same culture, should be considered Bronze Age sites. This culture survived from the middle to late period of the Western Zhou right up until Qin and Han times, and was founded in succession by the Tuoli and Fuyu people. Our city was already advancing at this time from primitive to class society, and these cultural relics, which show a relatively high level of craftsmanship, are an important indicator of social progress.

Among the "Baijinbao-Wanghaitun" relics unearthed in our city are some that have a style differing from that in the central plains region and with their own special characteristics. The pottery prop stand unearthed in the 1940s by the Russian L. M. Yakefuliefu [Yakovlev?] in Chenggaozi is one such example. The pottery prop stand, also called "pottery prop leg," with cut sides and a round awl-shaped body, was used to prop up the cooking utensil. This kind of stand was current in the central plains before the appearance of the *ding* and *li4* cauldrons and other cooking utensils, but later fell out of use. Within the confines of the "Baijinbao-Wanghaitun culture" it continued to be used for a long time, however, and furthermore "the pottery prop stands in this region have hollows on top that allow the legs of the *li4* cauldron to be placed securely. This is something not seen anywhere else."[2] In addition to this, the Russian V. S. Tashijin [Dashkin?] has also found in an area between Chenggaozi and the Shelitun station a pottery statuette of a wild pig and another of a bear. These statuettes, so full of local characteristics, obviously bear a close connection to the hunting life of the population and also reveal the artistic talent of the first inhabitants of our city.

Following on from them, the Wuji people established a new culture in the broad area of the Songhua River valley, which includes present-day Harbin. Many stone, pottery, and metal objects have been unearthed in places in the Harbin area such as Molijie, Gaotaizi, Beishanchengzi to the south of Huangshan, and Huangjiawaizi. The pottery includes such varieties as yellow-brown, black-brown, and plain pottery, while the metal objects include, among other things, copper rings and needles, silver bracelets, and iron arrowheads. Also found have been articles made of nephrite, each of them original and unique in style and color and offering evidence of the rather high cultural level at that time.

During the Liao and Jin dynasties, the Nüzhen nationality established a culture with a high level of civilization in the area of our city. The Jin dynasty was particularly outstanding and could rightly be called the most glittering period in our ancient history.

More than twenty ancient city walls have been discovered within the boundaries of Harbin, with the majority of them built during the Liao and Jin dynasties, as for example the ancient city walls of Wanbao, Pingle, Songshan, Sifangtai, Banlachengzi, Molijie, and Chenggaozi. A few of these walls are still preserved in a relatively intact state, although most of them have already crumbled away. The land in and around some wall sites is still scattered with a great quantity of woven-patterned cylindrical tiles, flat tiles, and broken bricks, these being the ancient building materials used for walls and houses. In all the walls one can collect or unearth many types of pottery and porcelain shards, as well as metal articles of all kinds (some of them tools for production and others articles for daily use), reflecting the rich and varied life-style of the people of that time.

The archeological site at the Jin dynasty's "Upper Capital" of Huiningfu, situated in Baicheng near the city of Acheng, is the most grandly spectacular site in the whole city area and is one of the most important cultural relic preservation units in the entire country. Construction began in the sixth year in the Huangtong reign of the Xizong emperor of the Jin dynasty (A.D. 1146) in imitation of the Northern Song capital of Bianjing (now Kaifeng), but it came to be destroyed while construction was still in progress, and work on it was not recommenced until the twenty-first year in the Dading reign of the Shizong emperor (A.D. 1181). In addition to all of the imperial palaces, there were also "the Emperor's Military Hall, a building for ball games and archery, the Cloud Brocade Pavilion, and the Ripple Viewing Pavilion, where hawks were kept."[3] Many of the foundations of palaces in the imperial city still survive, and a wide range of building materials has been excavated, including "cylindrical tiles, sheet tiles in all sizes marked on the inside with a coarse mesh pattern, fine square bricks, bricks inscribed with clouds and dragons, bricks with a striped pattern and coarse rectangular bricks. There are also plaster eaves tiles with animal, flower and dragon patterns, green glazed tiles, dragon-pattern eaves tiles, dragon-shaped dripcatchers, phoenix heads and much more."[4] On the evidence of these exquisite artifacts it is not difficult for us to imagine how impressive and magnificent the city must have been.

The architecture of the Jin capital provides just one small glimpse of the glorious culture of the Jin dynasty. Other areas, such as metal-melting technology, the minting of coins, weapon manufacture, the manufacture of daily articles and handicrafts, engraving, and calligraphy, made either their first appearance in this region or were vastly more developed than anything that had gone before. . . .

During the Yuan and Ming dynasties and the early Qing, the culture of the area now encompassed by our city was in a period of decline lasting several centuries. Having said this, it still could not be described as "culturally blank," however. The Yuan dynasty texts "The Seal of the Ningzhou Army Garrisons" and "The Red Seal of the Commoner Daluhua Who Is the Mongol in Charge of the Waters," written in the Basiba script, for example, give an indication of the relatively high cultural and artistic level of our region at the time, and the Islamic mosque built at Acheng during the reign of the Qing dynasty Qianlong emperor is a magnificent building resplendent with national characteristics.

To sum up, the historical culture of our city is one of great antiquity, continuity, and variety, and it forms an important constituent part of the glorious and outstanding historical culture of the Chinese nation. The people of our city should therefore increase their sense of national pride and historical responsibility and work even harder at building up Harbin into a modern city famed for its culture.

Notes

1. Wei Zhengyi, "Investigations into the Early Microlithic Site on the Banks of the Hulan River," *Heilongjiang Cultural Relics Series*, no. 3 (1982).

2. Si Jin, "Ancient Pottery Prop Legs of the Songnen Plain," *Northern Cultural Relics*, no. 1 (1986).

3. "The History of the Jin: Geographical Records."

4. Xu Zirong, "The Archeological Site at the Jin Upper Capital Huiningfu," *Heilongjiang Cultural Relics Series*, no. 1 (1982).

1B. When Writing History and Gazetteers, Make a Critical Reassessment of the Sources (Excerpts)

Shu Li

Harbin, a city situated on a river amid beautiful scenery, is one of our country's important industrial centers. It has a long history and glorious revolutionary tradition. In the first half of the century, deliberate falsifications and distortions by Russian and Japanese imperialists, together with the capricious conjectures and fabrications of Chinese scholars and writers, led to the existence of erroneous beliefs about Harbin on a whole series of questions, such as the meaning of the city's name, the city's historical course and development, and the organizational system of the city government. Because we have not laid sufficient emphasis on research into local history and gazetteers and because several comrades have irresponsibly occupied themselves with twisting the earlier distortions further, in the thirty years since the founding of the People's Republic, many of the imperialistically inspired fallacies and groundless myths have continued to be propagated. The study of local history has also tended not to pay attention to the verification or refutation of historical data, resulting in large discrepancies between the data cited and historical fact, which has also had an adverse effect on the writing of local history and gazetteers. Now that work on the compilation of gazetteers for the entire city is on the point of getting under way, the author considers it necessary to give his opinion on several questions that presently face us, and in so doing ask for guidance both from those involved in the compilation and from the general reader.

1. The Meaning and Origin of the Name "Harbin"

What "Harbin" means and how the name came into being are the first questions facing anyone researching the history of the city. During Harbin's period of Russian domination, this area was still very much uncharted territory, and people only knew that it was called Harbin, but not why. At the beginning of the 1920s, following the restitution of partial [Chinese] control over the Chinese Eastern Railway and the Harbin city government, attempts were made to provide an explanation of "Harbin," with backgrounds in a

---

Shu Li, "Bianshi xiuzhi zheng ben qing yuan," *Haerbin shizhi* [Harbin History and Gazetteer], no. 1 (1983), pp. 27–31.

wide variety of standpoints and interests. With regard to the meaning of the name, there were people who held it to be "fishing lake," "place for drying nets," "crossing place," "poor village," "good riverbank," and "large grave." As for its language of origin, there were claims for Manchurian, Mongolian, Chinese, and Russian. All in all, there were so many contradictory views being touted that it was impossible to sort out fact from fiction. Each of the contending parties, without exception, could provide only subjective conjectures, groundless hearsay, or far-fetched interpretations and analogies to support its view, and none of them could produce convincing evidence. The "place for drying nets" interpretation was the one with the widest popularity, gaining credence from the fact that there had actually been a "netting place" in Harbin at the end of the Qing dynasty. However, this "netting place" had been an area established by imperial edict for the catching of fish and was a basic unit in the collection of fish levies; not only is "place for drying nets" quite different from this in meaning, but the actual pronunciation of the expression has almost no resemblance whatsoever to that of "Harbin."

In the thirty years since the founding of the People's Republic, many of the groundless and absurd speculations about the meaning and origin of "Harbin" have not been repeated, but its interpretation as the Manchurian word for "place for drying nets" has spread so widely that it has even been cited in such publications as the *Cihai* encyclopedia, the *Atlas of Chinese Provinces,* and *The Traveler* magazine, and practically acquired the status of an indisputable fact.

An article entitled "Harbin—Celebrated City of the North" states: "According to a documentary account, the name 'Harbin' derives from a transliteration of the Manchurian 'Alejin,' which had the meaning 'fishing lake' or 'place for drying nets.' " Reading such an account leaves one quite speechless with astonishment. "Alejin" is not Manchurian, nor does it have the meaning "fishing lake" or "place for drying nets"; if one searched through all the relevant historical books and ancient records from cover to cover, one would not be able to find such a "documentary account." The present author believes that this irresponsible and sloppy style of writing is totally impermissible. According to the textual research of comrade Guan Chenghe, working in collaboration with scholars of the Nüzhen and Manchurian languages both in and outside China, such as Jin Qizong and Mu Yejun, the word "Harbin" is actually a transliteration of the village name "Alejin" recorded in the "History of the Jin Dynasty," having the meaning "glory," "honor," or "prestige," and being a place name of Nüzhen origin combined with elements of the Qidan [Khitan] pronunciation.

2. The Historical Development of Harbin

The historical development of the city and the meaning of its name are two closely related questions. The misinterpretation of its original name has by necessity led to misconceptions about its historical development. As with the name, the interpretation of the city's historical development has abounded with misconceptions and been the subject of fabrications and distortions by the Russian and Japanese imperialists as well as the inventions and exaggerations of a small number of scholars in the old China. Under their pens, Harbin was described as if it had been a scene of utter wilderness before the building of the Chinese Eastern Railway. As early as 1902, [Count Sergei] Witte, the Russian minister of finance, wrote in a memorial to Tsar Nicholas II: "an inspection of Harbin showed it to be an unpopulated wilderness."[1] In the beginning of the 1920s, local scholars also blindly engaged in phrase-mongering, saying: "In the period before the construction of the Chinese Eastern Railway, there was no more than a handful of fishermen who had gathered together on the banks of the Songhua River with their boats forming a cold and desolate settlement."[2] On the question of Harbin's founding date, the tsarist Russian colonialists expressed themselves even more flagrantly, brazenly taking as Harbin's "birthday" the day the first contingent of workers arrived in Harbin to build the Chinese Eastern Railway, June 9, 1898 (May 28 according to the Russian calendar). With a still greater display of chauvinism they conferred the title "founding father of Harbin" on Count Khilkov, section chief of the ninth section of the Chinese Eastern Railway construction project.[3] Although they fly in the face of the historical facts, many of these fallacies were still being widely circulated after Liberation, deluding the general opinion both at home and abroad. Right up to this very day there are still many comrades who consider 1898 the year of Harbin's founding and think that the city has less than ninety years of history. In *Buildings from Harbin's Early Period and the Local Architectural Style of Harbin*, published in 1980 (Guo Lin 1980), it was written: "Up until the end of the nineteenth century, [Harbin] was a small and insignificant country settlement." The title of this book could easily lead one to think that the author was going to discuss Harbin's architecture in the Liao and Jin dynasties, or else that he would discuss the techniques for the construction of cave dwellings employed by the even earlier Wuji people. This, however, is not the case. Reading the book reveals that Harbin's "early period" of architecture is no more than the rather few buildings, churches, and clubs constructed in the period of the occupation of the city by the Russian imperialists (some of them even a little later than this, being built in the 1930s). Furthermore, not one mention is made of Binjiang County, as if this area under Chinese sovereignty, as opposed to the Russian imperialists' "self-governing city," did not exist at all. Can it really be the case that the Harbin mentioned in this book is no more than the "self-governing city of Harbin," an illegal political authority set up in Harbin by the Russian imperialists? Is it also the case that Chinese buildings are not really buildings? That Chinese architectural styles are not also to be considered architectural styles? Can it really be correct that the "early period" of Harbin's architecture can be seen only from the viewpoint of Russian imperialists? The people of Harbin should take each and every one of these questions seriously to heart.

How far back does the history of Harbin actually go? With regard to this question, the great quantity of archeological finds has already provided incontrovertible evidence of Harbin's long history. There was human activity in Harbin in the late period of the Old Stone Age from 10,000 to 50,000 years ago. From ancient times this has been an area where all the ethnic groups of northern China have lived and labored. As explained above, "Alejin" is the earliest name for Harbin, having taken form as a village, which is found in the ancient records, and the year 1097 seems best qualified to stand as the founding date of Harbin.

Before the construction of the Chinese Eastern Railway, was it really true that Harbin was "small and insignificant" or a "cold and desolate settlement"? The answer must be in the negative. Disregarding for the moment the ancient past, the Harbin area has been since the time of the Qing dynasty in the province of Jilin and fallen under the administration of the subsidiary capital Alchuka. In the fifty-third year of the reign of the Qianlong emperor (1788), the area around Guxiangtun was already being cultivated by Manchurian and Chinese peasants. During the reign of the Jiaqing emperor, following the policy of "resettling the [Manchu] bannermen from the capital and letting them break new ground" and the ending of the "forbidden zone" policy [i.e., the ban on Han immigration], more banners and civilian villages were founded in Harbin's Pingfang, Nangang, and Guxiangtun districts. According to figures from the second year of the reign of the Guangxu emperor (1876), alone in the state villages around the Qing navy division's barracks (now the area around Shuangkoumian and the Qianjin people's commune in Daowai) there were 3,730 households and a population as large as 28,257.[4] Around the sixteenth year of Guangxu (1890), settlements such as Fujiadian, Gangjiadian, Wujiadian, and Sijiazi sprang up in what is now the Daowai district.[5] And at Xiangfang, "the more than 200 households in the surrounding area came to form a village."[6] In connection with the Tian Family Distillery alone there were "32 buildings, some of which were built of brick."[7] In 1895, an imperial Russian "inspection team" went up the Songhua River to make an illegal survey, drawing up a sketch map that provides us with more powerful evidence: the map records more than fifty settlements of various sizes along the river including Harbin, the Tian Family Distillery, the Yuanju Distillery, and the navy division's barracks at Chuankouzi and Shuangkoumian.[8] Therefore in 1898, when the first batch of construction workers on the Chinese Eastern Railway arrived in Harbin, they would have seen with their own eyes many villages, such as Qinjiagang and Majiagou, at what is now Harbin railway station, Majia Road in Nangang, Harbin Technical University, Huayuancun, Jiwuduan, Zhaolin Park, Zhengyang River, and Sijiazi. Moreover, near the present site of the Jihong Bridge there was a small temple, and on the banks of the Songhua River there was "a customs station with one hundred people. . . ."[9] There is a great amount of material proving that before the building of the Chinese Eastern Railway there were already many villages in all districts of Harbin, and these could be said to thickly cover the whole region like stars on the sky. How could such a dense distribution of villages be called an "unpopulated wilderness"? How could a village with "more than 200 households" become a "cold and desolate settlement"? How is it that the busy transit place of Fujiadian on the road from Hulan to Acheng could be termed "insignificant"?

The stratagem of the tsarist Russian imperialists of trying to wipe clean Harbin's long history was without doubt an attempt to prove that they were the "founding fathers" of this area and the "masters" of Harbin. The Japanese imperialists followed tsarist Russia's pattern in attempting to distort the history of Harbin and the Northeast, and this was also done clearly for the sake of their own political objectives. Even today, there are still those who ignore the historical facts and depict Harbin before the Chinese Eastern Railway as a desolate wilderness; what on earth can their motives be for doing this? . . .

In this essay, the author has not been able to avoid making some modest criticisms of the articles of others. This has been done with no intention other than that of helping in the correct compiling of historical records and of bringing about a thorough reassessment of the historical sources. All criticisms and corrections of mistakes or omissions will be received most gratefully.

Notes

1. Main points from the contracts and files of the Eastern Provinces Railway.
2. *The Harbin Guidebook* (Eastern Frontier Commercial Newspaper Office, 1922).
3. *The History of the Eastern Provinces Railway* (in Russian), pp. 84, 113.
4. *Heilongjiang Gazetteer Manuscript.*
5. *A Sketch of Manchuria's Cultural History* (in Japanese), p. 146.
6. *Record of the Bai Mountains and the Hei River*, p. 11.
7. *History of the Eastern Provinces Railway* (in Russian), p. 129.
8. *Rough Map of the Songhua River and Its Tributaries, the Bukui and the Hulan* (in Russian), 1895.
9. *History of the Eastern Provinces Railway* (in Russian), pp. 129–32.

2

The Era of Russian Influence: 1898-1932

After the arrival of the railway engineers in 1898, Russian influence in Harbin was indisputable and highly visible for several decades. The city was initially run directly by the Russian Chinese Eastern Railway (CER) management, but in the years 1907–17 its status changed to that of an "open city," with the Russians still playing the leading role. After the 1917 Russian revolution, Harbin remained dominated by its White Russian community for yet another decade (1917–26), while at the same time experiencing growing Soviet influence in the years following the 1924 Sino-Soviet treaty concerning the CER. The gradual dilution of Russian power in Harbin thus followed a complicated course: purely Russian rule gave way to a growing international presence, and after 1917 the Russian factor was itself split into "white" and "red" forces.

Thus things appeared to the European travelers, businessmen, diplomats, and missionaries who visited and reported on Harbin in the first three decades of the twentieth century, as well as to later Western and Russian historians. To the Chinese local historians, however, the crucial factor in Harbin's changing political and economic landscape during this period is the sinification of the city, the development and maturation of its Chinese population as well as the perennial struggle to re-establish Chinese sovereignty in the area. In the eyes of the contemporary local historians, this process of sinification is best brought out by focusing on the local manifestations of the great upheavals that shaped the Chinese nation during the period in a broad context of early industrialization, the rise of nationalism, and the emergence of communism as a political force.

The "Russian perspective" on early Harbin history thus differs fundamentally from the Chinese historians' approach. For the purpose of an outline, however, the structure of Harbin's political and economic history cannot be divorced from the larger political drama of wars and revolutions influencing the history of the Far East.

Direct Russian Rule, 1898–1907

The Struggle over Manchuria

Toward the end of the nineteenth century Manchuria had become the object of a tripartite race for control among China, Russia, and Japan. Far-reaching plans were being drawn up in Russia, where construction of the Trans-Siberian Railway was begun at Vladivostok in 1891. By 1894, survey crews were reporting that technical difficulties could be expected if the railway were routed north of the Amur River as originally planned (Wieczynski 1976, p. 49). The idea of running a line directly through Manchuria in order to save some 340 miles of railway is normally attributed to Count Witte, the highly influential Russian minister of finance from 1892 to 1903. The opportunity to force such a concession from China came with the Chinese defeat in the Sino-Japanese War of 1894–95. As part of the 1895 Treaty of Shimonoseki, China ceded the Liaodong Peninsula in southern Manchuria to Japan, but Russia took the lead in the Three Power Intervention that year, which persuaded Japan to accept retrocession of Liaodong to China. As payment for this service Russia demanded the needed railway concession in North Manchuria. To circumvent Chinese objections to the operation of the railway as a Russian government enterprise, in 1895 Witte set up a "nongovernment" subsidiary company of the Russo-Chinese Bank as a thinly disguised adjunct to the Russian treasury for the purpose of penetrating Manchuria and the whole of North China (Huenemann 1984, pp. 49–50). The contract between this company and China was signed on September 8, 1896. It covered an eighty-year period, after which the railroad would revert to China free of charge. After thirty-six years China would have the option of buying back the railroad at full payment of the invested capital. Construction work started the year after, and in 1898 Harbin was established as headquarters of the project. The line was put in operation in 1903, but in the meanwhile the teeth of the imperialist powers had been sharpened considerably.

In 1898 Russia forced China by gunboat diplomacy to accept a twenty-five-year Russian lease of Dalian and Port Arthur on the Liaodong Peninsula as well as a new railway concession, this time from Port Arthur to Harbin, creating the southern arm of the T-shaped Manchurian Railway. Russian designs in Manchuria and North China became more candid, and the Boxer Rebellion of 1900, which extended to most places in Manchuria, was followed by Russian intervention and full-scale occupation of Manchuria by an expeditionary force of about 100,000 men. By November 1900 the region was more or less under Russian military control. After the Boxer Protocol was signed Russia clung to Manchuria, demanding the virtual cessation of the region, but with the Anglo-Japanese Treaty of Alliance of January 1902 Russia was grudgingly forced to withdraw its forces. Russian procrastination in carrying out the evacuation from Manchuria was one of the direct causes of the outbreak of war between Russia and Japan in 1904. After the Russian defeat in 1905, the Russian possessions in the Liaodong area as well as the Port Arthur–Changchun railway link, henceforth known as the South Manchurian Railway (SMR), were surrendered to Japan, which now joined in the struggle for domination of Manchuria as a major player. The area was de facto divided into Russian and Japanese spheres of influence along an east-west line passing through Changchun.

Faced with the danger of losing its ancestral lands in the Northeast entirely, the Qing government employed the two related strategies of frontier management and self-strengthening (Hunt 1973, p. 86f.). But the disastrous effects of the 1896 alliance with Russia had demonstrated the limitations of the time-honored method of "using barbarians to control barbarians," and China observed strict neutrality in the Russo-Japanese War. The cautious approach was rewarded as the Chinese government regained much of its authority in Manchuria after the Russian military evacuation in 1905. As for self-strengthening, the strategy of promoting Chinese migration to Manchuria was further intensified during the 1898–1907 decade.

Harbin and the Chinese Eastern Railway

The Russian buildup in Manchuria during the 1896–1905 period was marred by a lack of overall strategy and purpose; by 1898 Russia had made clear to the other powers her ambitions in Manchuria and indeed in the whole of North China (Huenemann 1984, p. 51), but a strategy for this enterprise was never worked out and the Russian government was deeply divided on the issue. The legal basis for the Russian presence in Harbin reflected this ambiguity. Although Russian domination in young Harbin was a de facto colonial setup, the legal and political foundation of Russian rule in Harbin remained tied to the CER contract of September 1896 (the treaty is reproduced in MacMurray 1921, pp. 74–78). The stipulations of this contract regarding ownership of the railway, composition of the board of directors, military protection of the railway, and taxation and administration of the railway zone turned out to be—from the Russian angle —inadequate to secure undisputed control of Harbin, even when the interpretation of the stipulations was stretched to the very limit. The Chinese authorities never lost their foothold entirely in the struggle to maintain a measure of control in the Harbin area and the railway zone, even though a major Chinese effort to regain the initiative did not materialize until after the Russo-Japanese War.

The city of Harbin took shape in the quagmire of Sino-Russian disputes relating to the interpretation of the CER contract. Certain issues were of particular significance in determining Harbin's future development:

The Definition of the Railway Zone

Article VI of the contract stipulated that "lands actually necessary for the construction, operation and protection of the line, as also the lands in the vicinity of the line necessary for procuring sand, stone, lime, etc., will be turned over to the Company," but the contract provided neither clear limitations on the company's land acquisitions nor a method for resolving conflicts in this regard (MacMurray 1921, p. 76). From the outset the CER company occupied large tracts of land along the route of the railway far in excess of the actual need for railway construction, and even after the completion of the railway, this "zone" was continuously expanded by the company. The more important stations of the railway had large tracts of land set aside for them, with Harbin as the largest, eventually growing to 15,800 acres (Gladeck 1972, p. 43). Bordering this area, however, a Chinese settlement contiguous with Russian-built Harbin grew apace. A host of problems relating to sovereignty, jurisdiction, administration, and so on were inherent in this setup.

Jurisdiction

The problem of jurisdiction in the city of Harbin was compounded by a discrepancy between the Chinese and Russian versions of the relevant section in the CER contract. In the Chinese version of Article VI, the central clause reads: "all the land utilized by the said [CER] Company is to be exempted from land taxation and to be managed by the said company singlehandedly" (*you gai gongsi yishou jingli*).[1] The implication of this version is a businesslike relationship in a context of Chinese sovereignty. In the Russian version, however, the last phrase is taken out to form an independent sentence, and indeed an independent paragraph of Article VI: "The Company will have the absolute and exclusive right of administration of its lands."[2] The difference between these two versions of the contract is crucial, because the ensuing de facto Russian colonization of the railway zone, that is, the entire Russian system of judicial and police authority as well as the structure of municipal administration in the 1896–1907 decade, was based on the Russian version of Article VI.

As for the legal system, Russian subjects were directly under Russian courts. In 1904 the railway zone was made a separate judicial district with headquarters in Harbin. Jurisdiction over Chinese working for the CER or living in the railway zone was exercised by two "liaison offices" (*jiaoshe zongju*) covering the provinces of Jilin and Heilongjiang. Both offices were located in Harbin, and they were more or less under Russian control since they depended financially on the CER company, and the general manager of the CER had the right of consultation in the appointment of Chinese members.[3]

Military Control

Article V of the CER contract stipulated that "the Chinese Government will take measures to assure the safety of the railway and of the persons in its service against any attack" (MacMurray 1921, p. 76). When the Russians began organizing railway guards in 1897, supplemented later that year by several hundred regular troops (Gladeck 1972, p. 46), this was based on their interpretation of Article VI of the contract as discussed above. The presence of Russian railway guards and regular troops was never recognized by the Chinese side, which lodged several protests. The number of guards rose rapidly, and by the time of the Boxer Uprising they numbered 11,000 men (Tang 1959, p. 96). During the Russian military occupation of Manchuria the railway guards served as an auxiliary force to the regular Russian troops, and by 1905 their number reached 21,000 (Gladeck 1972, p. 47). In 1907 the command structure of these guards was formalized as they were put under the command of the general manager of the railway, D. L. Horwath. The Treaty of Portsmouth (September 1905), which concluded the Russo-Japanese War, provided the Russians as well as the Japanese with "the right to maintain guards to protect their respective railway lines in Manchuria," but China was not a signatory to this treaty and thus maintained its policy of nonrecognition (MacMurray 1921, p. 526).

Civil Administration

Civil administration in Harbin and the railway zone was closely related to the above-mentioned issues. Russian administration was an indisputable reality during the years of military occupation between 1900 and 1906.[4] There were initial discussions on the government system during that period. A town commission was first established in December 1903 (Zhu Xianping

1988, p. 49); in December 1904, ten Russian merchants were elected as its members, and a series of conferences was held to discuss the introduction of self-government for the town (Quested 1982, p. 189). Apparently the main objective of the CER management in this matter was to introduce taxation in Harbin to help finance city construction. The early efforts in this regard were overtaken, however, by the political effects of the Russian defeat to Japan in 1905, as well as the 1905 wave of political unrest in Russia itself.

Local historical studies of the CER and its significance for Harbin focus mainly on the political aspects of railway building, that is, the threat to Chinese sovereignty implicit in the CER project and the protracted struggle against this threat,' culminating in the years following the 1917 Russian revolution. But one can also find detailed studies of the first few years of the railway with more focus on technical, economic, and managerial aspects.[5] Local historians in Harbin are unanimous in their condemnation of tsarist Russia's self-proclaimed image as a "friend of China," which is seen as a thin disguise for the true purposes of the CER: the economic plunder of China, the annexation of Manchuria, and ultimately a position of hegemony for Russia in the Far East (Li Jitang 1987, pp. 56–57). The terminology used to describe the evils of imperialism often harks back to Maoist times, with frequent use of terms such as *fengkuang* ("mad, unbridled"), *lüeduo* ("plunder"), *qitu* ("to plot, scheme"), and so on. A more regrettable heritage from the history writing of the 1960s and 1970s is the habit of reproducing statements from historical persons without stating the source, date, or context. This style appears to be in decline during the 1980s, but some old habits die slowly.

There are remarkably few comments on the mistakes and failures of the Qing court in relation to the CER project; as a rule, all blame is concentrated on the Russian government and its local representatives in Manchuria. Only Li Hongzhang, who negotiated the CER contract with the Russians, is presented in an ignominious light, though explicit condemnation is avoided. When Qing officials did in fact strive to uphold Chinese sovereignty in relation to the CER, as they did sporadically in the 1898–1905 period and more consistently between 1905 and 1909, this is presented as a matter of course and typical of China's attitude to infringements of her sovereignty. But when the same officials failed or neglected to play this role, silence seems to be the preferred reaction. Truly positive comment is reserved for the popular struggles against the Russian presence in Manchuria, from the Boxer Uprising to the later strikes and nationalist manifestations.

Life in the City

In the 1890s, the main concentration of villages in the Harbin area was in Xiangfang, about 10 km south of the river. When the first batch of Russian railway builders arrived in April 1898 they initially tried to find suitable buildings near the river, at the designated location of the railway bridge, but they had to settle for Xiangfang, where they were able to purchase an abandoned distillery. This became the first headquarters of the railway enterprise, and despite the distance to the river a small Russian town sprang up here. Concurrently, the construction work attracted thousands of Chinese workers to the area.

The settlement grew at an astonishing pace. In 1899, after only a year, the non-Chinese population had grown to 14,000 people, representing twenty-eight nationalities of the Russian Empire (Melikhov 1990a, p. 68); many of these had not freely chosen Harbin but were forced to settle there after serving sentences in Siberia. A Railway Staff Assembly House with two rooms, opened in January 1899, served as the first community center in Harbin, and across the road a public garden was laid out. A small prayer-house had been built as early as February 1898.

A major interruption of the bustling activity in young Harbin came with the Boxer Uprising, which in Manchuria developed into a brief but regular war between Russia and China. The course of events in Manchuria differed from that in intramural China. The Boxers spread slowly in Manchuria, but in their place regular Chinese armies played a prominent role in what developed into a major, although poorly coordinated, anti-Russian effort. The most serious clashes took place in southern Manchuria, but the north also experienced significant confrontations in July 1900, with a Chinese attack on the northern line of the CER and a siege of Harbin, where refugees from Liaodong had swarmed in.[6]

An attack on Harbin was first expected by the Russians on July 10, 1900, and some families of railway guards were evacuated while able-bodied men were organized into a militia (Lensen 1967, pp. 142–43). The attack did not materialize, but with the influx of more refugees from Boxer-dominated regions in the southern part of Manchuria and with widespread dissatisfaction among Chinese servants and laborers, who worried about their pay, panic grew in the city. As the last Russian train left Harbin station on July 11, there was some looting of Russian homes by the Chinese, but no Russian was hurt during the disturbances. On July 22 a telegram came from Shoushan, the military governor of Heilongjiang, informing the Russians that military action against Harbin would begin shortly. He gallantly exhorted the Russians to fight bravely, because they were "going to be exterminated without mercy." Shoushan also offered safe passage out of Manchuria to all Russian women and children, and the next day some 3,000 women, children, and wounded left Harbin on two steamers with barges bound for Khabarovsk (Lensen 1967, pp. 146f.). The Chinese offensive started with an attack on July 26 and another on July 30. During the first offensive the Chinese forces managed to occupy the main railway depot as well as the railway connecting Old Harbin with the new sections of the city under construction near the river. But a Russian counterattack drove the Chinese forces away. The second battle on July 30 did not go quite as smoothly for the Russians, who suffered dozens of casualties before they assembled their forces for an orderly withdrawal. Finally, on August 3 massive Russian reinforcements arrived in Harbin by ship, and the next day a religious service was held on the city square to celebrate the salvation of the Russian community in Harbin.

In 1901 it was decided to move the railway headquarters to an area of elevation nearer to the river; this became the "New Town" (*Novy Gorod*), and the original settlement became "Old Harbin" or "Old Town" (*Stary Gorod*). At the same time a third settlement began to emerge on the riverfront. It was called Pristan and was located next to the rapidly growing Chinese village of Fujiadian. The area between these two riverside settlements was called "Mostovoy" or "Eighth Section"; it was home to the main concentration of CER tracks and depots, and it developed into a mixed Sino-Russian settlement, inhabited mainly by railway workers. "New Town," today called Nangang ("Southern Elevation"), became the center of officialdom. All the main CER buildings and institutions were established here, as well as villas for the Russian official elite. Pristan, called Daoli ("within the tracks") by the Chinese, became the commercial and recreational center of Harbin. The Chinese town Fujiadian bordering the railway zone, also called Daowai ("outside the tracks"), developed into a large residential area relatively untouched by foreign influence. These first four nuclei of Harbin, originally quite separate, gradually merged in the following years, but to this day they have retained the distinct differences related to their origins, from the stately buildings and government institutions concentrated in Nangang to the "bourgeois" Daoli and the "Chinese" Daowai. The name Harbin was first used in reference to the Old Town and soon came to replace the official Russian designation "Railway junction Sungari"; it later became the general name of the city (Melikhov 1990a, p. 160).

At the time of the first census in Harbin, held on May 15, 1903, Chinese outnumbered Russians two to one, even when the Chinese settlement of Fujiadian was excluded: 15,579 Russians against 28,338 Chinese (Melikhov 1990a, p. 174). The Chinese probably outnumbered the Russians in Harbin at any time of the city's history, but population figures for Harbin's early period are quite uncertain, with great variation between different estimates.

The young Harbin of the CER construction period (1898–1903) has been described as a "wild, wooden boom town" (Quested 1982, p. 100). The regular forces of the Russian army remained a visible part of town life until 1903, when the railway guards, whose reputation ranged far below that of the regular troops, resumed full responsibility for defense matters. The overall sex ratio was 14 women to every 100 men, and brothels flourished everywhere with the Japanese as the most successful operators (Quested 1982, p. 99). Harbin quickly became famous for its particularly wild night life, and this image stayed with the city well into the 1930s, surviving many dramatic changes. As for industry, the flour mills expanded rapidly, with seven modern enterprises equipped with machinery in operation by 1903. In 1902 the new CER headquarters and the new Railway Assembly House, located in Nangang, were completed, and the city also acquired its first theater around this time, as well as a library and an official Russian newspaper. A complete microcosm of Russian society thus emerged in Harbin with social differences ranging from the refined, cultured life in the villas and clubs of the CER top officials to the lowly taverns of the railway workers and guards. Ethnically, young Harbin was very heterogeneous, with a large representation of minority nationalities from all parts of the Russian empire, but social distinctions were highly visible, with each stratum living separately and with its own institutions such as clubs, restaurants, and baths.

Segregation between this miniature Russian class society and the equally stratified Chinese society was even more marked. Most Chinese lived in the Fujiadian settlement adjunct to the CER zone, and apart from shopowners Chinese were not allowed to reside in the Russian sections of the city within the zone. Nevertheless, at the outset of the CER project the attitude of most ordinary Chinese toward the Russians was rather positive, because the CER created economic opportunities for them rather than dislocating workers, as was the case with the European-built railways in North China (cf. Malozemoff 1958, p. 136). The Boxer confrontation and the ensuing military occupation hardened the feelings of the Chinese, and it was reported that "only the very lowest class of Chinese" would take domestic service in Russian homes (Quested 1982, p. 132). Large numbers of Chinese had to learn Russian for business purposes, and even more Chinese were affected by the Russian language in the curious Harbin-Chinese dialect laced with Russian loanwords and strange amalgamations (Li and Shi 1987, pp. 156–57), but the contact between the two cultures produced very few truly Russianized Chinese. Even the brothels were said to employ only few Chinese women during the first several years of Harbin history.[7]

When the Russo-Japanese War broke out in February 1904 the immediate effect in Harbin, at a safe distance from the zone of military combat, was a huge boost to the economy. As a center for food manufacturing Harbin became a vital supplier to the Russian army. The population leapfrogged from around 100,000 (60,000 in the Russian sections of the city and 40,000 in Fujiadian) on the eve of the war to a total of some 250,000 by war's end (Quested 1982, pp. 43, 100). Russian businessmen rushed to Harbin to grab a share of the boom, and Chinese entrepreneurs became noticeable for the first time. Prices skyrocketed, and a single room in one of Harbin's inns cost as a much as five rubles a day (Quested 1982, p. 143).

Naturally, after the Russian defeat the situation changed in Harbin. First came the tide of poorly organized and demoralized soldiers returning from the front; drunkenness and crime became rampant in the city. Then the effects of the 1905 political upheaval in Russia reached Harbin. A soldier's committee was formed in October 1905, and soon afterward a Menshevik organization was set up, rallying the support of intellectuals such as CER engineers and army doctors, as well as a Bolshevik organization based in the railway workshops (Quested 1982, p. 149). There was general excitement but no coordination among the various groups, and no leadership emerged during the movement. Destruction was limited in Harbin except at the CER headquarters, which were set on fire five times during the period from November 1905 to January 1906 (Li Shuxiao 1986, pp. 20–21). A general strike on the railway in December 1905 soon collapsed because of internal conflicts within the strike committee. Apparently the Chinese population in Harbin was not involved in the events. The movement in Harbin was finally repressed in January 1906, although more mildly than in Russia proper, and the restoration of order was accompanied by a reform program that produced some modest improvements for the CER workers.[8] For the Russian authorities in Harbin, the situation was saved for the moment, but in the wake of the military defeat to Japan, a major change of the status quo was on its way.

Local Historical Research

The closer one gets to the zero point of Harbin history in 1898, the less there is to say about the Chinese side of the story. For the first decade or more foreign sources are indispensable and very often the only to be found. This situation preconditions the Harbin historians' choice of subjects. Diplomatic history has come to play a large role in local historical studies, and the Harbin local history community is well equipped with people who are masters of the Russian and Japanese sources. It also draws on experts in diplomatic and other special branches of history in dealing with the Russian presence in Manchuria and with the larger political setting. Major articles and monographs cover topics such as the history of the CER (e.g., Zheng Changchun 1987) and the economic imperialism of tsarist Russia in Manchuria (Kong and Zhu 1986).

As for city history in a strict sense, coverage of the first decade is sporadic because of the obvious scarcity of Chinese source materials. In the case of the Boxer confrontation, a Russian text from that period was translated and published explicitly because of the scarcity of Chinese material on the topic ("A Record of the Participation of the CER Railway Guards in the Manchurian Incident of 1900," in *Haerbin shizhi*, no. 2 [1984]: 57–76). The Chinese translation was duly equipped with warnings regarding the imperialistic viewpoints in the text. Much work consists in the search for information on the origins of various institutions and enterprises in Harbin—"the first brewery (telephone, newspaper, etc.) in the city." Such data are ambiguous, however, being on the one hand early manifestations of modernization, on the other hand symbols of foreign presence. A genuine Chinese interest in positive Russian contributions is brought out mainly in articles and monographs on architecture, including the Russian churches, where foreign influence is presented in a favorable light.

One might have expected some interest in the revolutionary movement of 1905, particularly the Bolshevik organization in Harbin, but the topic is not very well covered by the local historians, who appear to regard such matters as belonging to "foreign affairs." A 1976 article in the leading historical journal *Historical Research* (Lishi yanjiu) described a strike in November–December 1905 by the Chinese CER workers in Harbin, taking advantage of the turmoil among the Russians to raise their own demands (Haerbin cheliang gongchang lishi bianxiezu 1976, pp. 84–89). The strike supposedly lasted for more than fifty days and was finally suppressed by the Russian military. In the 1980s, however, reference to this strike has been dropped, so in all probability it was actually a Russian strike, misinterpreted in 1976 as an example of the struggle of the Chinese workers.

Open City, Russian Domination: 1907–1917

The Political Framework

The Russian regime in Harbin survived the military defeat to Japan and the internal political turmoil, but in the larger picture the Russian presence in Harbin and all of Northern Manchuria was shaken at its very foundations.

As pointed out by R. K. I. Quested, the Russian plans in Manchuria had in a sense failed already *before* the Russo-Japanese War (Quested 1982, pp. 155–56). Economically the CER had been a very costly adventure for the Russian treasury, and the expected benefits in terms of trade had failed to materialize.[9] Military force had been relied on to a far greater extent than originally envisaged by Count Witte, who had hoped to nurture collaborationist forces within Manchuria and gain control by largely peaceful means. Russian migration to Manchuria was unorganized, and the attempts to attract Russian peasant settlers had totally failed. As for winning over the Chinese population in Manchuria through education and religion, once again very little had been achieved. The dream of a "Yellow Russia" had collapsed, and henceforth Russian policy in the region was to be mainly defensive, trying to save at least some of the CER investments, although the battle cry for annexation was occasionally heard, not least from the Russian population in Harbin.

For the Chinese, the Russian defeat to Japan offered new opportunities to enlist the support of the commercial powers, above all the United States, in the ongoing struggle to contain the territorial ambitions of Russia and Japan in Manchuria (Hunt 1973, pp. 119ff.). The Qing court tried to strengthen its position by turning the Northeast into a testing ground for administrative reforms, and it reorganized provincial governments in Heilongjiang and Jilin in 1908. At the same time preparations for constitutional government were initiated and "local self-government research bureaus" set up at various administrative levels in the two provinces.

The political struggle around the structure of municipal administration in Harbin 1905–9 became a test case of the new balance of power in Manchuria. After the Russo-Japanese War Russia started to take steps toward a formalized structure of Russian civil administration in the CER zone and in Harbin as a reaction to mounting Chinese pressure. In October 1905 a Chinese official, Du Xueying, was appointed to reside in Harbin (i.e., Harbin proper, not the adjoining "Chinese section" of the city) on a provisory basis (Li Shuxiao 1986, p. 20). He at once began to collect taxes from the Chinese in the CER zone but was stopped by the Russians. According to Quested, this official "spoke Russian fluently . . . and vigorously tried to uphold Chinese interests, although his powers were slight compared with Khorvat's [Horwath] within the railway zone" (Quested 1982, p. 183). By spring of 1906 there were reports of incessant disputes between the Russian and Chinese officials in Harbin. But Russian privileges were equally threatened by the provisions in the Treaty of Portsmouth, which stipulated that in Manchuria Russia had not "any territorial advantages or preferential or exclusive concessions in impairment of Chinese sovereignty or inconsistent with the principle of equal opportunity" (MacMurray 1921, p. 523). The United States had in fact advocated the "opening" of Harbin, among other Chinese cities, as early as 1903 (Hunt 1973, p. 70); and in December 1905 the opening of sixteen cities and towns in Manchuria, among them Harbin, was included in the Sino-Japanese Treaty of Peking (MacMurray 1921, pp. 549–53). On January 7, 1907, China officially declared the opening of Harbin along with several other Manchurian cities.

In August–October 1906, a series of conferences was held in St. Petersburg on the question of how to preserve Russian domination in North Manchuria, and in December 1906 a set of "General Regulations of Civil Administration" in the CER zone were published (Tang 1959, p. 74). Also in 1906, a committee of fifteen leading citizens, including two Chinese, was set up in Harbin to discuss the question of municipal administration. The Russian population in Harbin were initially opposed to the idea of a municipal government because they feared heavy taxes, but they were won over by an emissary from the Russian Ministry of Finance (Quested 1982, p. 189). In November 1907 the CER announced its intention of establishing its own local administrations in Harbin and other North Manchurian cities on the railway.

During this period the Russian authorities made a serious miscalculation when they decided in 1906 to site the new Russian consulate in Harbin itself rather than in Fujiadian outside the CER zone. When the U.S. consul arrived in October 1906, the Russians also made him open his office in Harbin, hoping to obtain de facto U.S. recognition of Russia's special position in the city (Quested 1982, p. 168). Only with the Chinese announcement of the opening of Harbin on January 7, 1907, did the Russian government realize its mistake: by siting the consulates, including its own, in Harbin, the Chinese argument concerning Chinese sovereignty in the city was reinforced. Soon the other powers also moved their consuls into Harbin.

The reform-minded general governor of the three northeastern provinces Xu Shichang had urged the Peking government to resist the Russian plans regarding municipal administration as soon as they were announced in 1907, and the Chinese Foreign Ministry sent its first note of protest in January 1908 (Tang 1959, p. 75). The disagreement revolved around the different Russian and Chinese interpretations of the CER contract mentioned above. The Chinese government managed to enlist the support of the Western commercial powers, who were going to be deprived of "normal" treaty port privileges by the Russian move. The U.S. State Department took the lead in marshaling Western opposition to the Russian plans, while striving to remain uninvolved in the sovereignty issue. The U.S. position was simply that it would prefer municipal administration "based upon extraterritorial rights under the treaties rather than upon an erroneous construction of the railroad grant" (U.S. Secretary of State Elihu Root, April 1908, quoted in Hunt 1973, p. 141). Japan did not join the protests, and the Japanese consul in Harbin chose to cooperate closely with the Russian authorities. Russo-Japanese relations in Harbin remained friendly throughout the 1907–17 period.

Despite the protests of the Chinese government as well as the Western consuls in Harbin, the Russian authorities proceeded with their program, and in March 1908 the first elections for the "self-administrative council" were held with 1,440 qualified (i.e., wealthy) Russian voters and 255 Chinese, who refused, however, to take part in the election (Quested 1982, p. 189). An ordinance was issued imposing fines or imprisonment on those who refused to comply with the new administration or to pay taxes. Many Chinese and Western residents in Harbin did in fact refuse to pay the taxes, and many Chinese shops were closed by the Russian authorities in retaliation (Tang 1959, p. 76). The Sino-Russian conflict on this matter rolled back and forth until a settlement was reached in May 1909, which provided for Chinese recognition of the Russian "self-administrative councils" in Harbin and other cities on the CER line in return for Russian recognition of Chinese sovereignty within the zone. The negotiations were complicated by internal Russian differences of opinion between the Russian Foreign Ministry on one side and the CER company backed by the Ministry of Finance on the other (Quested 1982, pp. 190–91). What emerged was a Russo-Chinese condominium—with Russia as the dominant partner—rather than a treaty port structure, leaving the legal status of Harbin as unclear as ever. The status of the heads of the newly formed Chinese provincial bureaus of foreign affairs was equated to that of CER General Manager D. L. Horwath, and the new Chinese chief magistrate in Harbin, Shi Zhaoji (Alfred Sze), was allowed to appoint three leading Chinese to join the Harbin municipal council (Quested 1982, p. 192). The Western powers did not readily accept this compromise, however, although in practice Western nationals in Harbin cooperated with the Russian authorities. Official recognition by the European countries of the power structure in Harbin did not come until around 1914, and the United States held out with its opposition throughout.

The Russian "self-administrative council" has been covered in two long articles by one of the most prominent experts on early Harbin history, Zhu Xianping of the Institute of Economic Management, Jilin University (Zhu Xianping 1986, 1988). His treatment is thorough and very reliable, although there are obvious differences of perspective compared to Russian and Western accounts of the matter. The leading role of the U.S. State Department in the Western opposition to the Russian strategy is conspicuously less emphasized, and the internal contradictions among the Russians are ignored. Furthermore, the 1909 agreement is considered a defeat for China, because it did not attain de facto political control of Harbin. The analytical model is the Leninist theory of imperialism, focusing on the intraimperialist rivalry.

The Russo-Chinese relationship was shaken by a new series of crises in 1910–11. In January 1910 the Chinese authorities banned the export of soybeans and wheat from Jilin and Heilongjiang. The purpose was to break the domination of foreign and Russian firms in Harbin's grain trade, and the embargo was initiated by a group of officials led by a Chinese businessman —soon to become the supreme Chinese official in Harbin—struggling to enter that market (Quested 1982, p. 197); the effort was given up after a month because of Russian pressure. This opportunity to study the brutality of cutthroat capitalist competition and the role of the Chinese in it is passed over by the Harbin historians, who see only a Chinese governmental effort to "prevent hunger among the local Chinese peasants"—the official Chinese reason for the ban—and the ensuing Russian trampling on Chinese sovereignty (Zhu Xianping 1985–86, pp. 100–101). A major outbreak of the plague in the autumn of 1910, killing around 7,000 Chinese and some 40 Europeans in Harbin, did not in itself harm relations, since Western and Chinese doctors cooperated in the fight against the epidemic, but it added to the general feeling of insecurity. Early in the spring of 1911 Russo-Chinese relations became very tense, and rumors spread of impending war. The war scare hit harder in Harbin than elsewhere, with mobilization of military reserves and evacuation of women and children in March 1911, but the crisis passed quickly. The collapse of the Qing dynasty at the end of 1911 had minimal repercussions among the Chinese in Harbin, and Sun Yat-sen's Tongmenghui (Alliance League) failed to realize plans for setting up a branch in the city (Zhang, Ma, and Li 1981, p. 81).

For a while in early 1913 Harbin became the stage for a Russian effort to pave the way for annexation of North Manchuria, and once again in February 1913 war rumors circulated in the city (Quested 1982, p. 239). In the end the degeneration of Chinese political power in the region offered to the Russians the far cheaper option of dominating northern Manchuria through the manipulation of Heilongjiang warlords, and when in 1915 all the CER guards were sent off to Russia's western front in World War I, Russia's own position was very much weakened. The logical outcome was an increasing Russian reliance on Japan in the last years of the tsarist East Asian adventure.

Life in the City

Harbin's economic vitality soon recovered from the slump of 1907–8 and developed by leaps and bounds in the 1909–17 period. Having lost their foothold in South Manchuria the Russians directed all their energy toward turning the CER, with Harbin as its center, into a profitable enterprise, while at the same time competition from the Japanese and Western businesses in Harbin as well as from the rapidly growing Chinese business community contributed to the economic vigor of the city. By 1909 Harbin was firmly established as the commercial center of North Manchuria with the grain trade—wheat and soybeans—as the backbone. The trade volume in Harbin doubled between 1908 and 1914. Light industry, banking, and other services followed suit. A Harbin Stock Exchange opened in June 1907, fulfilling also the role of a chamber of commerce; a Chinese stock exchange was established in Fujiadian as well as a Chinese commercial association.

Despite the redirection of the CER toward commercial purposes the company continued its poor economic performance, running at a loss until 1915. The main reason for this was the high cost of various CER institutions in the railway zone rather than the operation of the railway itself, but the company was also much criticized for its inefficiency and corruption.[10] In contrast, the southern section of the line, which was taken over by Japan in 1905 and renamed the South Manchurian Railway, soon became the most profitable railroad in China (Huenemann 1984, pp. 190–91). The fortunes of the Russian business community in Harbin followed a similar pattern, with a dwindling share of manufacture and trade relative to the Japanese, the Westerners, and the Chinese after 1908. For example, Russian-owned flour mills numbered fifteen in 1911 but just five in 1913; and only two Russian firms ventured into the profitable soy extraction business, while by 1917 there were seventeen other such enterprises, most of them owned by Chinese (Quested 1982, pp. 210–13). European companies made significant inroads in industry and commerce, but the Japanese took the lead with a trebling of the import of Japanese goods between 1911 and 1914. On the eve of World War I there were about 1,000 Japanese in Harbin, and Japan had emerged as the leading foreign business power. Russian enterprises remained by far the most numerous in the non-Chinese business world, but most of these firms were small-scale light industrial or commercial enterprises. Also on the eve of World War I, Harbin had 1,151 registered businesses with a capital of more than 1,500 rubles within the CER zone (i.e., excluding Fujiadian); Russian enterprises constituted 78 percent of these (Zhu Xianping 1985–86, p. 70). Further down the ladder there were some 800 Chinese businesses within the zone, the vast majority being small handicraft and commercial undertakings. Only some twenty Chinese enterprises could count as modern industrial units, and they contributed only 15 percent of the output value of Chinese manufacturing in Harbin (Zhao Dejiu 1986, pp. 45–46). Despite its humble beginnings the Chinese business community was highly dynamic; the ascendancy of Chinese entrepreneurs in the milling business, gaining further momentum with the outbreak of World War I, is reflected in Texts 2C and 2D.

Political life in Harbin remained dominated by the CER; the power of the company was in part delegated to the municipal council, and the CER leadership was anxious to enlist the involvement of the business community in local politics. This effort was only moderately successful, and the cost was increased friction and differences of opinion on issues such as municipal schooling. The Chinese boycotted the 1911 election as they had done in 1908, but in 1914 they filled two seats in a chamber of fifty-one members (Quested 1982, pp. 270–71).

R. K. I. Quested has pulled together from a large number of sources a rich description of social life in Harbin's Russian community from 1907 to 1917 (Quested 1982, pp. 255–79). Social divisions within this community remained conspicuous and were further complicated with the emergence of a Russian intelligentsia and a middle class. High society was tied to CER officialdom. Intellectual life was stimulated by the high standards of educational facilities and the fine library of the Railway Club, and several newspapers flourished. As for the middle class, the Jewish community played a large role with around 1,500 members in 1910, growing to a few thousand by 1917. There was a large Russian underclass, from the families of railway guards and workers of the railway workshops to servants and *droskhy* drivers. Russians and Chinese remained at a long distance from each other; it is remarkable that only a single marriage between a Russian man and a Chinese woman in Harbin has been recorded in the pre-1917 period (Quested 1982, p. 276). Relations were best at the highest social level, at least when pro-Russian Chinese officials were in office, and there was a growing interest in Chinese culture among Russian intellectuals, as indicated by the formation of a Society of Orientalists in 1909. But further down the social ladder racial hostility was evident, and the attitudes of the Russian population toward the Chinese gradually came to resemble the contemporary Western colonialist world outlook.

Local Historical Research

In local historical research the emergence of Chinese social forces, institutions, and enterprises is very closely covered. An example is Text 2E, "Harbin Workers Were the First to Commemorate May Day," a topic that has received particular attention because of the pioneering role of Harbin's Chinese population in what was apparently the first May First demonstration in all of China.[11] Equal attention is paid to the first Chinese entrepreneurs who began to expand their businesses during this period. The focus on Chinese entrepreneurship in the early part of the twentieth century became significant in Harbin historical research after the mid-1980s and is obviously related to the contemporary economic reforms. Much less is said about the industrial ventures initiated by the Chinese authorities in Harbin in fields such as electricity supply, shipping, and sugar manufacturing. The investments of Chinese "bureaucrat-capitalist" enterprises up to 1913 in fact surpassed private Chinese investments by 50 percent (Zhao Dejiu 1986, p. 46).

One of the significant recurring themes in Harbin local historical research is Russian economic imperialism. This topic involves the theoretical problem of the relationship between rapid economic growth in Russian-ruled Harbin and the "destructiveness" of economic imperialism, particularly vis-à-vis the "national bourgeoisie." There is no disagreement among Harbin historians on the issue of Russian motives, and condemnation of tsarist Russia's "rapaciousness" and "greed" is universal. However, the condemnation often seems formalistic, dodging the theoretical dilemma. A text may describe how a certain kind of business or social phenomenon emerged in the early days of Harbin, most often directly related to the activities of the Russian population. The concluding condemnation of "Russian imperialist aggression and plunder" seems to serve a ritualistic rather than an analytic purpose; without it the writer might be accused of presenting the economic activities of the Russians in a favorable light, contradicting the official line on "foreign economic penetration of China" before the establishment of the People's Republic.

The substance of the issue was confronted in the main journal of Harbin historiography, *Harbin History and Gazetteer*, which in its two first issues in 1985 and 1986 carried a long article aiming to prove that the Russian economic activity in Harbin was in fact destructive in nature and thus refute the "fallacy of a connection between the Russian imperialist investments and the economic development of Harbin" (Zhu Xianping 1985–86, p. 63). The author is again Zhu Xianping, who presents an orthodox Marxist-Leninist line of thought. Zhu's argument can be summed up in five main points:

1. The Russian investments in Harbin in the early part of the twentieth century were not a "decisive element" in the economic development of the city. There was already an internally generated, autonomous Chinese process of economic development in the making, an early stage of Chinese industrialization based on the already existing handicraft industries and the production of soybeans in the area. "If not for the penetration of imperial-

ism Harbin would have continued to develop in a normal way and would gradually have produced an independent capitalist transformation" (Zhu Xianping 1985–86, p. 65).

2. The Chinese national bourgeoisie in Harbin was in fact prevented by the Russians from expanding "in a normal way" because of discrimination, exorbitant taxes, expropriation, and so on. As a result, Chinese-owned enterprises in the city rarely made the leap from family-based small-scale operations to large-scale businesses.

3. The economic development of Harbin was "distorted" by the Russian presence to the extent that commercial capital won a domineering position over industrial capital.

4. The Russian influence laid Harbin open to a massive import of Russian merchandise, while at the same time raw materials from the Harbin region were exported in a big way, producing a colonial-type economic structure of dependency.

5. Private Russian investments in the early stage of Harbin's economic development "in no way originated in Russia. . . . The so-called spontaneous growth of Russian capital in Harbin without exception came from expropriation of Chinese property, either directly or indirectly" (Zhu Xianping 1985–86, p. 70).

Zhu's arguments presuppose a "normal development" of capitalism that appears highly abstract. One important aspect of the "Russian factor" that is excluded from Zhu's discussion is the CER. The railway was the original raison d'être of Harbin, and Zhu does not deny the significance of investments by the Russian *state* related to the railway, but he nevertheless leaves this aspect out of his argument, which deals only with *private* capitalist investments in Harbin. One might argue that this distinction is artificial. Zhu's first four points are all derived from Lenin's 1917 work, *Imperialism as the Highest Stage of Capitalism*, while the fifth point, explaining Russian investments as based on expropriation of Chinese property, draws on the theory of Karl Marx on the "primitive accumulation of capital," that is, an essentially precapitalist form of exploitation, which serves as a starting point for capitalist accumulation in the strict sense.

Zhu Xianping's orthodox Marxist-Leninist analysis was soon contradicted, however. A group of writers from the Harbin Trade Department argued that "the penetration of tsarist Russian imperialism constituted, on the one hand, a kind of aggression and national suppression, but on the other hand it also provided an impetus for the rapid development of capitalist economic relations in the Northeast and Harbin" (Wei, Yang, and Wang 1986, p. 23). The subjective purpose of Russian imperialism was the conquest of China, but "objectively it stimulated the opening up of the Northeast, the immigration of people, the development of a commodity economy, and a great upsurge in industry and trade" (Wei, Yang, and Wang 1986, p. 24).

The issue has been left open in Harbin historiography with no apparent intervention by higher levels, and the case demonstrates that Marxism-Leninism is in fact interpreted differently by individual researchers in the local historical community. As of 1989 the debate was still on, and in fact the issue is as old as Marxism itself is in Harbin.[12] But regardless of which view is taken on the effects of Russian economic imperialism, a basic difference remains between Chinese accounts of Harbin's economic history and Western interpretations: the Harbin historians tend to overlook the economic failure of the Russians relative to the Japanese, Westerners, and Chinese.[13] In Harbin historiography the economic might of the Russians is taken for granted. This blind angle seems dictated by frustrated nationalist feelings rather than imprinted by the theoretical heritage of Marxism-Leninism.[14]

Whites and Warlords: 1917–1932

The Political Framework

In the period from the 1917 Russian revolution to the Japanese conquest of Harbin in 1932 the political framework became extremely complex because of fundamental internal changes affecting the key countries with an interest in Manchuria as well as changes in the international political system. After the Russian revolution Harbin became a point of contention between Russian revolutionary and counterrevolutionary forces; Chinese political efforts in Harbin became confused with the emergence of distinct and competing policy-making arenas, from the level of the Peking government to the regional power of Zhang Zuolin in Manchuria and the rivaling warlord cliques in northern Manchuria. Japan emerged with an even larger potential power in Manchuria after World War I, but internal political democratization and the effects of international cooperation in the 1920s moderated Japanese imperialism for a period of time after 1922.

The 1917 Russian revolution had an immediate and powerful impact in Harbin (see Quested 1982, pp. 295–324; Gladeck 1972, pp. 63–139; Tang 1959, pp. 114–21). When news of the establishment of the provisional government in St. Petersburg reached Harbin in March 1917, an executive committee was immediately formed, seriously weakening the authority of CER management. A soviet (Russ., council) was also formed by the railway workers. During the summer of 1917 a power triangle between General

Manager Horwath, the executive committee, and the soviet emerged. The crisis escalated during the autumn of 1917 as wealthy Russians began to move to Harbin from Russia while left-wing émigré Russians made stopovers in Harbin on their way back. News of the October Revolution reached Harbin on November 7. Bolsheviks gained a majority in the Harbin soviet in late November, and on December 4 they were instructed by Lenin to seize power from Horwath, who was under pressure from the Western consuls to invite Chinese troops into the city in order to subdue the Bolsheviks and at the same time forestall a Japanese occupation of the railway zone. When the Bolshevik proclamation of power in Harbin came on December 12, that was in fact the outcome: on December 26 Chinese troops disarmed some 2,000 revolutionary Russian militiamen, who were packed onto trains and sent back to Russia. For the moment—and for the first time ever—the Chinese were in control of the CER zone. A Chinese president of the CER was also appointed in December. This post had been vacant since 1900, when the first Chinese president of the CER had been executed by the Boxers and Russia had refused to accept the appointment of a successor.

The struggle for control of the CER became even more complex in the following years as Horwath joined forces with the anti-Bolshevik leaders Aleksandr Vasil'evich Kolchak and Grigorii Mikhailovich Semenov, while Japan strove to increase its power in North Manchuria through the Allied intervention in Siberia in 1918–22. In October 1918 Japanese troops had de facto control over Harbin and the railway zone, and to counter a possible Japanese annexation of North Manchuria the United States took the lead in establishing the Inter-Allied Committee entrusted with the supervision of the Siberian railway system and the CER. The Technical Board associated with the committee was led by the American railway engineer J. F. Stevens and had its headquarters in Harbin. The CER remained under the supervision of this structure from early 1919 to late 1922, when the last Japanese soldiers were finally evacuated from Siberia. In the meanwhile Horwath lost the last vestiges of power in 1920 after a general strike among the CER workers in March 1920 as well as pressure from the Jilin governor, who was concurrently serving as president of the CER. Forces loyal to Zhang Zuolin disarmed the Russians in the railway zone—whites as well as reds— and Zhang gained military control of the CER, although technical management of the railway was entrusted to White Russian experts, who concentrated on making the line profitable.

Soon the Soviet Union emerged as a new player in Manchuria. Soviet overtures toward China regarding the CER in the 1918–24 period have been analyzed in several studies. A Soviet offer of July 1919 for the return of the

CER to China without compensation created a stir in China, but the offer was restated in September 1920 as a proposition for a "special treaty" between China and the Soviet Union (Whiting 1953, pp. 24–33, 142, 149; Tang 1959, pp. 137–40). Protracted negotiations led to the establishment of Sino-Soviet diplomatic relations in May 1924 and an agreement providing that "the rights of the two Governments arising out of the Contract of August 27, 1896, for the construction and operation of the Chinese Eastern Railway . . . shall be maintained" until the various questions relating to the CER could be settled at a special conference (Whiting 1953, pp. 278–79). The instability of the Peking government prevented this conference from producing any results. Sino-Soviet joint management of the CER, with the Soviet Union as the dominant partner, was inaugurated in October 1924, but on a shaky legal foundation.

Within the CER zone the new Soviet general manager, A. N. Ivanov, was quite successful in stamping out White Russian influence during 1925, but less effective in securing a working relationship with his Chinese partners. In January 1926 the Soviet CER managers were arrested on the order of Zhang Zuolin because they refused to transport Zhang's troops on credit (Lensen 1974). They were soon released, but Chinese efforts to shake off Soviet domination of the CER continued with new crises and clashes every year. After the break in diplomatic relations between China and the Soviet Union in 1927 the Soviet position in Manchuria was still strong enough to avoid the breakdown that befell Soviet interests elsewhere in China. But Zhang Xueliang, having taken over in Manchuria after the Japanese assassination of his father in 1928, continued the harassment of the Soviet representatives, culminating in the "little war" (also known as the "CER Incident") of 1929. On May 27, 1929, Manchurian police raided the Soviet consulate general in Harbin, arresting dozens of Soviet consular officials, and in July the CER was seized by Zhang Xueliang's military forces while the Nanjing government on July 20 announced its decision to break off relations with the Soviet Union. A vigorous but limited Soviet invasion of Manchuria in November 1929 quickly crushed the resistance of Zhang Xueliang's troops, forcing the Chinese to restore the *status quo ante*.

The fighting did not reach Harbin, although one source claims that there were some acts of Soviet sabotage against the telephone network and local railway tracks during the summer of 1929 (Tang 1959, pp. 207–8). The foreign consuls in Harbin were apparently far more worried about an outbreak of looting by demoralized retreating Chinese soldiers than about Soviet attacks (Lensen 1974, p. 72).

Despite Soviet military victory the Zhang Xueliang regime continued its opposition to Soviet influence in North Manchuria. An even more important concern for Moscow, however, was avoiding conflict with Japan. When the Japanese Guandong Army unleashed its forces on Manchuria in September 1931 the Soviet Union declared its neutrality and eventually sold its stake in the CER to Japan in 1935.

Life in the City

The turbulence and revolutionary fervor of the 1917–20 period shook the foundations of Harbin. The city was inundated with refugees from Russia, and the Russian population swelled, according to one source, from 34,200 in 1916 to 120,000 in 1922, adding a large and volatile element to the urban population (Stephan 1978, p. 40). The Chinese population also experienced a rapid increase, from around 45,000 in 1916 to 94,000 in 1918 (Lee 1983, p. 27). A number of strikes have been put on record during this period, and often the Russian and Chinese workers joined forces, re-establishing a link that appears to have been inactive in the years from 1908 to 1917. Chinese workers were involved in protests and strikes from early 1917, and during the years 1917 to 1919 a total of thirty-six strikes has been recorded in Harbin (Liu Shaotang 1989, p. 148; for an overview of important strikes in Manchuria 1905–25 see Lee 1983, pp. 29–31), culminating in the March 1920 general strike that helped unseat Horwath.[15] In October 1918 the first Chinese labor organization, the "Industrial Peace Preservation Association" (Gongye weichihui) was set up in the CER workshops, and despite the "official" character of this organization it played a significant role in the strikes of 1919 and 1920 (Zhang Fushan 1984). The immediate cause of these strikes was economical, the workers protesting payment in prerevolution rubles, which were rapidly losing their value. But nationalist sentiments also became visible in the agitation among the Chinese workers at this time (Lee 1983, p. 32).

Industry and commerce suffered no less from the chaotic currency situation, and the frequent stoppages of CER transport as well as anti-Japanese boycotts added to the economic woes in 1917–19. There was a modest recovery from 1919 to 1921, but the postwar depression hit Harbin very hard in 1922–24 with a grave slump in the grain trade (Teng 1986, p. 41). According to one source, the Harbin oil mills suspended production in 1921, and by 1923 half the city's flour mills were said to be bankrupt (Sun 1969, p. 62). A recovery followed in the 1925–28 period, spurred by a new wave of foreign investment, but the revival was sluggish compared to industrial development in Japanese-dominated South Manchuria (Sun 1969, p. 63).

Beneath this sluggishness, however, the advances of the Chinese business community continued unabated. Bankrupt Russian firms were bought up by Chinese entrepreneurs, who also fanned out into new trades such as shoe making and printing while consolidating their position in the oil and grain milling businesses. Some 400 private Chinese firms were established in the 1914–22 period, and by 1931 their number had grown to 1,200 (Zhao Dejiu n.d., pp. 197–98). The technological level of these enterprises was generally low; Harbin nevertheless emerged as the leading city of Chinese entrepreneurship in the Northeast. By 1929, 57 percent of the combined product value of the Manchurian national capitalist enterprises was created in Harbin, compared with only 17 percent in Dalian and 7 percent in Changchun (Zhao Dejiu n.d., p. 203). Chinese entrepreneurs thus successfully moved into the vacuum created by the demise of Russian influence. The Japanese managed to maintain their position as the leading foreign business community, but their investments and trade in Harbin were increasingly challenged during the 1920s by Chinese nationalist movements and campaigns, which in this way served as a supporting force for the Chinese industrialists.[16]

Administration and local politics in Harbin became very complex and fluid in the 1920s. The Municipal Council, dominated by the White Russian émigré community, was shaken by the 1924 Soviet takeover of CER management, but it continued to operate within the original CER zone in Harbin until 1926, while the other sections of the city fell under the control of competing warlord groups. The Municipal Council was defeated by a combination of local opposition and Chinese authorities, as described in Text 2C. The council was replaced by a Self-Government Committee, and the districts within the former CER zone were placed under the supervision of an Executive Bureau of the Special Region of the Eastern Provinces controlled by Zhang Zuolin (Zou 1985, p. 78). Elections were held for the newly established Self-Government Committee in October 1926 with 6,682 qualified voters. Two Russian representatives were allowed to join the committee, and in 1928 a Japanese representative was also admitted (Zhang Chunlin 1986, p. 115).

Despite the growing force of the Chinese in the city's economic and political life, the large Russian community remained the most conspicuous feature of Harbin during the 1920s, and a number of travelers' reports from that period focus primarily on the tragic decline of this relic of prerevolutionary Russia.[17] Wealthy refugees continued their aristocratic lifestyle as long as their money lasted; eventually many of them joined ranks with the rapidly growing poverty-stricken Russian underclass. The city was thick with political intrigues and competing anti-Bolshevik organizations, all of them infiltrated by Soviet agents (Stephan 1978, pp. 43–45).

Social relations between foreigners and Chinese took a new turn under these circumstances. As the Russian refugees gradually came to realize that their exile was permanent, some chose to accept living among Chinese. The 1920s were also the heyday of the Christian mission in Harbin. This was primarily a European and American endeavor, as the Russian Orthodox church had never occupied itself much with proselytizing among Chinese. But the Western missionaries in Harbin often saw their efforts frustrated by growing Chinese national sentiments.[18]

The great nationalist movements and campaigns of the 1920s were all echoed in Harbin, but after the chaos of the 1917–20 period Harbin became tightly controlled by reactionary warlords, and progressive movements in the city only developed slowly and under the shadow of powerful repression. A Guomindang (Nationalist Party) branch was not established until September 1925 (Lee 1983, p. 53), and the Harbin branch of the Chinese Communist Party (CCP), although established as early as 1923, went through a number of crises and reconstructions during the decade.[19] The above-mentioned Chinese trade union in the CER workshops degenerated after the strike wave of 1917–20 into a "yellow" organization allied with the CER management. The difficulties of the CCP in gaining a strong foothold in Harbin, which had 65,000 workers by 1922 with fresh experiences of strikes and revolutionary struggle, may be ascribed to a combination of neglect and political misguidance. Soviet representatives and Russian workers employed by the CER failed to support the local Chinese Communists, who in 1927 complained about the "obstinacy" and "unreasonableness" of their Russian comrades (Lee 1983, p. 66). Until 1928, the national leadership of the CCP also assigned low priority to Manchuria, which was seen as far removed from the main centers of revolutionary activity. Conditions for revolutionary work in Manchuria differed from other parts of China; CCP cadres sent to the region reported back that the struggle against Japanese imperialism, implying a broad united front, should be the main task in Manchuria, but the CCP leadership urged them to concentrate on organizing the industrial proletariat (Lee 1983, p. 61). In 1927 the CCP membership dropped from 130 members to only 30, and organizational activities came to a temporary halt.

In the late 1920s the credibility of the local Communists was further weakened by the Sino-Soviet conflict over the CER. Adhering to the party line of "defending the Soviet Union against imminent imperialist attack" amounted to calling for a Chinese defeat in the conflict. A glimpse of this dilemma is provided in Text 2F, which narrates the political development of a young girl in Harbin. A Communist-controlled trade union was organized in the "thirty-six barracks" attached to the CER workshops in 1930, but on the eve of the Japanese occupation it had only seventy-one members (Lee

1983, p. 137). The efforts of the CCP cadres were undermined by internal conflicts and mutual accusations, including the defection to "Trotskyism" by one of the leading CCP labor organizers in 1930.[20]

Local Historical Research

Insignificant as the results of the CCP's efforts in Harbin during the 1920s may appear it is nevertheless one of the most important topics of contemporary Harbin historiography. The activities of the early CCP organizers are covered in great detail interspersed with significant omissions. The general tone of uninterrupted victorious advance is misleading, and political analysis is remarkably scant. Immaturity and rashness is conceded to, such as the case of Chen Weiren—one of the two CCP organizers sent to Harbin in 1923 to start up a party branch there—who wrote a jubilant editorial in the local progressive newspaper *Dawn* (Chenguangbao) on the occasion of the 1923 Tokyo earthquake (Han Tiesheng 1980, p. 35). But the fundamental issue of how to develop revolutionary struggle under the special conditions in the Northeast is not discussed. The conflicts between Soviet representatives and Chinese Communists in Harbin, although clearly expressed by Chen Weiren in a 1927 report, go unmentioned in contemporary scholarship. The political difficulties regarding the CER issue after 1927 are not analyzed although they are closely related to the emergence of the "Li Lisan line" in the CCP national leadership 1929–30 and could have provided a fine opportunity to explain the substance of that matter. Even the treatment of the rather clear-cut case of "Trotskyist deviation" in 1930, described in several sources, docs not divulge what "Trotskyism" actually means.

The overall impression of early CCP activity in Harbin, as described by the local historians in available sources, is one of many promising beginnings with nothing in between. The political gropings of the first generation of CCP activists in the city are reduced to a question of "implementing the party line" (or failing to do so), and the issue of the specific conditions of Manchuria does not enter the picture. There is nothing surprising in this, and presumably more thoroughgoing research is actually taking place behind tightly closed doors. Nevertheless one can find a wealth of information on the social milieu of the 1920s in the available sources, particularly in the memoirs of old revolutionaries. As for the Sino-Soviet conflict in 1929, there were signs of a change of attitude in historical circles toward the late 1980s. A more critical view of Soviet policies was emerging, but signs of this change were more visible in general history writing than in party history.[21]

Local historical studies of the development of Chinese private capitalist enterprises in the 1920s conquered the stage after 1984, and the topic is today the single most covered in all the branches of local history. The general tone is matter-of-fact, focusing on technical and economic aspects, with explicit praise reserved for the anti-imperialist implications of early Chinese entrepreneurship. There is, however, an obvious intention of pointing out managerial and technical "lessons for the present" that might be of use in the current economic reforms, as reflected in Texts 2C and 2D on two successful Harbin entrepreneurs. In this matter the local history writing in Harbin faithfully follows a general trend in contemporary Chinese historiography.

Another important topic in the study of the 1917–32 period is the sovereignty issue and the struggle of the Chinese to regain control of Harbin and the CER. Several carefully researched studies cover themes such as the political control over currency issue, customs, and the legal system. But the towering topic is the CER, which involves sensitive political questions regarding the role not just of the Soviet Union but also of Zhang Zuolin and the Manchurian warlords, as well as the activities of the various foreign powers.

This debate opened in Harbin in 1984 with the publication of a provocative study by the historian Zhang Tong, covering the struggle for control of the CER in the 1917–24 period. On the politically sensitive issues, three of Zhang's conclusions merit attention:

• The role of the U.S. in the Inter-Allied Committee (1919–22) should be appreciated. Thanks to "vigorous U.S. opposition to Japan, the Chinese military gained control of the CER" (Zhang Tong 1984, p. 29).

• Zhang Zuolin objectively played a "certain role" in gaining control of the CER through his resistance to the Japanese-sponsored White Russian warlord Semenov (Zhang Tong 1984, p. 30).

• The 1924 Sino-Soviet Treaty on joint management of the CER was "a step backward compared with the first Karakhan Manifesto [of 1919]," which must be attributed to the feebleness of the Peking government (Zhang Tong 1984, p. 32).

Each of these points conflicts with official Chinese views held for decades. As could be expected, a reaction to Zhang Tong's article appeared the following year—without a direct reference, however—in an article by Lü Lingui. The main topic of Lü's article is the 1929 Sino-Soviet conflict, but he also covers the prehistory of that event, thus allowing a comparison of the two writers' accounts of the 1917–24 period. Simply put, Lü negates the three points in Zhang's article emphasized above. As for the 1924 Treaty, Lü sees it as a victory of the progressive forces over the reactionaries and imperialists. In Lü's account the main imperialist powers tried to prevent China from coming to terms with the Soviet Union, and the reactionary Peking government would gladly have succumbed to this interference had it not been for the "pressure of the Peking students and the firm attitude of the Soviet government" (Lü Lingui 1985, p. 48). Lü also emphasizes the great improvements for the Chinese CER workers during the period of Soviet management. Regarding the 1929 conflict Lü basically restates the time-honored formula of "defending the Soviet Union," quoting from the resolution of the CCP Central Committee of July 12, 1929, on the matter and concluding that the "true cause of the CER Incident is by no means the Soviet Union; the incident was caused by imperialism and the counterrevolutionary policy of the Guomindang" (Lü Lingui 1985, p. 51).

The crux of these disagreements is the relative weight of arguments relating to *nation* and *revolution*. The standard solution—in Maoist as well as in post-Mao historiography—is to see these two dimensions as essentially identical. But sometimes identification is impossible, as the case of the CER demonstrates, and differences of opinion are unavoidable. The trend in Harbin local historical writing during the 1980s is to choose nation rather than revolution, when a choice has to be made, but disagreement persists, as the Zhang vs. Lü debate illustrates.

Notes

1. Bu Ping et al. 1987, p. 136. The complete Chinese version of the CER Contract is reproduced on pp. 134–38. A discussion of the difference between the two versions can be found in Tang 1959, pp. 55–59.

2. MacMurray 1921, p. 76. According to Peter S. H. Tang, the English version derives from the Russian version, Tang 1959, p. 56.

3. Gladeck 1972, p. 51; Tang 1959, pp. 70–71. These local agreements in the Northeast were made during the Russian military occupation of Manchuria in the wake of the Boxer Uprising, and they were apparently not fully reported to the Peking government. The Chinese government did protest in 1902, however, against granting consultation rights to the Russians with respect to appointment of Chinese officials to the liaison offices.

4. According to the strongly nationalistic account of Peter S. H. Tang, the Russo-Chinese disputes over civil administration in Harbin began as early as 1898, when the Chinese Imperial Court dispatched Governor Xu Shichang to Harbin to organize a "self-administrative government" there to counter a series of municipal rules and regulations promulgated by the local Russian CER officials; Tang 1959, pp. 72–73. Tang's account appears flawed, however; it presents D. L. Horwath as the general manager of the CER as early as 1898, but that position was not established until 1902.

5. The construction work of the CER in Harbin is covered in Zheng Changchun 1988. In a study by Li Jitang (1987), professor of history at Harbin Normal University, Russian and Chinese sources are pulled together to produce a survey of the strategic, legal, and economic implications of the CER up to 1917.

6. The siege of Harbin in July–August 1900 has been described in great detail by G. A. Lensen, based on Russian sources, in Lensen 1967, pp. 140–59.

7. These features of Russo-Chinese social relations in the early years of Harbin contrast with Quested's general observation about "free and easy mixing of the lower-class Russians with the Chinese" in Manchuria in contradistinction to the racial segregation typical of Western imperialism in the nineteenth and twentieth centuries (Quested 1982, p. 329). It appears that "free and easy mixing" in Harbin never developed to any high degree, and in fact Quested's claim is contradicted by many writers, e.g., Owen Lattimore, who found that "[i]n the Russians, the remarkable Chinese faculty for absorption, which for many centuries has disposed of a succession of alien conquerors, appears to have met its match. The Russian exile community . . . remains stubbornly ignorant of China and uninterested in China." Lattimore 1975 [1935], p. 247.

8. According to Quested this mildness was the outcome of CER General Manager Horwath's personal insistence; Quested 1982, p. 152.

9. In fact the CER turned out to be more valuable to the Chinese as well as to Japanese, American, and British exporters than to the Russians. For an account of the Russian financial disaster in Manchuria in general and regarding the CER in particular, see Romanov 1974, pp. 31 ff., and Malozemoff 1958, pp. 186–96.

10. Quested 1982, pp. 222–31. For a statistical presentation of the CER's economic results, see Tang 1959, pp. 433–55.

11. According to Text 4A the first May Day demonstration in Harbin with Chinese participation was in 1907; there was in fact a small-scale demonstration that year, but the events described in Text 4A seem to have taken place on May 14, 1908, if we are to believe the Russian sources (Quested 1982, p. 179) and most other Chinese accounts (e.g., Li Shuxiao 1986, p. 30).

12. One of the first CCP organizers in Harbin, Li Zhenying, wrote in a 1923 report that the Northeast "developed into an area where culture is backward and where industry and commerce developed in a warped fashion by yielding to imperialism"; quoted in Lee 1983, p. 60.

13. One exception to this trend is Zhang Tong 1984, p. 26.

14. One can find a close parallel to the contemporary Harbin historians' view on Russian economic imperialism in the description by Peter Tang—by no means a Marxist-Leninist—of Russia's "excessive advantages in political, military, economic and cultural influences derived from the Chinese Eastern Railway" (Tang 1959, p. 112). Like the Harbin historians, Tang is inclined to exaggerate the Russian "successes."

15. According to the 1976 *Lishi yanjiu* article on the revolutionary activities of the Chinese CER workers, the Chinese workers in the main repair workshop joined in the revolutionary fervor of the time by setting fire in April 1917 to a garage building with fifteen newly repaired passenger coaches; Haerbin cheliang gongchang lishi bianxiezu 1976, p. 87. A strike in 1917 by Chinese restaurant waiters had a more comic note to it. At the height of the supper hour, the waiters would "storm into the restaurants, throw food on the patrons, and argue heatedly with the owners"; Gladeck 1972, p. 68.

16. The memoirs of first-generation Harbin activist Han Tiesheng provide an interesting account of how in 1923 the first nucleus of radical intellectuals in Harbin managed to enlist crucial economic support from a local businessman by helping him forestall aggressive Japanese competition in his trade through anti-Japanese agitation (Han Tiesheng 1980, pp. 33–34).

17. A description of the Harbin Russian community after the 1917 revolution, based on a number of travelers' reports, is provided in Hinrichs 1987, pp. 18–21. For a fascinating account see Stephan 1978, pp. 39–47.

18. The frustrations of the missionaries are fully reflected in the annual reports of the Danish mission in Harbin to the Danish Missionary Society. In 1925 most of the mission's work collapsed because of the Chinese congregation's objections to foreign domination; Madsen 1926, pp. 75–86.

19. There is a large body of studies in Harbin local history of the first years of the CCP branch in the city. An authoritative summary of this scholarship is Liu Shaotang 1989. Chong-sik Lee has drawn on a mass of Japanese and Chinese sources, providing many insights into the CCP activities in Harbin; Lee 1983.

20. The "Trotskyist affair" is described in Haerbin cheliangchang, Haerbin shifan xueyuan lishixi bianxiezu, 1980, pp. 130–33.

21. We were told in an interview that the "traditional view" of the 1929 conflict, i.e., the "need to defend the Soviet Union against imminent imperialist attack," was losing out to a new consensus regarding the Soviet CER policy, seeing it rather as a continuation of pre-1917 Russian policies.

Texts

Foreign Economic Activity

Harbin historians have very little good to say about the foreign business-
men who operated in the city before 1949. The first article in this section is
a general review of foreign involvement in Harbin written with the explicit
purpose of learning from the past. The authors describe all types of foreign
economic activities, even the building of power stations, as imperialist plun-
dering and attempts at monopolizing the resources of the area. The under-
lying assumption is that the foreigners kept the Chinese entrepreneurs out
and blocked the development of native Chinese industrial and commercial
enterprises. Written in the period of the "open door," the article still rec-
ommends increased economic interaction with the outside world. Its uncon-
ditional praise of the national capitalists can be read as a statement of
support for the private entrepreneurs of the 1980s.

The second article, 2B, offers an account of the history of one of the
major foreign businesses in the food processing industry, the British
"Chicken and Duck Company." Foreign-owned factories have played a
crucial role in the development of Harbin's industry, and many large indus-
trial enterprises in Harbin today have European, Japanese, or Russian
roots. However, the attitude of the Harbin historians toward the foreign
industrialists is almost exclusively negative. Whereas portraits of the na-
tional capitalists focus on their contributions to economic development
while downplaying or blankly ignoring their exploitation of the workers, the
opposite perspective is used in stories about capitalists of foreign origin.
Text 4A in Chapter 4 tells the story of the same plant after the Communist
takeover.

2A. The Historical Lessons of Harbin's Foreign Trade in Modern Times (Excerpts)

Lin Huanwen and Zhao Dejiu

In the summer of 1858 the Russian steamship *"Mutebieyefu"* [?] bustled down the Sanxing stretch of the Songhua River, thus bringing to an end the river's millennium-long peace and serenity. In 1872 the "Heilongjiang Steamship Company," set up by British merchants, established the Khabarovsk-Harbin route under the protection of the Russian government, opening a gateway to the northern part of the ancient Northeast of China. After 1895 Russia engendered a great "steamship fever" and eventually superseded British shipping influence (according to the 1903 Japanese Ministry of Foreign Affairs publication "Siberia and Manchuria"). This brought Harbin into the world capitalist market system, thereby raising the curtain on the recent history of Harbin's relations with the outside world.

1. The Imperialists' Frenzied Export of Capital to Harbin

The Sino-Japanese Treaty of Shimonoseki signed in 1895 was yet another heavy imperialist yoke set on the shoulders of the Chinese people: a large piece of Chinese territory was taken over by Japan, increasing the damage done to Chinese territorial integrity and sovereignty and adding to the arrogance of all the imperialists scrambling to divide China. Tsarist Russia saw that Japan had seized China's Liaodong Peninsula, which it had long coveted, and wasted no time in colluding with Germany and France to put pressure on Japan. Because Japan had been worn down by the 1894–95 war with China, after extorting a ransom payment of 3 million taels of silver from the Qing government, it had no choice but to reach a temporary compromise with Russia, Germany, and France and hand the Liaodong Peninsula back to China. This "Invention of the Three Powers for the Return of Liaodong" set the scene for the partition of China by the large imperialist powers after the Sino-Japanese War. As Lenin pointed out, "The governments of all European countries (first among these, I am afraid to say, being Russia) have already begun to carve up China" (*Selected Works*

Lin Huanwen and Zhao Dejiu, "Jindai Haerbin duiwai maoyi de lishi jiaoxun," *Haerbin yanjiu* [Harbin Research], no. 4 (1987), pp. 42–45.

of Lenin, Volume 1, p. 214), which serves to show that tsarist Russia was the leading henchman in the imperial dismemberment of China. In 1896 tsarist Russia enticed the Qing government into signing the "Secret Sino-Russian Treaty" and the "Contract for the Joint Sino-Russian Eastern Provinces Railway," in which it took over sole rights for the construction and operation of the Chinese Eastern Railway from Manzhouli, through Harbin, Mudanjiang, and right up to the Suifen River. In the 1898 "Lüda Land Rental Treaty," tsarist Russia also took control of the construction of the Chinese Eastern Railway branch line running from Harbin, via Changchun and Shenyang, to Lüda, as well as the right to all the rail income from the points it passed through. The "treaty" and the "contract" stipulated that tsarist Russia had all kinds of special privileges in Harbin and the Northeast. In 1907 Harbin was opened up as a "trading port" and became to tsarist Russia "the Moscow of the Far East." The other imperialist countries, citing the "principle of equal benefit" of the unilateral most-favored nation clause, also awarded themselves the right to carry out various kinds of economic plunder in Harbin. The gate had now been well and truly opened to the northern part of the Northeast and the imperialists dramatically stepped up their export of capital to Harbin and tightened their control over the city's economic lifeline. The main methods by which this was achieved were:

1. The Establishment of Banks. After the Russian "Sino-Russian Daosheng Bank" opened a branch in Harbin in 1898, banks became the "nerve center" of the imperialist economic invasion of the city. From 1903 to 1916 the Russian ruble exclusively dominated the financial markets in Harbin and northern Manchuria and had a stranglehold on economic life. Although it was no longer possible to redeem the ruble during World War I, a large quantity of ruble banknotes still flowed into the northern part of the Northeast, and these were still used for trading activity by the businesses along the route of the Chinese Eastern Railway, as well as by Chinese and Russian citizens. Statistics show that in the early period of the world war a total of 1,660 million Russian rubles were issued, and in the area of Heilongjiang 100 million rubles were in circulation. Out of this figure, about 60 million rubles were in circulation in the area along the Chinese Eastern Railway, and approximately 40 million rubles in Harbin. In 1917, at the time of the Russian bourgeois democratic revolution in February and the socialist revolution in October, [Alexandr] Kerensky's provisional bourgeois government and the Siberian government recklessly increased the supply of banknotes in order to consolidate their control and maintain funds for the army and government, but without regard for a resulting collapse in the living standards of the people. In consequence Harbin was awash with a veritable flood of "yellow strips" (this was the popular name for the long, broad yellow banknotes issued by the Siberian government). After World War I ended, the ruble suddenly became worthless, and the people of Harbin suffered heavy losses. The Japanese imperialists were not affected, however: after the outbreak of the Russo-Japanese War in 1904 the Yokohama Specie Bank issued notes for military use, which were based on the silver standard and appeared in denominations from 10 *fen* to 10 yuan, with a total issue of 150 million yuan. In 1906 and 1915 they issued four additional types of banknotes and three kinds of gold notes, monopolizing the funds for trade in Harbin's local products and funds for remittances. Investment in Harbin's industry and mining, railway building, and import and export businesses as well as other activities were all carried out with the help of the banks. In order to deepen their aggression further, Russia, Britain, France, the United States, and Japan joined together to form the "Harbin Foreign Bank Society," which with its control of public finance and the monetary system assumed the role of "overlord" of Harbin.

2. *Investments in Commerce.* After the Russo-Japanese War ended in 1905, Japan seized all Russian rights and interests in the southern part of the Chinese Northeast. In March 1906 the tsarist Russian Eastern Railway Land Department began furiously selling off land in Harbin at low prices, leading hordes of businessmen, both Chinese and foreign, to flock to Harbin, where they opened shops and established chambers of commerce. To give a few examples, such companies as the Japanese Mitsui, the British Sino-British Company, and the Danish Siberian and East Asiatic Companies set up branches in the city. In 1920 the population of Harbin reached 300,000, of which 72,000 were Russians and 84,000 foreigners of other nationalities. There were at that time more than 1,700 foreign stores, a chamber of commerce for each nationality, seven giant import and export companies, and sixteen international banks. The commercial groups of Harbin were all branch organizations attached to each of the major cities of the world, and each group had its own radio communication network enabling direct contact with head offices in such places as Moscow, London, New York, Tokyo, Osaka, Paris, and Berlin. All these foreign commercial organizations made large-scale investments in Harbin's commercial sector, completely monopolizing the city's import and export trade. The total value of exports from Harbin in 1928 was 105 million customs taels, making it the city with the seventh-highest figure in the whole country.

3. *Investments in Industry and Mining.* In the years before 1913, the imperialists started up more than 100 factories in Harbin, with a total investment of more than 50 million Japanese gold yen. After 1914 the number of factories rapidly increased to a total of around 400, and investments

increasing to more than 100 million Japanese gold yen. Tsarist Russia alone set up nine power stations, monopolizing the supply of electricity to the whole city; it built the "First Manchurian Flour Mill" in Harbin in 1900; by 1913 it was operating a total of twenty-four flour mills in the city; it also set up oil-extraction plants, distilleries, tobacco factories, and so on. It made use of the rich natural resources of Harbin and the surrounding area, as well as the cheap labor and raw materials; relying on special privileges, it directly exploited the local working people, extorted enormous profits, and inflicted great harm upon Harbin's national capitalist industry.

4. *Control of Communications and Transport.* After the Russo-Japanese War ended in 1905, tsarist Russia took exclusive control of the land and resources along the railways of the northern part of the Northeast, turning Harbin into a leased territory both in name and in reality. At this time de facto sovereignty was lost over the whole of the Harbin area apart from Binjiang County, which measured 30 *li* from east to west and 20 *li* from north to south. Using the Chinese Eastern Railway as an important tool in the invasion of the Northeast, tsarist Russia turned the land attached to the railway into a "country within the country." First of all, tsarist Russia barbarously seized Chinese territory. In August 1907 Russia forced the Qing government to sign successive contracts selling land to the Chinese Eastern Railway Company in the provinces of Jilin and Heilongjiang: in Heilongjiang 126,000 *shang* of land were opened up and in Jilin 55,000 *shang*.[1]

As a part of this land, Harbin was the home of the Chinese Eastern Railway Company and also the site of the key railway junction. After three acquisitions of land, tsarist Russia was in occupation of 10,394 *shang* of Chinese territory. Resentment increased because the land Russia had forcibly occupied was then sold off cheaply. Tsarist Russia sold off plots in Harbin three times, causing Chinese people to lose their land and become homeless. Next tsarist Russia relied on its military forces to encroach on Chinese territory, stationing 70,000 troops along the line of the Chinese Eastern Railway as well as positioning police there. On the first of October 1903 a police station was opened in Harbin under the jurisdiction of the civil administration department of the railway company. In 1908 a secret service agency was set up, suppressing the Chinese people's resistance struggle, as well as a law court, the latter representing a severe infringement of Chinese sovereignty. Before 1917, shipping on the rivers Songhua, Heilong, and Wusuli was under the monopoly control of Russian steamship companies. Tsarist Russia had previously stipulated in the Treaty of Aihui [Aigun], which the Qing government had been coerced into signing, that shipping on the Heilong and Wusuli Rivers was restricted to China and Russia. The Chinese Eastern Railway Company set up a shipping office, buy-

ing nineteen steamers and thirty-seven cargo boats, which then plied the
Heilong and Wusuli rivers, as well as working illegally on the Songhua
River in an attempt to stifle the Chinese shipping industry.

On February 5, 1932, Harbin was occupied by the Japanese. Via the
puppet government they issued a law on monetary reorganization and a
bank law, in so doing wrecking the national capitalist private banking
houses, seizing control of the financial institutions, and establishing a monopoly on the import and export trade. In 1935 Japan bought up the Chinese
Eastern Railway and established complete monopolistic control over Harbin. The Japanese imperialist economic invasion of Harbin was intensified
during the period of Japanese puppet government control. Before 1931,
Harbin had always had a positive balance of trade with foreign countries. In
the period 1935–43, however, the city had for the first time a negative
foreign trade balance, and this was at a time when Japan occupied the
leading place in the import and export business. The Japanese invaders
were in complete control of the city's economic lifelines; the main imports
into Harbin were consumer goods and the main exports secondary agricultural products, making Harbin a market for Japanese imperialist products
and a supplier of raw materials.

At the same time, the Japanese were in control of the currency of the
Northeast, and they passed laws to introduce a colonial-style foreign currency standard, replacing the silver standard in the so-called Manzhouguo.
This meant that the currency had a direct and fixed link to the Japanese yen
and therefore the Manchurian puppet regime's currency became nothing
more than a lap-dog of the Japanese yen, allowing Japan complete control
of the financial market in Harbin.

In the Northeast the Japanese used Dalian as their base, Shenyang as
their axis, and Harbin as an outpost, forming an integrated system for
military production and military offensive made up of points, lines, and
areas. In Harbin they established heavy industries directly serving the war
effort such as airplane, motor vehicle, and cement production, as well as
monopolizing light industries such as flour production, brewing and distill-
ing, oil extraction, and sugar manufacture. Pursuing policies to stifle nationalist commerce and industry in the city, the Japanese imperialists first
established joint organizations such as "The United Association for Corpo-
rations in the Manchurian Cotton Industry," "The Central Association for
Manchurian Special Products," "The United Association for Tobacco Manufacturers and Traders," and "The United Association for the Manchurian
Rubber Industry," thereby establishing monopolies in cotton goods, hemp
goods, and other industrial materials and gaining complete control of the
import and export markets. The second method they employed was to work

through the local sales offices of the puppet administration's central monopoly sales bureau, in this way establishing a unified management of the buying of raw materials for, as well as the processing, allocation, and retailing of, such commodities as table salt, flour, matches, and paraffin. Finally, by the use of companies such as "The Manchurian Cereal Administration Joint Stock Corporation," "The Manchurian Livestock Products Joint Stock Corporation" and "The Japanese-Manchurian Commercial Joint Stock Corporation," they gained strict control of key commodities such as grain, daily necessities, iron and steel, coal, timber, and cement. It is not difficult to see, therefore, that Japanese monopoly capital had by this time already taken a stranglehold on political life, the economy, the military, and culture in Harbin and had plunged the city's inhabitants into an abyss of suffering.

2. The Historical Lessons of Harbin's Foreign Trade

1. The development of Harbin's trade with foreign countries is an inevitable historical tendency. . . . For a long time the Qing court operated a "closed door" policy in the Northeast, limiting and severing all types of foreign contact with the area in order to preserve its status as the "land of imperial origin." The consequence of this was to plunge the whole of the Northeast into a state of dormancy, leaving it lagging behind the rest of China in development and even further behind the Western countries. History has shown that sealing a country off from the outside world is a policy that only preserves a state of underdevelopment and serves only to make the nation ignorant and backward. Harbin became "open" under unjust conditions with its loss of sovereignty and by necessity had to suffer oppression at the hands of the invaders. However, the good and honest people of Harbin broke through the obstructions placed by Chinese and foreign reactionary forces and after coming into contact with the world once again they broadened their horizons, studied advanced Western science and technology, and urged the city on to progress. And it was in this way that Harbin gave rise to new social forces: the birth of the capitalist and proletarian classes and the development of national capitalism. . . .

2. In economic dealings with foreign countries it is imperative that policies opposing foreign expansionism and preserving Chinese sovereignty are adhered to. . . .

3. The potential of the national capitalists should be brought as fully into play as possible. Harbin's national entrepreneurs, financiers, and businessmen combined their study of the advanced science and technology associated with Western societies with a vigorous development of their industries

and a transformation of the face of Harbin society. They worked for a resurgence in the city's economy based on a fair and just "open door" policy to the outside world, which included "the retrieval of rights and powers" and "opposition to foreign interference.". . .

4. In Harbin's economic dealings with foreign countries it is necessary to uphold internationally recognized laws and to employ them adeptly. . . .

Note

[1. The indignation of the authors is hard to understand in this case. In fact the 1907 land agreement *reduced* the area allotted to the CER, in the case of Heilongjiang from over 200,000 *shang* to 126,000 *shang*, as compared to the 1904 agreement, which had been exceedingly advantageous to the Russians.]

2B. A Brief Introduction to the Binjiang Products British Import and Export Company Ltd. —The Chicken and Duck Company (Excerpts)

Wu Dongsheng, Jiang Haozhi, and Yu Wenzhang

It is the autumn of 1913. In Harbin, where the lower part of Qinjiagang (Nangang) meets the southwestern part of Fujiadian (Daowai), a British flag flutters under the murky sky, and shabbily dressed Chinese bricklayers sweat feverishly away at the construction of a new factory building under British supervision. This is to be the "Binjiang Products British Import and Export Company Limited" founded by the British to plunder the animal products of the Northeast of our country. It was commonly known as the "Chicken and Duck Company" and was the forerunner of the Harbin Meat Products United Processing Plant.

1. The Period of British Business Control: 1913–1941

A) British Production Management

The British businessman Maqian [?] and others made an investment of £55,000 sterling, spent partly on construction of the plant and partly on starting up their business with the purchase of domestic chickens, domestic ducks, pheasants, etc. The staff and supervisors hired by the company were all foreigners, among them Indians, Russians, and Germans.

In 1915 the engineering office of the Chicken and Duck Company completed the building of their three-story slaughterhouse, four-story refrigerated warehouse, cutting plant, chicken farm, and egg-beating plant. The British businessmen hired Chinese workers to install the freezing equipment, electrical generator, and large boiler, all of which had been shipped in from England. The refrigeration plant could accommodate more than 4,000 tons of meat. By that time the British company had employed more than 700 workers, and it had begun to exploit its Chinese labor force even more ruthlessly and to carry out wide-scale plundering of Northeast China's wealth of animal products.

Wu Dongsheng, Jiang Haozhi, and Yu Wenzhang, "Ji-Ya Gongsi jianjie," *Haerbin shizhi* [Harbin History and Gazetteer], no. 2 (1983), pp. 17, 48–53.

Beginning in 1916 the company expanded the scope of its operations and started to purchase pigs, cattle, sheep, eggs, and other commodities besides chickens and ducks. The Chinese compradors bought up chickens, ducks, eggs, and pigs in the neighboring districts of Harbin such as Shuangcheng, Wuchang, and Lalin, and these were then transported to Harbin by horse-cart or by rail. There is a description of the method used to transport chickens and ducks by rail: "they were bundled into baskets twenty at a time, eighty-five baskets could be crammed into an awned railway carriage, making a total weight of about 8,500 *jin* (5 tons)."[1]

Every year from August to December the British purchased cattle and sheep directly from Inner Mongolia, Manzhouli, Hailaer, and other places:

> They sought out well-to-do merchants in the regions of Mongolia and pro-
> ceeded to exploit them. Three or four British staff accompanied by hired
> Chinese went in person to these locations and made purchases from the
> powerful merchants, or made the merchants buy on their behalf.[2]

It was reported that the Hake station near Hailaer: "often has large consignments of livestock, the majority of them destined for the slaughterhouses of Harbin and subsequent export. The enterprise transporting most of the livestock from this station is the British Export Company."[3] And at the Manzhouli Station:

> the goods dispatched are extremely varied, the most important among them
> being livestock, meat, hides, furs, fish and pelts, as well as timber and coal
> transported from the Trans-Baikal. The livestock, meat and pelts are destined
> for export. All of the livestock is transported to Harbin to be slaughtered (it is
> delivered to the British Export Company's slaughterhouse).[4]

The British businessmen bought up large quantities of pigs, cattle, and sheep at a cheap price [in 1916]; utilizing the company's slaughtering facilities, they hired Chinese workers to slaughter 600 pigs, 200 head of cattle, and 2,000 sheep.

The British company slaughtered 22,756 pigs in 1917, 48,092 in 1918, and 9,300 in 1919.[5] The meat was first frozen and then exported. The chickens and ducks were fattened up after they were purchased and were then slaughtered, frozen, and packed into wooden boxes holding 25–30 birds. Poultry was exported throughout the year, averaging 100,000 birds a year.[6] Pheasants were also exported in wooden boxes; before the birds were packed their wings were bound tightly to their sides so that their feathers could be smoothed down and any bloodstains removed. Their heads were jammed in under the left wing, wing feathers and tail feathers were pressed tightly into the body, and they were finally wrapped up in paper. Each box contained twenty-four birds: twelve cock and hen pairs. In the spring eggs were packed and exported directly; in the summer they were beaten in the egg-beating plant and packed into 20 kg tubs; whites and yolks were mixed together and frozen. The hides were shorn and then dried in the sun, wool from the sheep being used to make coarse knitting wool. Intestines from the pigs, sheep, and cattle were subject to a preliminary processing to produce sausage casings, which were then exported to the United States via Vladivostok; all other products were loaded onto ships in Vladivostok and shipped to England. Counting beef exports alone, there were 18,000 head of cattle exported in 1923, and 10,000 in 1925.[7] Only a small quantity of heads, hooves, and offal was sold locally in Harbin.

In 1920 the British built a large goods and materials store, where such things as spare parts for the installations and packing boxes were kept. There was a fire that year in the cutting plant, and the electric generator, hacksaws, and plant building were reduced to ashes. The company rebuilt the plant immediately, finishing it before the end of the year.

Although the Chicken and Duck Company's products were selling well in far-off Europe and America, this was not enough to satisfy the obsessively greedy British businessmen, and in 1922, bemoaning the scrawny condition of the Mongolian sheep, they started up a new operation. They bought six pure-bred Romney Marsh sheep from New Zealand and crossbred them with the native Mongolian sheep. The Romney Marsh rams were hornless with a snowy white fleece, and by the age of five they could weigh as much as 82 kg and reach a length of 94 cm. The British hired Chinese workers to raise the sheep.

In the autumn of 1926, to test the results of their experiment, the British slaughtered 250 of the crossbred sheep (seven-month-old lambs) and found that on average they gave over 20 kg of meat, the biggest of them giving 24 kg. Thereupon, the British began to raise them on a large scale. It was said of these crossbred sheep that "after they were slaughtered, the meat was sent to London for trial sale and was universally praised for its high quality; it was said to fully satisfy the demands of the market."[8]

In 1927 the business activity of the British-run Chicken and Duck Company contracted drastically, and much of it was transferred to Zhangjiakou and Tianjin, because the rail transport taxes and levies in the region of Hailaer and Manzhouli were extremely high.[9]

The Manzhouguo puppet government was set up in 1932. After the Japanese army of invasion occupied Harbin it took strict control over animal products and the slaughter of livestock, imposing heavy taxes on the slaughterhouses. The livestock transport duty levied by the Eastern Provinces Railway was also increased. The British-run Chicken and Duck Company's activities waned with each passing day.

In 1935 the Japanese forcibly bought up the Chinese Eastern Railway, after which the company's products were exported through the port of Dalian.

The Japanese began their all-out invasion of China in 1937, and they also violated the British imperialists' rights and interests on Chinese soil. British businesses were on their last legs, and so in order to make up for their own losses they did their best to squeeze even more surplus value out of the bodies of their Chinese workers.

2. The Workers' Resistance Struggle

The British businessmen were interested only in profits and treated their Chinese workers with the utmost mercilessness. The workers were given no form of safety precautions, and they even had to pay the British a fee to rent the tools they used. Every single copper coin in the hands of the British businessmen was drenched in the blood of Chinese workers. The company workers had to pluck chickens and ducks by hand in the hot water boilers, where the temperature was 75° Celsius. When slaughtering the cattle, pigs, and sheep, they had first to give the animals a violent blow to the head with a hammer, which was both highly exhausting and also extremely dangerous. Often working barefoot and stripped to the skin, the workers shaved off pig bristles with a hand-plane and used a large meat-chopper to divide the carcasses into sides. The workers in the cold storage plant had to bring their own cotton-padded trousers when coming to work, and they labored the whole year round in a temperature of −18° hanging up and taking down the carcass sides; they were not given any contribution toward health care expenses and were not even allowed any breaks. The labor conditions for workers at the Chicken and Duck Company were abominable, and the working day was at least twelve hours long. This cruel exploitation by the British businessmen "should raise the wrath of the Chinese, who are renowned for their gentle natures."[10] Under the period of British control the company's workers rebelled many times by holding strikes.

On the evening of December 6, 1916, after a hard day's work, the company's workers headed in twos and threes toward the main gate (the north gate) preparing to go home. When they reached the gate the Indian sentries hired by the British barred their way on the pretext that it was not yet time to stop work and forced them to return to the factory building with blows from their rifle butts. A quarrel started, the Indian overseers began punching a number of the workers, and a fight broke out between the two groups.

With a thunderous noise, the Indian guards opened fire with their rifles. According to a contemporary report:

> There was suddenly the sound of gunfire in the southwestern part of Fujia-dian. Investigating the matter, it was reported that the Chinese hired by the Chicken and Duck Company wanted to leave the factory site at the end of their working day. The gate sentries barred their way, however, as the time was not yet up, whereupon there followed a verbal confrontation. After both sides resorted to physical violence, the British guards fired warning shots. Fortunately, the manager of the company heard the shots and came out, immediately ordering them to desist. There were by this time already many injured. We do not yet know how the situation was subsequently dealt with.[11]

By the time the British manager Maqian arrived on the scene four workers had been shot dead and seven were seriously injured. According to a report:

> At the Binjiang Products British Import and Export Company Ltd. (Chicken and Duck Company) the Indian sentry guards were involved in a conflict with the Chinese workers. The Indians opened fire, killing four and wounding seven of the Chinese. The Chinese workers resisted strongly, beating to death three Indians and injuring another four.[12]

The workers were seething with anger and yelled at the British manager Maqian: "You will pay for the death of our brothers with your own life!" That night the workers, together with relatives of the victims who had rushed to the scene, smashed up the British company's office. They burned paper offerings at the company gates for the victims' families and held a memorial ceremony for the dead, mourning them with a mixture of grief and anger in an unbearably tragic scene. The British manager Maqian was so frightened he fled to his residence in Nangang and did not dare return to the company. The next day the Binjiang police station and the Binjiang County office sent people to the Chicken and Duck Company to investigate the incident. They checked the name register of the Chinese workers, but did not attempt to affix any blame to the British company. Seeing how the impotent Chinese officials had failed to punish the British, the workers immediately got together and organized a general strike. No smoke issued from the company's chimneys and the refrigeration equipment came to a halt. The water and electricity supply was cut, chickens and ducks careered around the factory yard, and cattle and sheep tore madly about. The workers maintained the strike for three days, by which time the British had become very uneasy as their economic interests were in serious peril: the boiler could freeze and crack if out of operation for such a long time, and if the livestock were not slaughtered then they had to consume fodder and many of them could die. And so in the end Maqian agreed to the workers' demands: (1) that the company should pay for the burial of the fallen workers and make compensation payments to their families; (2) that they should pay for the treatment of the injured and dismiss all remaining Indian overseers; and (3) all workers should receive a payment of 3 yuan as compensation for their shock and distress. The Chinese returned to work only after these conditions were met. The workers subsequently held several other strikes documented in the historical records:

In 1917 there was spiraling inflation and a slump in the value of the ruble. On August 3, workers at the Chicken and Duck Company held a general strike.[13] On May 3, 1918, "the Binjiang Products British Import and Export Company (the Chicken and Duck Company) without cause or reason reduced the wages of the workers, who then went on an all-out strike."[14] On December 28, 1924, "at the Binjiang Products British Import and Export Company (i.e., the Chicken and Duck Company), more than 200 workers in the chicken feathers department went on strike demanding a pay increase."[15]

Workers at the Chicken and Duck Company were blessed with a spirit of revolt, and the glorious history of their struggle added one more glistening page to the annals of the Harbin workers' movement, as well as offering a mighty blow to the aggression and plunder of British imperialism. . . .

Notes

1. The Eastern Provinces Railway Economic Investigation Bureau, *North Manchuria and the Eastern Provinces Railway* (1 vol.), published in December of the sixteenth year of the Republic of China (1927), p. 111.

2. Eastern Provinces Economic Monthly Editorial Department, "Economic News Magazine," in *Eastern Provinces Economic Monthly*, December 15, fifteenth year of the Republic of China (1926), p. 36.

3. *North Manchuria and the Eastern Provinces Railway*, p. 360.

4. Ibid., p. 358.

5. Cf. *The Harbin Japanese Trade Council Times*, October, twelfth year of the Taisho era (1924), issue no. 10, p. 4.

6. See note 1.

7. *North Manchuria and the Eastern Provinces Railway*, p. 89.

8. Eastern Provinces Economic Monthly Editorial Department, "Livestock Breeding in the North Manchuria Region and Its Improvement through the Installations the Eastern Railway," *Eastern Provinces Economic Monthly* 5, no. 1, p. 30. Issued on January 15, eighteenth year of the Republic of China (1929).

9. *North Manchuria and the Eastern Provinces Railway*, p. 198.

10. *The Selected Works of Lenin*, vol. 1, p. 215.

11. *Far Eastern Reporter*, December 8, 1916, p. 7.

12. Li Shuxiao, *Local Historical Materials*, vol. 2, p. 72 (published in 1980 by the Harbin Local History Research Unit).

13. *Far Eastern Reporter*, August 4, 1917, p. 3.

14. Li Shuxiao, *Local Historical Materials*, vol. 2, p. 88.

15. Ibid., p. 167.

The National Capitalists

In the mid-1980s Chinese historical research witnessed a growing interest in the contributions of the Chinese bourgeoisie to pre-1949 economic development. There was an obvious link between this trend and the concurrent economic reforms, particularly the 1984 decision on industrial reform. The increasingly positive evaluation of earlier Chinese capitalists not only reflected post-Mao perceptions of market forces and entrepreneurship in general; it also served the purpose of digging for valuable experience in fields such as market awareness, management, investment planning, and technical planning, thus providing contemporary Chinese management with role models within a nationalistic framework (Wright 1993).

Harbin local historians from the outset welcomed the new interpretation of pre-1949 Chinese capitalism, and they could draw on rich material: As early as 1913 Harbin was the leading industrial city in the Northeast, and although most industrial enterprises were foreign-owned, Chinese entrepreneurs rapidly built a strong base, particularly in light industries such as flour and oil mills.

The foremost Chinese industrial group in Harbin was the Shuanghesheng Company, led by Zhang Tingge, whose biography is found in the first text. The author's evaluation of Zhang is highly positive, and he is obviously impressed by Zhang's talent for making money, even when the methods seem dubious, to say the least. It is interesting to note that this text has little to say about Zhang's post-1949 career. When a more official biography was published in May 1989 in Harbin Biographies, *the following paragraph in an otherwise positive evaluation described his attitude in the 1950s:*

> But Zhang Tingge still measured everything with his old standards. He supported only those of the CCP's policies which were to the advantage of Shuanghesheng, and was very calculating. He became particularly quarrelsome when his liberal capitalist economic ideas were met with restrictions. He stopped caring about the quality of the products, as they would all be sold to the state anyway. (*Haerbin renwu* 1989, vol. 1, p. 32)

It seems that the historians realized by the late 1980s that the relationship between private entrepreneurs and the party was not unproblematic, and the description of the capitalists of the 1920s subsequently became less hagiographic.

The second article provides a close view of an early modern Chinese capitalist enterprise. It is written by a descendant of the Shao family, which played a significant role in the Northeast before 1949. It is a good example of the memoir genre typical of the Historical Text Materials publications (cf. Chapter 5).

In the narrative of Shao Yueqian one senses self-criticisms and "struggles" of the past, thus the article provides echoes of earlier attitudes to Chinese capitalism. But the main value of the text is the detailed account of management and work conditions in the Tianxingfu Company, and the clear picture of the importance of family and native place ties in a city of immigrants, a topic that is understated in the writings of the professional historians.

Both texts cut across our chronological divisions as they cover the entire history of the early Harbin bourgeoisie until its demise in the early 1950s. As the main sections of the texts fall within the 1898–1932 period, they have been included here.

2C. A Biographical Sketch of Zhang Tingge

Jin Zonglin

Editor's note: Zhang Tingge was one of the leading national capitalists in prerevolutionary Harbin. He traded in Vladivostok during the closing years of the Qing dynasty and the early years of the Chinese Republic and became one of the city's most prominent wealthy Chinese merchants. On the eve of the outbreak of World War I, Zhang decided to return to China and establish his business operations there. Beginning in 1914 he founded in succession such concerns as the Peking Beer and Soda Plant, the Harbin Shuanghesheng Flour Mill, the Shuangchengbao Flour Mill, the Harbin Shuanghesheng Oil Mill, the Harbin Shuanghesheng Tannery, and the Fengtian Navigation Company. He transformed himself from an overseas Chinese merchant into a distinguished industrialist in the Chinese homeland. The enormous size of the Shuanghesheng organization and its huge capital resources meant that it had a great influence on Harbin and Northeast China. In the mid-1920s, Zhang was elected leader of the Harbin Chamber of Commerce and continued to serve in this post for over twenty years. During this time, he also concurrently held other posts such as leader of the Eastern Provinces' Special District United Chamber of Commerce,[1] leader of the Harbin Special City Self-Government Committee and acting mayor of Harbin. He made a great contribution to the development of the national economy of the Harbin area. This article sets out the details of Zhang Tingge's life as an aid to those colleagues researching into and trying to understand the history of the development of national industry and commerce in Harbin.

Zhang Tingge (assumed name [*hao*] Fengting) was born on October 4, 1875, in the village of Zhulan in Ye County, Shandong Province, into an ordinary, relatively impoverished, peasant family. At the age of eight or nine he began to attend a private school in the village, but subsequently had to give up his studies and start working in the fields because his father died. In 1896, together with several other young villagers, Zhang left the village and went out to look for work; after a long, roundabout route, he eventually ended up in the Russian Far Eastern port of Vladivostok.

When he first arrived in Vladivostok, Zhang had no money and no one to turn to for support. Later, after an introduction by one of his fellow villagers, he entered the employment of a certain Fuchangxing plant nursery and started to study business. This is where he began his business career.

Jin Zonglin, "Zhang Tingge zhuanlüe," *Haerbin shizhi* [Harbin History and Gazetteer], no. 2 (1985), pp. 28, 89–91.

In the three years Zhang was in training there, not only did he acquire inside knowledge of the principles and secrets of commerce, but he also learned to speak fluent Russian. This was to give him great advantages in both the purchasing of merchandise and the retailing of products. Through his commercial activities he soon became acquainted with Hao Shengtang, manager of the Shuanghesheng General Store. Hao was also a native of Ye County, Shandong. He had arrived in Vladivostok at a relatively early date and had started out peddling from a street stall. Later, in 1889, after saving up some capital, he joined together with his fellow villager Fang Laiyun to open the Shuanghesheng General Store. On account of slack business, Fang Laiyun later sold his share in the store and started out on his own. Hao Shengtang then found two other men from his home district to enter the partnership: Li Mengling and Du Shangzhi. It was at this time that Hao Shengtang's attention was called to Zhang Tingge. Originating from the same county, they soon formed a close and confidential friendship. Upon Hao Shengtang's warm invitation, Zhang resigned from his position at Fuchangxing around the year 1898 and entered the Shuanghesheng General Store.

After his arrival at Shuanghesheng, Zhang soon gained Hao's confidence and high regard, and Hao asked for his opinion on several large transactions. The company's important trading deals were arranged through Zhang Tingge's personal negotiations, and within a relatively short period of time Zhang pulled off many big deals relying on his facility in Russian as well as the business acumen he had picked up from his years studying commerce. Before long, Hao Shengtang promoted him to Shuanghesheng's deputy manager and granted him full power to carry out business on behalf of the Shuanghesheng Company. There was a marked improvement in business following Zhang's promotion. On the eve of the Russo-Japanese War a great number of Russian soldiers were garrisoned in Vladivostok. Zhang used all his ingenuity to secure contracts for supplying daily articles to the Russian army and made enormous profits from them. After the war broke out, Zhang, seizing his chance, again made several large speculative deals and in so doing turned the Shuanghesheng General Store into a highly successful enterprise in Vladivostok. After the war ended, the Shuanghesheng Company immediately rented land in Vladivostok's commercial district and built new premises. They expanded their range of merchandise and turned themselves into a large-scale general bazaar, second to none in the city. Zhang was subsequently elected to the post of leader of Vladivostok's Chinese Chamber of Commerce.

In 1911, the feudal rule of the Qing dynasty was overthrown by the Xinhai revolution. The triumph of China's national bourgeois revolution created conditions for the development of national commerce and industry.

Under the influence of the call to "save China through industry," Zhang Tingge also began considering returning to China and establishing businesses there. From the year 1912 onward, after discussions with Hao Shengtang and others, he gradually transferred all of the Shuanghesheng Company's assets to start up business in China. By 1919 he had brought the company's business activities in Vladivostok to an end.

In 1914, Zhang bought a Swiss-founded beer and soft drinks factory in Peking and changed its name to the Peking Shuanghesheng Beer and Soda Plant. This was the first concern founded by the Shuanghesheng Company in China. In 1915, it bought the Russian-run Diliejin [Telegin?] Steam Mill in Harbin and renamed it the Harbin Shuanghesheng Flour Mill. In 1916, Zhang bought a steam mill in Shuangchengbao, which had been run by the Yangsheng Company. In the same year, Shuanghesheng's central accounting office moved to Harbin, Zhang was promoted from deputy manager to general manager of Shuanghesheng, and he took up permanent residence in Harbin. Hao Shengtang settled in Peking and took special responsibility for the Peking Shuanghesheng Beer and Soda Plant.

The first years of Zhang's return to China coincided with the period of World War I. Shuanghesheng's two flour mills were in operation day and night, but were still unable to keep up with demand. Large consignments of flour were sent via the Trans-Siberian railway to the battlefields of Europe, and the Shuanghesheng Company derived enormous profits from them. After the war ended, Zhang bought an oil mill at Xiangfang in Harbin. Subsequently, in 1920, he bought 43,000 square meters of land on the banks of the Songhua River in the eastern suburbs of Harbin and established what was then the largest mechanized tannery in the whole of China. In the same year, Zhang spent 1,300,000 Harbin dollars on an order for a complete oil hydrogenation installation from Germany, and tried, without success, to set up a large-scale oil hydrogenation plant. In 1924, Shuanghesheng invested 210,000 Harbin dollars in the founding of the Fengtian Navigation Company. In 1925, the Shuanghesheng organization was officially registered and became known as the Shuanghesheng Company (Unlimited) with Zhang Tingge as the company's general manager. By this time, Shuanghesheng was already Harbin's largest national capitalist organization and Zhang was the city's commercial and industrial giant.

Zhang Tingge showed great originality with regard to the management and organization of production. He placed great value on the use of modern machinery and advanced production techniques, and did not hesitate to spend large sums of money on the purchase of imported machinery and the hiring of foreign technicians with specialized knowledge. The equipment for his flour mills, tannery, and later the oil hydrogenation plant were all shipped halfway around the world from Germany and Switzerland. The brewery and tannery were similarly staffed with expert foreign technicians, who had been hired at great cost. In terms of output and quality, therefore, each of Shuanghesheng's factories held a lead over its competitors. Zhang laid special emphasis in his management on product quality. He checked the quality of the flour in his flour mill nearly every day for thirty years. Amid intense competition, products such as Shuanghesheng's "Five Star" beer and "Red Cockerel" flour always stood head and shoulders above rival brands and built up a high reputation in the eyes of consumers.

Zhang Tingge had an extremely strong sense of devotion to his work and an unquenchable thirst for building up enterprises. There were many among China's national capitalists who failed to be aggressive enough when it came to the development and expansion of their businesses. This was especially the case for joint stock companies, where shareholders were eager to share the dividends, but were not interested in building up capital and expanding production. In this respect far-sighted Zhang Tingge stood out from the crowd. By taking measures such as boosting accumulation funds and reducing visible profits and dividend payments, he accelerated to the greatest possible extent the accumulation of capital, which he then proceeded to use to expand production. This allowed the Shuanghesheng Company to develop rapidly year after year, so that other companies of comparable strength had great difficulty keeping up in the development of production. No one was ever entirely certain of the capital value of the Shuanghesheng Company at any stage in its history; even long-serving senior employees in the accounts department were unable to say for sure. This was because Shuanghesheng's actual capital was several times higher than that shown in the account books: a "secret," which was in fact common knowledge. From the figures below, however, one can see that Shuanghesheng developed exceedingly rapidly. In its first period in Harbin, Shuanghesheng's registered liquid assets were 270,000 silver dollars. In 1927, according to the accounts, the total liquid assets of all its enterprises combined were 1,820,000 silver dollars. By 1930, this had increased to 2,470,000 silver dollars. In fact, the installations at the five Shuanghesheng-controlled factories, the ships and docks of the two navigation companies, the oil-processing machinery (worth over 1 million Harbin dollars), together with a large amount of real estate and shares etc. far exceeded in value that of their official assets. Under the puppet Manzhouguo regime, the puppet Bank of China carried out an assessment of Shuanghesheng's assets (with the exception of the Peking Beer and Soda Plant) and calculated them to be greater than 10 million Manzhouguo yuan, far surpassing any other national capitalist organization in Harbin and making it the richest national capitalist group in the city.

Zhang Tingge held many public posts in the old China. As early as 1914, he held the post of leader of the Vladivostok Chinese Chamber of Commerce. In 1918, after his return to China, he was elected to sit as a member of the Harbin City Council and in 1925 was elected leader of the Harbin Chamber of Commerce. In 1926, he was also elected leader of the Eastern Provinces' Special District United Chamber of Commerce. In November that year, at the inaugural meeting of the Harbin Self-Government Committee Council, Zhang Tingge was elected chairman of the council. In the period of the Japanese puppet regime, the Japanese invaders endeavored to draw Zhang over to their side not only by allowing him to retain his position as leader of the Harbin Chamber of Commerce, but also by arranging for him to hold several other posts in the business world, such as leader of the Harbin Branch of the puppet Manzhouguo Innovation Committee and member of the main Asian section of the puppet East Asian Consultative Committee. After the Japanese surrender in September 1945, the Soviet Red Army appointed Zhang acting mayor of Harbin. He was also at this time involved in other organizations such as the Harbin Political Consultative Conference and the Sino-Soviet Friendship Association.

Some of the positions that Zhang held were of a purely nominal character, while others carried with them a certain responsibility. This was something that Zhang himself understood very well. In the era of the Japanese puppet administration, his chief concern was to safeguard his own, and Shuanghesheng's, economic interests. At the same time he tried as far as he was able to use his influence to protect the interests of other national industrialists and business people. To give an example, in Harbin the Japanese invaders, using the excuse of clamping down on economic crime, ruthlessly persecuted national businessmen. Together with several other figures from the upper echelons of the commercial world, Zhang Tingge, under cover of "donating money for the country's defense," bribed the Japanese puppet government and in so doing put a stop to continued persecution of national businesses. He frequently made use of his influence in other ways to carry out acts of benefit to the people and the nation and in several important affairs fully lived up to his obligations. For example, in 1926 the Russian members of the Harbin City Council, using their majority in a high-handed manner and with disregard for Chinese sovereignty, overturned a proposal made by the Chinese delegates that the Chinese language should be used in the debating chamber, and thus provoked the indignation of Harbin's citizens. Zhang Tingge was also enraged and, together with Fu Runcheng and others, he signed a petition to the senior government office demanding the withdrawal of powers from the municipal administration, the reorganization of the City Council, and the establishment of a Self-Government Committee consisting entirely of Chinese members. The senior government office subsequently adopted their proposal, reorganizing the City Council and setting up a Self-Government Committee, of which Zhang was elected the first chairman. In November 1931, Commander Ma Zhanshan led his troops in resisting the Japanese invaders, which resulted in the famous "Battle of the Bridge" [The Nonni River Battle]. Support for Ma Zhanshan's fight against the Japanese was widely expressed at all levels of Harbin's masses. In the world of commerce, Zhang Tingge took the lead in making donations, and he anonymously presented a large amount of money to the liaison office stationed by Ma Zhanshan in Harbin. Zhang also anonymously contributed large sums to the many collections organized by the Red Cross for the relief of disaster victims. In April 1946, when the Guomindang officials in charge of taking control of Harbin were pulled out, Zhang Tingge together with Xie Yuqin and over a hundred other well-known people from all walks of life jointly sent a telegram to the commander of the Northeastern National United Army asking on behalf of the 800,000 residents of Harbin that the National United Army occupy the city. They also did much preparatory work to enable the Northeastern National United Army to enter the city.

After the liberation of Harbin, Zhang Tingge at once set about restoring production at Shuanghesheng. In the first instance, because of a lack of capital, he had to resort to borrowing money to get his factories up and running. Later, with the assistance of the people's government, the economic climate took a turn for the better. In this period, the main task of the Shuanghesheng Flour Mill was to receive government orders for the processing of goods, and, in turn, Shuanghesheng's other plants followed the same pattern. Shuanghesheng was one of the very first privately run enterprises to process products for the government.

By the time of the liberation of the whole country, Zhang Tingge was already getting on in years, but he was nevertheless in possession of an honest patriotic ardor. In 1951, he donated, on behalf of the Shuanghesheng Company, an airplane to help in the War to Resist U.S. Aggression and Aid Korea, and he played a very positive role in the Harbin business community.

In 1954, the Shuanghesheng Flour Mill was seriously damaged by fire, and the Harbin Insurance Company accordingly paid Shuanghesheng compensation of more than 700,000 yuan. That year, Zhang Tingge passed away after an illness. He was seventy-nine years old.

Note

[1. "The Eastern Provinces" (*Dongsheng*) was the late Qing and early Republic appellation for what is today known as Northeast China (*Dongbei*)].

2D. The Founding and Development of the Tianxingfu Company (Excerpts)

Shao Yueqian

1. The Origin of the Shao Family's Capital

This article has been pieced together on the basis of my father's recollections, from the things that I have personally seen, heard, and experienced, and also from the reminiscences of surviving senior employees of the Tianxingfu company, such as Li Jinzuo, Zhao Zikuan, and others. The main narrative is composed of three sections: the source of the Zhao family's wealth and its subsequent growth (the period of prosperity), the breakup of the Shao clan, and finally the story of the Tianxingfu No. 4 Flour Mill. The evolution of the Shao family's capital took place over a period longer than a century, and it is therefore difficult to narrate its course with any great accuracy. Luckily many of my relatives and other people with knowledge of these matters are still alive and well, and they are most welcome to send criticisms and amendments.

To allow the reader to form a clear picture of the rise in wealth of the Shao family, I will begin with a rough outline:

Tianxingfu was founded in 1861, the final year of the Xianfeng emperor of the Qing dynasty. It was at this time that they borrowed the sum of 200 dollars and opened a small stall selling general goods. During more than twenty years in business they were unable to expand their operations to any extent and were only able to make enough to support their own family. Later they made their fortunes during the 1894–95 Sino-Japanese War and the Russo-Japanese War; their business developed into a medium-size general store, and in 1904 they also opened a branch in Dalian. In 1907 they set up the Tianxingfu No. 1 Oil Mill in Dalian and in the same year established the Tianxingfu grain warehouse in Changchun. Because of their capable management the businesses made good profits. In subsequent years their enterprises expanded rapidly, and they went into the oil-manufacturing and flour production businesses. In 1918 they built the Tianxingfu No. 1 Flour Mill and began to produce flour under the "Tianguan" brandname. In Octo-

Shao Yueqian, "Tianxingfu de chuangli he fazhan," *Haerbin wenshi ziliao* [Harbin Historical Text Materials], vol. 4 (1984), pp. 22–53.

ber 1921 they started the Tianxingfu No. 2 Flour Mill in the Eastern Xiang-
fang district of Harbin, in 1923 the Joint Tianxingdong Flour Mill in Vladi-
vostok in collaboration with a friend Yang Hanchen, in 1924 the Tianxingfu
No. 3 Flour Mill in Kaiyuan, in the same year the Tianxingfu No. 2 Oil Mill in
Dalian, and in 1926 the Tianxingfu No. 4 Flour Mill in the Daowai district
of Harbin. In 1928 they bought the Fuxingheng Flour Mill in Harbin's
Guxiangtun district, and changed its name to the Tianxingfu No. 2 Branch
Plant. In the same year they bought the West Xiangfang Manchurian Flour
Mill from Harbin's Zhengjin Bank and changed its name to the Tianxingfu
No. 4 Branch Plant. During this period they also started the Tianxingfu No.
3 Oil Mill in Dalian, opened the Tianxingfu Private Bank and the Tianxingfu Hospital, planted large-scale fruit orchards in Jinzhou County, and established more than a dozen grain warehouses in the provinces of Jilin and
Heilongjiang. They also bought almost 10,000 *qing* (66,666 hectares) of
cultivated and uncultivated land in Zhaodong County, Heilongjiang. The
combined value of their property was more than 8 million yuan, and their
liquid assets were almost 2 million yuan (silver dollars). After half a century of hard work in business they had developed into the Shao family
capital group worth more than 10 million yuan, making them one of Northeast China's foremost families in the national capitalist commercial world. . . .

3. The Harbin Tianxingfu No. 4 Flour Mill

The splitting of the family in 1924 was an enormous blow to my father,
Shao Qianyi; he had never imagined that members of his own family could
destroy the family business. For many days he did not eat or sleep properly,
and all of us felt that he had lost the will to continue after this huge setback.
Who could have thought that his determination to revive the Shao family's
fortunes had not been lessened in the least. In 1925 he went to the Daowai
district of Harbin and bought a building plot at Neishi Alley, off Beima
Road, together with a nearby railway siding. He then energetically set about
building the Tianxingfu No. 4 Flour Mill, employing exactly the same
methods as had been used before: while constructing the factory buildings
he had the eight large American milling machines apportioned to him in
Changchun transported to Harbin. Working day and night at the construction site, my father had the factory buildings ready and the machinery
installed in only six months; and after a test run, he began producing flour
in 1926 with a daily output of 2,000 sacks. Due to market demand, he later
went to the Hengfeng Company in Shanghai and bought six more American
milling machines, increasing output to 4,200 sacks a day and making the
plant one of the largest flour mills in Harbin.

When the Tianxingfu No. 4 Flour Mill began operations its assets amounted to no more than 500,000 silver dollars. As business prospered the plant began making large profits, and in order to increase production my father let the total assets grow to 1 million silver dollars. In 1928 the Bank of Korea in Harbin took possession of the West Xiangfang District Japanese-Manchurian Flour Mill, and we took it over on the basis of a loan of 256,000 yuan in gold currency notes, with repayment over five years, repaying a sum of 50,000 yuan each year. It became the Tianxingfu No. 4 Flour Mill Branch Plant, and its daily production of 5,400 sacks of flour was marketed, together with that from the No. 4 Mill, under the "Tianguan" brand name.

The combined flour production of the two plants thus reached almost ten thousand sacks per day. This had a great effect on maintaining the momentum of production development and on revitalizing the Shao family's great enterprise. On account of a protracted illness, my brother was at this time sent back home to Jin County to assume personal command of the old store, becoming manager-in-chief of the Tianxingfu Jin County General Store, and he was also put in charge of the Tianxingfu Dalian Agency Store as well as the Jinzhou fruit orchards and real estate. An additional 800 *qing* of cultivated land and over 2,000 *qing* of uncultivated land was purchased in Zhaodong County as a contingency nest egg.

Organizational Format and Management Methods

On paper the Tianxingfu No. 4 Flour Mill was controlled by the general manager, but in fact it was under the direction of Shao Qianyi alone, and its senior employees were each charged with specific duties. The plant was divided into sections for business, general affairs, industrial affairs, insurance, purchasing, and marketing, among others. Each section chief had individual responsibility; senior employees directed the workers under them in the execution of their professional work. With the exception of the technicians in the industrial affairs section, all those in positions of authority (i.e., managers) in the other sections received personal shares. Employees at all levels, right down to the workers, maintained close links with our family; a number of them were relatives, and a majority of the senior employees had worked for many years in the original general store. With the exception of temporary labor they were all old acquaintances or else people recommended by family and friends from the same home district. It could indeed be said that it was a family work force from top to bottom.

The labor force at Tianxingfu No. 4 Mill could be divided into seven levels: (1) the proprietors: capitalists; (2) managers: representatives of capitalist interests and senior employees, both groups holding personal shares; (3) "salaried employees" (*laojin*): ordinary employees who had worked a certain number of years and with a certain capability; (4) young employees: shop workers who had served less than three years, those studying business or apprentices; (5) technicians: operating engines and millstones; (6) workers: both foremen and production workers (including temporary seasonal labor); (7) miscellaneous labor, canteen staff, nightwatchmen, and cleaning workers.

These seven levels of labor were divided into two distinct strata, basically, into those working in the accounting office and those working in the factory. The proprietor treated these two groups quite differently with respect to wages, living conditions, and recruitment procedures.

1. The recruitment of personnel:

a) The employment of new accounting office staff was decided personally by the manager, and there were three conditions that had to be satisfied: the first condition was that they had to be relatives, friends, or people from the same home district; the second was that they be recommended by some creditable person (such as a colleague, relative, or a distinguished person in society) who would stand as guarantor; the third was that they had a certain level of education, in no case lower than that of higher primary school. Normally, the accounting office staff, therefore, had a strong connection to the capitalist, either by blood or through friendship, and thus formed a group structure held together by a sort of kinship bond. People who were unable to claim a close relation to the Shao family had great difficulty making their way into the family enterprise.

b) The employment of new factory workers was based on a joint decision by the factory head and the technicians, the status of the person who had recommended them was unimportant and it was not necessary to have a guarantor. However, at that time the factory head and the technicians functioned as feudal labor contractors and they held great power. My father was well aware of what they did but could not interfere, wanting to use them to ensure that the labor force did its work.

2. Remuneration conditions: the general policy was one of low wages and high bonuses, which had the aim of stimulating production and mitigating the antagonisms between labor and capital.

a) The staff received remuneration in the form of an annual salary and a yearly bonus. In addition to the salary there was a share-out bonus dependent on profits, and extra payments could also be made for weddings and funerals.

b) Workers received monthly wages: it was only possible to let one's wages accumulate, not to receive advances, and bonuses were not given.

c) The treatment of technicians, cooks, nightwatchmen, and others differed from that of workers, as it did from that of the accounting office staff.
Because the majority of them were employed as hired labor, their wages
were not docked for absence due to illness, and in addition to their wages
they received bonuses, the size of which depended on the economic performance of the company and the personal inclinations of the proprietor. Otherwise conditions were the same as for the workers.

3. Living conditions:

a) Accounting office staff had an official holiday enabling them to make
a trip to their family home once a year for a period of forty days. For
persons who had served more than two years, the period of leave was three
months. In this period wages were paid in full and return travel expenses
were also given. In the case of absence through illness, full pay was given,
but treatment costs were not covered. Workers did not enjoy the same
conditions: they were docked a day's pay for each day missed and had no
holiday entitlements.

b) Meals for accounting office staff and technicians were paid for by the
company. Senior employees, foremen, and engine and mill technicians were
given top-quality food and for lunch could get two bowlfuls of rice and four
different dishes. Lower-quality food was provided for the ordinary staff,
trainees and odd-jobmen, and they were given rice and one dish from the
communal pot. Piece-work laborers ate their own food in a separate canteen, the company providing them with flour at half-price.

4. The demands placed on employees also varied: accounting office staff
had to observe the company rules strictly, everyone from workers in the
workshop to managers without exception had to observe three prohibitions:
they were not allowed to spend the night away from their living quarters,
they were not allowed to visit prostitutes or gamble, or to acquire dissolute
extravagances. However piece-work laborers were not subject to these restrictions, and after finishing work and returning home they were free to do
as they wished. By these means it was possible to enforce the strict separa-
tion of the staff and the workers, thus ensuring that the accounting office
employees felt that they occupied the same position as the managers: that
they were the proprietor's own men, thus giving them a white-collar
worker's feeling of superiority and a lack of respect for the workers. The
desired result was to confuse class relations so that they would side both
ideologically and emotionally with the capitalists and earnestly strive to
serve their interests.

5. The management of workers: The flour mill work force was divided into millers, steam power technicians, electricians, foremen, sieve tenders, mesh tenders, oil burners, packing workers, mechanics, and others. With the exception of the technicians, ordinary skilled workers would progress in stages from sweeping the floor to oiling machinery, before finally reaching their technical position. This was essentially for the purpose of seeing how industrious the new employee was, and not a case of the factory following a deliberate policy of worker training. The turnover of workers was very high; they would often switch factories from one day to the next. By 1944 the livelihood of the Chinese people was impoverished in the extreme as a result of galloping inflation, and the turnover of workers increased still further. In order to stabilize the labor force, No. 4 Mill supplemented the workers' wages, improved their welfare conditions, increased their food allowances and subsidies, and even gave a bonus of two months' wages. All these measures, however, were still not enough to put a brake on the rate of turnover. With the long working hours at the flour mills, the day being divided into two twelve-hour shifts, the workers were heavily exploited and they had a very hard life. The Shao family's earlier wage system had not been carried on very well at the No. 4 Mill, and in the later period the company began to reduce their once-high yearly bonuses or defer their payment altogether. As a consequence, Tianxingfu No. 4 Mill became one of Harbin's low-paying flour mills. A manager at the Shuanghesheng Flour Mill, for example, would be paid 600 silver dollars a year, whereas a manager at No. 4 Mill would receive only 300 yuan. And the yearly bonus payments would also be considerably lower than at other factories.

The pressures of the times caused changes as well in the organizational structure. In 1938, after the Japanese imperialists had turned the screw on the economy, the Tianxingfu No. 4 Mill was unable to pay the exorbitant taxes and levies calculated on the basis of the value of goods sold, and as a result decided to transform itself into a joint stock company. Its assets were initially fixed at 500,000 yuan (in the currency of the puppet regime), but this was later increased to 1 million yuan and documents made out with each investor's contribution. In this way the company would be levied a tax only at the end of year based on the net profit. The shareholders were as follows: my father, Shao Qianyi, 400,000 yuan; my elder brother Shao Jiuqing, 300,000 yuan; and myself, 300,000 yuan. This structure was adopted chiefly to deal with the Japanese puppet government; in reality this sum of money was still less than half the total assets of the Tianxingfu No. 4 Mill. A shareholder's association and section share organizations were also established in accordance with the laws governing company organization. These structures functioned solely as a smokescreen, however; it was actually still a one-man business, in which my father, Shao Qianyi, made all the decisions.

Machinery

The machinery at the Tianxingfu No. 4 Flour Mill was comprised entirely of machines from the American Hengfeng [?] company together with machines made by the Swiss Bila [?] brothers. They could be divided into the three main categories of power supply, corn cleaning, and flour milling machines. There was in addition a subsidiary ironwork department, which was responsible for simple mechanical repairs. Before the "September 18 incident" [in 1931], the main supply of power at the Tianxingfu No. 4 Flour Mill came from a gas boiler, which produced steam power by burning lump coal and gave coking coal as a by-product, making it very economical. After the "September 18 incident," the mill replaced its steam-driven machines with electric-powered ones, buying a 50-horsepower Mitsubishi brand electrical generator from Japan, and later a 400-horsepower Fushi brand electrical generator in addition.

The Tianxingfu No. 4 Mill had in all eighteen American large-scale milling machines, which could produce on average 333 sacks of flour per day. The machines were not installed strictly in accordance with their mechanical specifications, but rather with the aim of producing as much flour as possible, and the life of the machinery was consequently shortened. At that time my father drew up an itemized account: a milling machine installed according to the normal specifications could only produce 200 sacks of flour a day and, comparing the price of machinery with the price of the flour produced, it was still advantageous to do it his way. He said that if the machines were not installed according to the specifications, it did not necessarily mean that his installation did not in fact conform to their real mechanical performance. . . .

The foreign engineers told my father that if the machines were not installed according to the blueprints, the load on them would be too great and their operational life would be reduced. The Shuanghesheng Flour Mill installed their machines according to the regulations, and on average it produced 200 tons of flour per day; fifty machines could therefore produce 10,000 tons, and their operational life would be extended. My father would not listen to this, saying that the mill merely wanted more machines and not more money: the more flour produced, the higher the profits, so why not do it! And so he did away with all the foreign rules and regulations and, together with the milling machinery technicians and the team leaders, repeatedly tried to work out a production schedule that corresponded to No. 4 Mill's technological process. . . .

This attitude was borne out by the results: the operational efficiency of the machines was very high, the output rose from 3,800 to 4,200 sacks and the bran was also relatively clean. . . .

Management of the Company during the Darkest Days of the Manzhouguo Puppet Regime

In 1931, after the "September 18 incident," the Japanese militarists invaded the Northeast and subjected the countryside to terrible destruction. In 1932, the river basin of the North Manchurian Songhua River flooded heavily and the northeastern wheat crop failed for a second successive year, making the economic outlook for the flour milling industry extremely grim indeed. In 1934, the Manzhouguo puppet government introduced a new customs duty in order to meet its military requirements. It was a policy of encouraging the export of wheat and flour and restricting its import, with every sack of imported flour being subject to a heavy customs duty of 0.367 yuan. As a result the marketing opportunities for flour in the Northeast took a temporary turn for the better, and the flour mill owners were stimulated to buy up more wheat, produce more flour, and increase their sales. In 1936, a new policy was taken up, permitting the import of foreign flour and the northeastern flour industry was hit once again.

By 1938 the Japanese puppets had by and large completed their military operations in the whole of Northeast China. With the support of the Japanese Guandong Army, Japanese financial groups set about a vigorous development of the sector of the flour industry controlled by Japanese capital. To take one example, the Manchurian Flour Company, the Ookura Commercial Affairs Company, the Mitsui and Mitsubishi companies, among others, joined together to form one large company, the Japanese-Manchurian Joint Stock Flour Corporation, which made investments and bought up flour mills all over the Northeast. Making use of their special position and powers, they attacked the Chinese national capitalists, bleeding them dry, squeezing them out of markets and coercing them to go over to the Japanese side. In April of that year, I returned to China after graduating from Tokyo Central University and the puppet government intended to assign me to Changchun (then called Xinjing by the puppet regime) to serve as a general affairs official in the puppet Ministry of Foreign Affairs. When my father heard of this he firmly refused to allow me to serve as an official in the puppet government and bade me return obediently to Harbin and help him run the Tianxingfu No. 4 Mill. This was the start of my career in the flour industry.

In October of that year the Federation of Manchurian Flour Producers was formed and fixed prices were introduced for wheat and flour. Flour producers were free to buy in raw materials within the set price limits, but flour could only be sold to the federation at the fixed price and could not be sold freely on the open market. This measure helped the Japanese mills to elbow the Chinese out of the market; Japanese mills would scramble to buy up wheat, ignoring the fixed price and offering the suppliers a higher price, whereas the Chinese mills were forced to follow the rules. The Japanese spent a bit more on the purchase of raw materials, but they could recoup this when it came to selling the flour and even make high profits. The Japanese introduction of fixed prices was no more than a despicable method of gaining economic control, and it was the first nail in the coffin for the Chinese-owned mills. On December 6, 1939, the Manzhouguo puppet government issued a new law controlling the wheat and flour industry. The next day it issued a monopoly law covering the sale of wheat and flour. The gist of these laws was that the wheat produced in each region was to be bought up entirely by a regional grain company, which would then allocate it at fixed prices to the flour mills in accordance with their production capacity, and the flour produced by the mills was to be bought in its entirety by the monopoly office, again at fixed prices. Two links in the mills' production chain, those of purchasing and selling, thus came under the control of the puppet government.

The monopoly office's requirements for flour quality were very high. If the output from a mill met or exceeded the standards of the monopoly office's chemical tests, it would receive bonuses and also be allocated more raw materials to process, thus increasing the mill's income from processing and helping it to keep its head above water. If the output failed to meet the standards, however, the mill was not only fined, but its processing allocation was reduced, making it virtually impossible for the mill to survive. With the aim of increasing the processing allocation to the Tianxingfu No. 4 Mill, I played the card of being a graduate of Tokyo Central University and paid frequent visits to the monopoly office to see Mr. Tamura, who was in charge of the flour industry, asking for his patronage and help in making our allocation a little larger. At the same time I worked together with the technicians to improve our technological and operational methods in order to ensure that the required standard was reached. Even though we did make a small amount of money in processing fees, it was very hard to survive. The tax bureau raised taxes based on the sales revenues with complete disregard for the ability of the business to pay. To alleviate the problem, I tried in many ways and sought the help of many people in sending presents and dinner invitations to Liu Guangyi and others at the Daowai customs bureau, but this did not succeed in helping matters. Furthermore, we still had to put up with the puppet regime's apportioning of government bonds, shares, savings and national defense contributions, as well as extortion and blackmail from collaborationist agents. The accounts of the Tianxingfu No. 4 Mill show that up until the eve of the revolution these items accounted for more than 470,000 yuan, equivalent to 50 percent of the net value of the mill's assets. My father was very unhappy that I had spent so much money in this way and accused me of being too generous. He put a stop to my having any more control over Tianxingfu's affairs and sent me off to the Dalian branch store where I was to be assistant manager. Later, my father was no longer able to run the No. 4 Mill properly because of large changes in the internal staffing, and so he brought me back from Dalian to act as manager. . . .

In 1944, the Japanese puppets once again advocated enlarging the area sown with soybeans and various other grains. They reduced the area sown with wheat, and combined with the poor wheat harvests of the previous years, the result was a year by year decline in flour production with some mills standing idle for long periods and others going over to the processing of maize. The Tianxingfu No. 4 Mill was also forced to turn to maize processing, and it remained in operation for less than sixty days of the year. The processing fees earned were extremely small, the price of goods rose incessantly, and the drain on the company's resources grew and grew, resulting in the almost total depletion of liquid assets. In order to survive, the company went to the Japanese Zhengjin Bank and took out a loan of 250,000 yuan with the flour mill as security; it was essentially bankrupt.

The Twisted Road to Development after Liberation

On August 15, 1945, the Japanese invaders surrendered and Harbin was regained. The United Democratic Army entered Harbin on April 28, 1946, and established the people's government. Thanks to the concern of the new government, the flour mills, which were hovering on the verge of bankruptcy, all came back into production after a short period of preparatory work. All the mills were in a bad way; after fourteen years under the ruthless Japanese puppet regime their capital had been eaten away. The Tianxingfu No. 4 Mill took in outside money in order to come back into production, and it went into a temporary four-month period of collaboration with the Harbin businessmen Dong Yanheng and Bai Yanwen. Only five milling machines were put into use because of the shortage of raw materials.

There were very large fluctuations in the price of goods during this period, which meant that cash reserves were not as important as having inventory. Some grain merchants exploited this situation by stockpiling flour and so creating conditions where demand far outstripped supply, leaving the residents of the city queuing up to buy all they could lay their hands on. Like other mill managers, I took advantage of this opportunity; we bought up as much grain as possible, increased our production of flour, and then adopted the method of selling in advance, first receiving payment and delivering the flour at a later date. And we made enormous profits in this way. During this golden period, our No. 4 Mill not only paid off the 250,000 yuan loan from the Zhengjin Bank, but the company and the employees also shared a profit bonus.

After the arrival of the United Democratic Army in Harbin, the people's government issued calls for an increase in production and economic prosperity and support for the war of liberation. Because of my ignorance about the Communist Party, however, I did not dare expand production any further, fearing that if the company became bigger it would be expropriated and the family fortune would be lost.

In 1947, the tide of the land reforms arrived and peasants from outlying counties came to Harbin and began seizing landlords. The Shao family had bought a lot of land around Zhaodong. There were 800 *qing* of cultivated land standing in the name of my father, Shao Qianyi, alone, and he had returned to his original home in Jin County before Liberation. I was afraid of being seized by the peasants and consulted with Deputy Manager Gao Xiangchen, asking him to take over full authority for the management of the Tianxingfu No. 4 Mill. I hurriedly left for Daoli and went into hiding at the house of my relative Lin Weiqing, who lived on China Second Street. Only after the land reforms had stabilized did I dare return to the mill, which shows how hazy my ideas were about the party. In October 1947, the government-run Dongxing Company abolished the practice of using grain merchants as agents for the selling of rice and flour and completely changed over to a system in which it was sold by district consumers' cooperatives on a commission basis. These measures were a direct assault on the illegal practices of the grain merchants and at the same time limited the speculative behavior of the flour mills. The flour industry was still able to stir up trouble in the marketplace, however, by manipulating the trade in flour and raising prices for the New Year's Festival, when demand exceeded supply, in order to skim off enormous profits. During the 1948 New Year's Festival, taking advantage of the fact that the state enterprises were running short of flour, I took part in an open meeting led by the Shuanghesheng and Yichangtai companies, which organized a joint stockpiling of flour and a raising of the price. This was an act of direct economic opposition to the state-run sector, and it led to chaos in the marketplace. Later, as the economic strength of the state sector rapidly increased, the scope of the private companies in production and sales was gradually narrowed. They were never again able to put up opposition to the state sector.

In 1949, after the founding of New China, the people's government adopted a policy of utilizing, restricting, and reforming private industry and commerce. The line taken toward private business in Harbin involved a combination of help, reform, support, and management, thus utilizing the initiative of the flour industry, but restricting its speculative tendencies.

In 1950, with the assistance of the government, all the flour mills voluntarily combined to set up a united administration center, which brought in the raw materials and sold the flour centrally; businesses supervised one another, and were able to see that their colleagues obeyed government directives. The market became generally more stable. There was a poor wheat harvest that year and, as there was a shortfall of grain to process, the government called on the mills to "help themselves by engaging in production." The Tianxingfu No. 4 Mill made use of their Eastern Xiangfang branch plant warehouse, which had fallen into disuse under the Manzhouguo puppet regime, and opened a chicken farm and a chemical factory (making electric plugs and buttons for clothing among other things), and the factory yard was used for raising pigs. These steps were taken in the interests of maintaining the wages of the staff and workers. That year the state built a large bearing plant in the Xiangfang district and found it necessary to occupy the factory building of No. 4 Mill's Branch Plant. This was achieved with the agreement of the city administration, and the chicken farm was transferred to the Xicheng district of Peking, where it continued in business. In an attempt to expand our own family enterprise, I also started up a timber company in Tianjin in partnership with an old friend. The chicken farm lasted less than two years; nearly all the chickens died from pestilence due to poor management, and the business was closed down. Not long after, the Tianjin lumber company also folded with losses of several hundred thousand yuan.

After Liberation, the employees of the Tianxingfu No. 4 Mill suggested that production could be expanded by repairing the abandoned milling machines. I rejected their suggestion, however, giving the excuse that there was insufficient capital. Nevertheless, the laboring masses gave free rein to their creative spirit and collective wisdom and they restored the machines themselves without recourse to investment. This unselfish act was a great lesson to me and made me realize the greatness of the working class. After the campaign against the "Five Evils,"* the government actively encour-

[*The "Five Evils" were bribery, tax evasion, stealing state property, fraud, and theft of economic information, as defined in the "Five Evils" campaign (wufan yundong) of 1952, which served to bring private business under effective government control.]

aged the processing of ordered goods, following the principle of "stabilizing morale and restoring production," and the Tianxingfu No. 4 Mill was soon restored to normal production.

The relationship between labor and capital changed after Liberation, as did the living conditions afforded employees. The working day was reduced in October 1946 from twelve to ten hours, and this was later reduced further to eight hours. This was the same for office staff and workers, with both groups clocking in and out at set times. The cost of medicine was now borne by the enterprise, wages were not docked for absence through illness, and even medical costs were covered by the employer. After 1947, temporary workers and laborers were reclassified as belonging to the enterprise's permanent work force, and the proprietor could no longer fire them at will; at the same time, the exploitation at the middle level by the labor contractors was also abolished. The workers were now provided with food as was the office staff, and there was no longer division according to status, now everyone ate the same. Conditions and hygiene in the employees' dormitories were also improved, and facilities such as showers and a barbershop were added. Recreational activities and places for study were provided for the employees, with the cultural and sporting supplies purchased by the company on their behalf. Moreover, wages for office staff and workers were reformed, and the factory set up a union controlled by the workers themselves. On July 1, 1955, the government ratified the Tianxingfu No. 4 Flour Mill's new status as a joint state-private enterprise and appointed me vice-director of the factory. Ever since then I have been walking down the bright road of socialism.

After the mill became a state-private enterprise, its production capacity rose from 120 tons of processed maize to 193 tons and, after technological reform in 1958, to 250 tons. Later the factory employees created an automatic conveyer belt and an automatic stacking machine, which replaced heavy manual labor as well as reducing transport costs. By the second half of 1959, the daily output of the Tianxingfu No. 4 Mill was up to 374 tons, and not only did the volume of production increase, but product quality remained up to standard. The Tianxingfu No. 4 Flour Mill continued in business right up until the beginning of the Great Cultural Revolution in 1966.

(edited by Mu Zhi)

The Early Labor Movement

The Chinese workers, and particularly the revolutionary among them, are the natural heroes of Marxist Chinese historiography. In works on the labor movement the writing style characteristic of the pre-1978 era is still in wide use, as in this article, written by veteran historian Zhang Fushan, who is now on the Party History Committee, but who has also written extensively on other aspects of Harbin history in the early twentieth century.

The dramatic narrative form of this piece, which even describes the inner feelings and facial expressions of the protagonists during the 1907 May 1 general strike narrated in the following article, became the exception rather than the rule in the 1980s, when most historians aimed at achieving a more objective tone. But the overall purpose of the text is fully in line with the whole local history project in demonstrating that Harbin compares favorably with other urban centers also with regard to the development of a labor movement, and that historians in intramural China tend to forget this fact.

An important point in Zhang's text is that the Chinese proved decisive in the outcome of the strike by backing their Russian colleagues at a critical time. In this way they can step out of the younger brother's role often assigned to them.

It is strange that Zhang seems to stand rather isolated in dating the event described in this text to 1907. In Russian accounts, as well as in the writings of other Harbin historians, the year is set at 1908, which would still, however, make Harbin first by a large margin.

2E. Harbin Workers Were the First to Commemorate May Day

Zhang Fushan

Much has been written in recent years on the question of in which year our country's working class first commemorated the May 1 International Labor Day. Opinions have varied, with a majority of people proposing that it occurred in 1920, when the occasion was marked by the workers of Peking. According to our information, however, workers on the Chinese Eastern Railway in fact began to commemorate the event in Harbin as early as 1907. This can be documented both from written records and from the eyewitness accounts of workers who personally took part in the activities. What follows is an account of the circumstances of this first commemoration based on relevant historical records and the recollections of old workers.

In 1898, at the same time as it was forcibly constructing the Chinese Eastern Railway in the Northeast, tsarist Russia decided to establish the railway's administration in Harbin, and it also built there a subsidiary plant to the Chinese Eastern Railway for the assembly and repair of locomotives and rolling stock—the Harbin General Plant (later called the Thirty-six Barracks General Plant). Because of this, Harbin became the location along the Chinese Eastern Railway of most production workers and where these workers were most concentrated. After the railway was completed in 1903, the General Plant had more than three thousand workers, both Chinese and Russian, and including other units such as the Harbin Locomotive Stockyard (i.e., the Maintenance Section), the Rolling Stock Section, the Industrial Affairs Section, the Station Goods Office, and the Railway Printing Works, the total number of workers employed was more than ten thousand. Apart from the Russian workers, who were recruited by the tsarist government in Russia, the majority of the work force were destitute peasants and small handicraftsmen recruited from Shandong, Zhili (now Hebei Province), Jilin, and Fengtian (now Shenyang). Receiving minuscule wages, these Chinese worker recruits slaved like mules year in and year out under the lash of tsarist Russia, and their lives were miserable in the extreme.

In August 1905 the Russo-Japanese War, which had lasted for one and a

Zhang Fushan, "Haerbin gongren zui zao jinian 'wu-yi' jie," *Heilongjiang wenshi ziliao* [Heilongjiang Historical Text Materials], vol. 16 (1985), pp. 9–15.

half years, ended with the military defeat of tsarist Russia and the signing of the Treaty of Portsmouth. The Northeast was divided between Japan and Russia. The area of southern Manchuria to the south of Changchun became the Japanese imperialists' zone of influence, while northern Manchuria to the north of Changchun was tsarist Russia's zone. The Russian imperialists increased their colonial domination of the area along the Chinese Eastern Railway in order to enforce tight control and oppression on the broad masses of the Chinese people in the northeastern region: after 1905 they added in Harbin and other places institutions such as administrative police stations, law courts, prisons, and espionage and surveillance offices. At the same time, they also pulled back Russian forces totaling 80,000 men from southern Liaodong and stationed them at areas along the Chinese Eastern Railway, with Harbin being the focal point. In addition to their plunder of the Northeast, the tsarist Russian invaders also brought in military administration of the Chinese Eastern Railway and assigned armed military police to watch over and suppress the workers. In an attempt to make up for the losses it suffered in the Russo-Japanese War, tsarist Russia increased its pillage and exploitation of workers on the Chinese Eastern Railway, plunging the broad masses of the Chinese workers yet further into the living hell that was their lives.

The broad masses of the Chinese workers never gave up their attempts to wrest themselves free from their position of servitude, however. From beginning to end they carried out a ceaseless struggle against the tsarist Russian invaders. At the same time more and more of the Russian workers, under the influence of the vigorously developing revolutionary movement inside their own country, began to intensify their struggle of opposition against the tsarist ruling forces. Thereupon, the Chinese and Russian workers of the Chinese Eastern Railway, with the Thirty-six Barracks Plant as their center, united even more closely in a struggle against their common enemy: tsarist Russian imperialism.

In the middle of January 1907 the Russian workers at the General Plant were organizing a strike to commemorate the second anniversary of the massacre of striking workers in St. Petersburg. The news leaked out, however, and ten Russian workers' leaders were arrested by the tsarist military police, leaving some of the Russian workers with no idea what to do next. After the Chinese workers heard about what had happened, they immediately went into action. They harbored an immense hatred of the tsarist invaders as well as sympathy for their Russian brother workers, and they decided to join the ranks of the Russian workers' struggle. The Chinese workers said indignantly, "The Russian tsarist government has butchered our Russian brother workers, so we should stop working for them." The leader of the Chinese workers at the time was Wu Tai, who before entering the factory had worked as a coolie in Russia and could speak Russian. He had been chosen by the workers as their leader because of his enthusiasm and his previous experience of workers' struggle. As a representative of the Chinese workers, Wu Tai consulted with the Russian workers and they decided to hold a strike on the morning of January 22 to commemorate the massacre in St. Petersburg and to demand the release of the imprisoned Russian workers, the strike not being lifted until their objectives were met.

Not long after the workers had arrived at the factory on January 22, white steam was emitted from the steam whistle of the Electric Lamps Branch Plant in a stream that cleaved the clear sky, and gave out an ear-piercing screech: this was the signal that had been arranged for starting the strike. Upon hearing this, workers from all the branch plants headed for the main accounting office, and, in a short while, all of the thousands of workers from the entire plant were gathered there. The workers were extremely angry, and the yard in front of the main office was about to boil over. The general manager of the plant Bakhilov, known to all the workers as "tub of lard" on account of his corpulence, had thought that by seizing the ten Russian strike leaders he would be able to prevent a strike. Seeing that the workers had now surrounded the main office so that not a mouse could slip out, he was frightened out of his wits. He was just about to report the matter to his boss, Horwath, chief of the Railway Bureau, when the door suddenly burst open with a crash and several representatives of the workers rushed in, giving Bakhilov such a start that the color drained out of his face. The representatives demanded, "Immediately release the arrested workers and do not attempt to interrupt the meeting we have convened today." With his hands clasped together Bakhilov answered, "Bureau Chief Horwath is holding the arrested men with him, I don't have any say in the matter." The representatives replied, "Ring Horwath and tell him to release the men at once, or you will never get us back to work." Bakhilov picked up the receiver and was about to dial the number when he suddenly stopped and put the receiver down again. Slyly he said, "I'll go over to see Bureau Chief Horwath this minute and get him to release the men, please wait a while." Having said this, he got into a horse-drawn carriage accompanied by some of his underlings and left the factory. The Chinese and Russian workers were afraid that General Manager Bakhilov would play a trick on them, so they at once decided to assemble their forces and head directly for the Railway Bureau. When the workers arrived at the office gates, Bakhilov was just coming out of the main railway administration building. He got into his carriage and, dissembling, he told the workers, "Bureau Chief Horwath has agreed to release the men, but everyone must return to work at once." The workers' representatives at once declared, "We won't go back before we see the workers released." This was quickly followed among the workers by a chant of "Set them free! Set them free! Set them free now!" Seeing that the workers would not go along with it, Bakhilov had no alternative but to go back and consult with Bureau Chief Horwath. After about a quarter of an hour, Bakhilov came out again and said, "The Bureau Chief has already sent the order to the Headquarters of the Outer Amur Military District that the men be released, so please return to the factory." The Outer Amur Military District Headquarters was a garrisoned body of the tsarist invasionary army and situated close by the Railway Bureau (at what is now the Harbin Railway Health School). The workers therefore immediately headed over to it, and when they arrived at the gates they saw the arrested workers actually being released. The striking workers rushed forward one after the other and embraced the men fervently. Everyone cheered in acclamation, "The strike has won, we won!" One of the Russian workers' representatives said with feeling, "Our Chinese brother workers supported us like true friends, and it was only with their help that the strike could be victorious . . ."

The Chinese and Russian workers established a deep militant friendship during the course of this struggle. In the days that followed many Russian workers would often set out to the Chinese workers the state of the proletarian and peasant masses' revolutionary struggle inside Russia and in other countries, and in this way Chinese workers, engaged in the struggle, gradually began to learn some new facts about the international proletarian revolution. May Day was something that the Chinese workers heard about from the Russian workers at this time. They learned that the first time the Russian workers had commemorated International Labor Day on May 1 was in 1893, when it was held in secret in St. Petersburg. By way of this introduction, the horizons of the Chinese workers were widened, and their struggle against the oppression of tsarist colonialism reached ever greater heights.

In April 1907, on the basis of their previous action, the Chinese and Russian workers consulted many times about holding a strike and some collective activity to mark the May 1 International Labor Day. The Chinese and Russian workers at the Thirty-six Barracks Plant took the initiative, and established contacts with workers at other plants such as the Maintenance Section, the railway station, and the printing works in order to plan a joint May 1 celebration. On April 30 the representatives of the Chinese and Russian workers at the main plant went to see the general manager of the plant Bakhilov and announced gravely, "May First is a festival for working people over the whole world, and we demand a day's holiday in order to celebrate it." The general manager rejected the workers' proposal, however, and with his corpulent body swaying he said unhurriedly, "According to the railway's regulations there is no such thing as a 'May First' holiday. Hurry back to your work and don't make any more absurd demands." Indignantly, Wu Tai told the general manager, "If there isn't going to be a holiday then we're going on strike!" Bakhilov quickly brought a document out of one of his drawers and raised it in the air, shouting out, "This is Bureau Chief Horwath's newly issued order No. 68, you just take a look at it, you don't want . . ." Without waiting for him to finish what he was saying, Wu Tai and the other representatives turned and left. The general manager thought that they had been frightened off, but in fact the representatives paid no attention to his trickery, and they decided to convene a meeting immediately in order to discuss how to deal with the general manager. Besides representatives of workers in the main plant, representatives were also invited from other places such as the Maintenance Section and the railway station, and it was decided at the meeting that on the morning of the next day (May 1) a rally would be held on the banks of the Songhua River to solemnly commemorate the May 1 International Labor Day, and if the Railway Bureau did not agree to this the workers would strike. The workers' representatives then disseminated this resolution individually to all their worker comrades. As soon as the news became known, it was greeted with enthusiasm by workers everywhere, and when general manager Bakhilov heard about it he fumed with rage, threatening to take countermeasures. That afternoon he posted a "proclamation" at the gate of each of the branch plants. The proclamation contained Bureau Chief Horwath's "order No. 68," written in both Chinese and Russian, which thundered that, "Anyone who deserts his post without permission will be held criminally responsible under Article 384 of the penal code and liable to imprisonment of a period from four to eight months. . . ." The workers did not pay a bit of attention to the proclamation, however. Bakhilov then tried more of his tricks and vainly attempted to buy people over and lure them onto his side. He sent out several of his tsarist overseers to proclaim "those who work normally will get a raise in pay," and "those coming to work on May 1 will receive double pay" and so forth. The majority of the workers could see through these tricks of his and rejected them on the spot, leaving only a small number who were unable to make up their minds. To deal with the latter, the strike organizers sent around handbills, calling on the workers to unite and fight for their common interests.

    May 1 arrived, bringing with it exceptionally fine weather, and morale was high among the Chinese and Russian workers at the main plant. A minority of workers still intended to go to work, but they were persuaded otherwise by the striking workers before they made it through the factory gates, and they then took their place in the ranks of the strikers. At the same time workers at other plants such as the Harbin Maintenance Section, the Rolling Stock Section, the Station Goods Office, the Railway Printing Works, and the flour mills also took part in the strike and thronged forward to take part in the rally to commemorate International Labor Day. Early that morning workers had come from all corners and now they streamed toward the Songhua River, some of them bearing red flags. The Russian workers at the Maintenance Section had gotten an orchestra together, and it arrived at the banks of the river in a four-wheeled horse-driven carriage. In addition to the workers, there were also many students, business people, and ordinary citizens who had heard the news and come along to join in the May Day rally.

As the workers were congregating at the riverbank, the Railway Bureau Chief Horwath was at that very moment moving up the tsarist military police to suppress the rally by violent means. When the strike organizers found out what was happening they immediately decided to change their intended site, moving it from the south bank to the north bank of the river and instructing the workers to cross over the river at once. There were not enough small boats at hand to carry everyone across, and so contact was made with some of the cargo ships that were moored on the river. When the sailors on the ships heard that the workers wanted to hold a May Day rally, going against the objections of the shipowners, they resolutely took upon themselves the task of ferrying them across, even taking part in the May Day rally themselves. The whole gathering was quickly ferried over the river in all different kinds of vessels, and by the time the entire force of the tsarist military police arrived they were already too late.

After crossing the river, the workers selected a high, sloping piece of ground by the riverside as a site to hold their rally, and a hillock served as a natural speaker's platform. Red banners were unfurled on all sides carrying slogans such as "Long Live May Day," "Labor is Sacred," and "Proletarians of the World Unite." The rally was officially declared open at nine o'clock that morning, and many of the Chinese and Russian workers vied with one another to give speeches, using their own numerous personal experiences to lay bare the terrible crimes of the tsarist Russian invaders. The Chinese workers from the Thirty-six Barracks Plant accused the tsarist government of building railways and factories on Chinese soil; of treating the workers in an inhumane manner, as was the case with General Manager Bakhilov and others; of consuming the lifeblood of the workers and gorging themselves fat on it, while the workers went hungry; of living in large Western houses, while the workers had to live in the cold and dark Thirty-six Barracks. They lambasted them for failing to do a scrap of work all day long, but spending their time instead bullying and spying on the workers, while no one was concerned if the workers were being worked to death. These speeches with their vivid comparisons had a powerfully moving effect on everyone present and drew fervent applause. The Russian workers gave an introduction to the situation in their own country where the tsarists had bloodily suppressed the workers' and peasants' revolutionary movement, and they told of the deeds of the people in their struggle against the tsarist government. Speeches were also made by the flour mill workers, dock workers, transport workers, and workers who had come from areas along the line of the railway. While the meeting was in progress, peasants from all the villages close to the north bank of the river also came over to take part and all in all there were more than ten thousand people gathered there, with the rally lasting for six hours. To close, the gathering called on the workers to unite in order to improve their living conditions and fight for an eight-hour working day. The tsarist military police standing on the south bank of the river could only watch open-mouthed, since it was impossible for them to cross the river and break up the rally. The boats were all moored on the north bank, and even if they had wanted to come across there was no way that they could. That the workers had actually been able to hold such an extraordinary event as a May Day rally in Harbin, where antirevolutionary forces were rampant, was something that not only frightened Horwath witless but even startled the tsarist government. The prime minister of the tsar's cabinet charged the minister of finance, [Count V. N.] Kokovtsov, who was in charge of the Chinese Eastern Railway, to make a "special report" on this affair. In his report, Kokovtsov was forced to admit that: the meeting had taken place on the north bank of the Songhua River; more than ten thousand people had taken part from the main plant, the Chinese Eastern Railway, and other places, and the majority of them were Chinese; if military force had been used to suppress the event it would have served only to inflame the situation. The Jilin provincial police also treated this affair as a very serious matter, sending policemen to conduct an investigation, but they too did not dare to take any ill-considered action.

The 1907 May 1 general strike left a deep and glorious impression on the minds of workers on the Chinese Eastern Railway.

Social Conditions

The following texts represent two of the main types of writings on social history. Wang Wen's story is that of a poor child who receives an education through the efforts of Communist Youth League activists, enters upon the revolutionary path, and begins a glorious career. It is a rags-to-riches tale in a Communist setting, typical of the "recalling past sufferings" (yiku) genre so common in Maoist times.

Elements of this genre can also be found in the second article, which deals with prostitution in old Harbin, but here it is supplemented with features typical of the gazetteer project, such as quantitative data and more detached accounts of the location of brothels, the different classes of prostitutes, and so on. The extent in Harbin of social problems like prostitution, gambling, and opium smoking shocked even callous observers, and such topics receive a great deal of attention from the historians.

2F. A Harbin People's Night School in 1928

Wang Wen and Liang Fushan

Editor's note: In her childhood Comrade Wang Wen was a family servant in a comprador capitalist household. With the help of Yang Diankun (i.e., Yang Zuoqing, after Liberation assistant secretary-general of the Harbin Municipal People's Congress) she studied revolutionary theory and cultural knowledge at the People's Night School of the Harbin Eastern Provinces Special Zone First Middle School (now the Harbin First Middle School), which set her on the revolutionary path. In 1935 she left Harbin for Beiping. In 1936 she worked for the Northern Bureau of the Chinese Communist Party at the Xi'an Communications Station and in the Shaanxi Provincial Party Committee. During the War of Resistance she held in turn the posts of head of the Women's Section of the Liquan County Party Committee, member of the Provincial Women's Committee, and secretary of the Cadre Section of the Provincial Party Committee's Organization Department. During the War of Liberation she held the post of secretary of the Party's Northwestern Bureau. After Liberation she was head of the Discipline Inspection Unit of the Shaanxi Provincial Party Committee and a member of the Provincial Political Consultative Conference. In 1979 she was transferred to become a member of the Committee for Historical Text Materials of the National Political Consultative Conference.

In 1928 the warlords were carving up the country, and the Guomindang had betrayed the revolution. The entire country was engulfed in "white" terror, and the forces of revolution were temporarily at a low ebb. In that deep gloom of the old society I was spending my bitter childhood days in the city of Harbin. Because of the hardness of life, I lost my parents at an early age and was sold as a servant to the wife of a comprador capitalist.

I was just fourteen years old at the time. Although I was still only a child, every day I was made to do all kinds of manual labor such as heat water, wash dishes, wash clothing, and other housework. I also had often to do odd jobs for my mistress and in the evenings had to wait on her until she went to sleep before I could get any rest myself. There were times when the old comprador woman was in a bad mood and then she would take out her anger on me: for small things she would give me a heavy scolding and in more serious cases she would beat me senselessly. As my old wounds

Wang Wen and Liang Fushan, "Yijiuerba nian Haerbin de pingmin yexiao," *Haerbin shizhi* [Harbin History and Gazetteer], no. 2 (1985), pp. 75–77.

healed up they would be replaced by new ones; I cannot count the number of times I wept in those unbearably bitter days.

When I was sent out with the trash, I would often take the opportunity to hurry over to the Harbin Eastern Provinces Special Zone First Middle School (now Harbin First Middle School), climb up the iron gates, and look over into the school, thinking to myself: when will I be able to be like them, able to study, play games, and have sports lessons without a care in the world?

In that period, I often used to go over to the school gates to take a look at what was going on, and once, while watching the pupils playing basketball, I got so carried away that I forgot about everything else, about all my cares and worries. Suddenly I felt a kick from behind, which left me sprawling on the ground, and before I could figure out what had happened, I heard my mistress scolding: "Worthless wretch, I give you your food and your clothes, but do you do any work for me at home? No, you come out here and stand around gaping!" She lifted her bamboo stick and began to hit me on the head. Luckily some of the school pupils came over and wrested the stick from her, leaving me to run off home sobbing.

I did not dare go there again after that. But when I got out again I would always walk on tiptoe past the schoolyard and feast my eyes on what went on. Once I was looking into the school grounds when someone tapped me lightly from behind. Turning around, I saw that it was one of the pupils who had come to my defense earlier. He was tall and handsome, with a large squarish face. He asked me in a kind voice, "Would you like to go to school, little sister?" I shook my head. He asked again, "Is it that you don't want to go to school, then?" I shook my head once more. "Well, that's all right then," he continued happily, "there is a people's night school here, this evening I'll come and take you to start lessons."

I hesitated for a while, and shaking my head again, said, "It's no good, I don't have any money!"

He replied with a laugh, "Don't worry about money, we run classes especially for poor children, you don't have to pay!"

"But it's still no use, my 'mother' wouldn't let me, I've got work to do!"

"I'll go and explain to her for you. If you have work we can help you do it!"

I later learned that the person who persuaded me to begin studying was called Yang Diankun, that he studied in the second year of the senior section of the First Middle School and was then a member of the Communist Youth League.

They were very concerned at the time about poor children like myself, and they did everything they could to mobilize us into studying at the night schools they ran. Studying was something I had dreamed about night and day, but in those days I was not a free person!

And so they came time after time to my "home" to do work for my comprador mistress. They told her that after I had studied a little I would be able to do the household accounts, and so she would be able to employ one person less and save herself some money. The mistress thought it over and, reckoning that it would be worth her while, she agreed.

This made me at once indescribably happy; from now on I would have the great joy of going to school. How could the old woman have known that she had made a big mistake in her calculations, and that from the day I entered the school the party began to train me to be a gravedigger for her entire class!

The evening school had been set up in late 1928 following a directive of the Chinese Communist Party's Manchurian Provincial Committee. It was situated on the first floor of the south building of the First Middle School, and had two large classrooms, one for male and one for female students. The teachers included Li Zepu, Yang Diankun, Hou Qitian, and Zhao Qingwen, who at the time were all second- or third-year students in the senior section of the First Middle School, and there were also students from the junior section; some of them had already joined youth organizations led by the underground party.

The school's revolutionary education was finely woven into the cultural education, lecturing, and recreational activities; extracurricular extensive reading and organizational work for the school itself all had their place in the lessons.

The entire cost of the night school, from the textbooks we used to the books in the library, was met by voluntary contributions. The teachers received no money for teaching, and indeed contributed money to the school themselves whenever they had a little to spare. The poor children were always treated with the utmost solicitude. In the old society, where money was the only thing that counted, this method of running a school was a complete and utter revelation for us students.

We girl students were separated into a lower and a higher elementary class. These both took place in the one classroom, which was divided up for this purpose; when the teacher was giving a lesson to one group, the other group would be doing exercises, and vice versa. Since we all had such a strong desire to learn, we did not let this disturb us. There were three general subjects: Chinese, arithmetic, and Russian. I was quite good at my studies, outstripping the planned study schedule, and this was soon discovered by my teachers. Thereupon, after teaching the two groups of students, they would teach me on my own, giving me assignments and assessing them individually. The teachers would often work until they were exhausted. We saw this and remembered it in our hearts, becoming ever more assiduous in our studies, and so doing all we could to lighten their heavy burden.

Every Saturday there was a lecture meeting or an evening of entertainment. The lectures were organized according to subjects, and there were two main areas: the first was basic knowledge about theories of social science, especially the history of social development, and natural science; and the second was current events.

Under the "white" terror, the lectures could not mention Marx, the theory of surplus value, or any such words, but nevertheless the teachers were able to explain in detail the basic content of both the theory of surplus value and historical materialism. After we had learned to read a bit, we poor children found these theories very easy to accept. Because all that our teachers talked about were things that directly touched our lives, I had a sudden feeling of being able to see the light when I listened to these lectures, my heart and mind opened wide, and sometimes I was so excited that I could not sleep at night. Only later did I learn that these ideas were Marx's great discoveries.

The current affairs talks covered a wide range of topics, including atheism, national liberation, women's liberation, and the Soviet October Revolution, as well as the things we saw every day on the streets of Harbin. On November 9, 1928, Harbin's middle school and university students took to the streets to protest against the Japanese imperialists' attempts to force through the building of five railway lines in the Northeast. At that time the situation in the Northeast was very complicated, with both revolutionary and antirevolutionary propaganda trying to win over the masses, and the reactionaries were capitalizing on the Chinese Eastern Railway in order to attack the Soviet Union. The average student had trouble understanding the true state of affairs: many of them were hoodwinked and brought out by the warlords to agitate against the Soviet Union. Under cover of the noisy anti-Soviet propaganda, the Japanese imperialists had stealthily plotted to build five railways in a vain attempt to take control of the whole of the Northeast. Under the leadership of the Manchurian Provincial Party Committee, party organizations at all levels exposed this plot to the masses through widespread propaganda, and organized and led the massive November Ninth Movement opposed to the construction of the railways. Afterward the party organizations carried out a great deal of propaganda concerning this movement in the night schools, and the First Middle School's night school put together a propaganda booklet and a collection of photographs of students who were in hospital after having been beaten, and these were eagerly passed around. The teachers gave talks, and we wrote essays; this incident was a vivid and enlightening lesson to us on questions such as national liberation and the class struggle, one that we would remember our whole lives.

At that time, the confrontation between old and new ideological trends was very intense, and to carry on the struggle for progressive thinking against the feudal, backward, ignorant, and foul ideology that had held sway for thousands of years was far from easy. I had been a Buddhist since childhood, and in that period everyone, rich and poor alike, believed in Buddhism. The rich hoped for promotion and riches, while the poor hoped for a bright future. In those days Harbin had the Temple of Extreme Happiness, and I was taken along every year at the time of the temple fair to prostrate myself and pray to Buddha. In 1928 I was still a believer, but in 1929, after receiving education, I stopped believing and no longer went to kowtow to Buddha to improve my fate. When the comprador mistress returned she scolded me for being an atheist and gave me a ferocious beating. At that time being an atheist was practically synonymous with being a bandit, and it was seen as a terrible offense. In anger I wrote a long essay, which was much praised by my teacher and for which I was commended in front of the composition class.

The evenings of entertainment were mainly given over to the performance of plays, which were also very substantial in content. I particularly remember "The Seventy-two Martyrs of Huanghua Hill" and "Autumn Jade," and there were rewritten versions of famous Chinese and foreign literary works. It was all written, directed, and acted by the teachers and students themselves; everything was warm and friendly and the feelings of the actors and the audience blended into one.

The place I was most fond of at that time was the night school's small library, where within the cramped confines of its walls I could wander through the boundless universe, find out how to gain knowledge and how to walk along the path of life. Here it was that I read enlightening works such as *Primeval Society*, Darwin's *Origin of the Species*, as well as the novels of Jiang Guangci, Lu Xun's *Diary of a Madman*, Guo Moruo's *The Goddess*, and many others. These books were the spiritual food of my whole generation of revolutionary youth.

The night school ran for less than two years, but this period proved to be one of paramount importance for my whole life. For more than a year, even though I was beaten and scolded during the day, as soon as I got to the school it was like entering a different world. I began a new life there, I began the transformation from a slave to a revolutionary fighter.

After graduation from night school, in order to train me yet further the party did everything it could in order to get me through the entrance examination to the girls' middle school. Going to middle school was something I had not even dared dream about, and this gives a full embodiment of the party's meticulous concern for us poor children.

Later, with the help of the party organization, I was finally rescued from my hell on earth. I escaped from those jaws of death and ran off to Beiping, where I passed the examination for the Liangji Middle School for Girls and later served as a member of the presidium of the students' committee.

In 1935 I took part in the December Ninth Student movement, which shook the whole country. I was tempered and grew up during this struggle, and I became a member of the Chinese Communist Party. Not long afterward I was transferred to work for the Beiping Municipal Party Committee, and since then I have been walking the revolutionary road.

2G. The Brothels of Harbin in the Old Society

Song Shisheng

In the period of warlord domination before 1926, the area of Fujiadian had already more or less taken shape. (It lay in the Daowai district, originally under the administration of Binjiang County in Jilin Province and later falling under the Binjiang municipality). In those days, brothels, bane of so many women's lives, were increasing in number and beginning gradually to concentrate themselves in definite neighborhoods, which finally came to be rated in class according to a fixed hierarchy. For instance, the Pingkangli neighborhood, which the Binjiang government office planned and built (at what is now an area to the east of South Sixteenth Street in Daowai) was first generally called the "Sheep-Pen" neighborhood and this was later changed to "Luxuriant Fragrance." The "New World" hotel was also built at this time (now a ward of the Fourth Municipal Hospital), as well as the "Merry China Stage" amusement palace (southern neighbor to the Fourth Municipal Hospital on South Sixteenth Street). Two-story buildings were erected nearby. Some of them were used for living quarters for the theater actors, while others served as high-class brothels. This was the area where the high-class brothels had congregated, there being the "Virtuous Wind Inn," "Suolan Inn," "Baosheng Inn," and "Red Eagle Inn." The prostitutes here had all come from the Jiangsu and Zhejiang region; they were young and pretty and attracted men visiting the city. The "Luxuriant Fragrance" neighborhood had been built with the sole intention of being an area for brothels: in those days there were thirty-nine of them there including the "Welcome Spring Courtyard," "Heavenly Treasure Group," "Rich Spring Tower," and "Peach Garden Bookhouse." Another district was the "Northern Market," also known as the "Daguan Court" and by some as the "Eighteen Turns," which was situated in Daowai to the west of North Seventh Street and east of North Fifth Street, between Fujin Road and Qiantang Road; there were eighteen third-rate brothels here, the best-known of them being "Heavenly Happiness Hall," "Lucky and Merry Hall," "Golden Sage Hall," and "Richness Hall." Other districts were the "Baza Market," "Peach Flower Alley," "Trouser-crotch Street," "Eastern Market" (west of North

Song Shisheng, "Jiu shehui Haerbin de jinüyuan," *Haerbin shizhi* [Harbin History and Gazetteer], no. 2 (1988), pp. 52–54.

Twelfth Street and north of Qiantang Road), "Southern Market" (west of South Sixteenth Street and north of Taigu Road), and "Old Beancurd Lane" (west of North Fifth Street and north of Changchun Road). In addition, there were also a small number of brothels in the Xiangfang, Guxiang, and Taiping districts. Daoli was also home to many brothels started up by foreigners, the greatest number being Japanese-run, then Korean, and the least common were those run by Russians. In those days the Japanese brothels were concentrated on Diduan Street and Commercial Street among others; there were sixty-four of them, including "Kaijin Mansion" established by Ikeda Kunitaroo, Kanzaki Shinzoo's "New Happiness Mansion," Ikeda Mitsuo's "Sunrise Mansion," Honda Sakutaroo's "Benjin Mansion," and Fukugawa Imataroo's "Fragrance Mansion." There were sixteen Korean brothels in Daoli on Commercial Street and Shuidao (Zhaolin) Street, the biggest concentration of them being in "Willow Town" to the west of Commercial Street. In all, 510 Japanese and 240 Korean prostitutes were employed. The Russian brothels were on Factory Road, Tiandi Road, China Seventh Street (East Seventh Street), and China Third Street (East Third Street), and in all there were more than one hundred Russian prostitutes.

After the Japanese invaded Harbin in 1932, the number of brothels and the number of prostitutes increased rapidly and exorbitant taxes were placed on them. In January 1936 (third year of the puppet Kangde emperor), a tax on prostitutes of 4,414 yuan was imposed, and there were 1,435 prostitutes. Taxes were fixed according to the class of the brothel.

In 1939 (sixth year of the puppet Kangde emperor) the greatest number of prostitutes registered was 1,971, of which 1,162 were Chinese, 467 Japanese, 230 Korean, and 103 Russian.

It can be seen from the above figures that in the three short years from 1936 (third year of the puppet Kangde emperor) to 1939 (sixth year of the puppet Kangde emperor) the number of prostitutes increased by 536.

Not long after the Japanese bandits had invaded Harbin, they began to increase their bullying and oppression of the Chinese population, greatly raising the price of the Japanese prostitutes and no longer admitting Chinese into their brothels. At the same time they also included Korean prostitutes in the same category as Japanese, stopping them from receiving Chinese customers and reserving them solely for the service of Japanese.

From 1935 (second year of the puppet Kangde emperor) to 1939 (sixth year of the puppet Kangde emperor) the brothels were open twenty-four hours a day. Life in the old society was indeed a hell on earth.

The majority of the prostitutes in the brothels had been abducted or purchased as young girls or young women from the Jiangsu and Zhejiang region and later sold in Harbin to the procuresses who ran the brothels. Later, after they had been brought up and trained, they would be forced to begin working as prostitutes. In the spring of 1931 (the twentieth year of the Republic), a girl of only six years of age by the name of Li was sold by her stepfather to a trader in human beings; she was then brought in a round-about way to Fujiadian, where she was sold to a brothel in the "Luxuriant Fragrance" neighborhood. At first she followed the everyday life of the brothel madam and would go on trips out of the brothel. At the age of fourteen, thanks to her brothel upbringing, quick wits, and talent for musical instruments, conversation, and singing, she became an "honest official" (a girl who merely conversed, sang, and played music for the guests), a role for which she had been specially trained by a celebrated prostitute. When she was sixteen, however, the brothel madam forced her to spend the night with a rich shop proprietor, who was more than fifty years of age. The madam had previously told her many times that if she upset the customers in any way, she and her pimp would beat her mercilessly. This was what she had also heard from the other girls, and her best friend among them had secretly warned her about this. During the long years when she had been learning to sing and "converse," she would often be beaten black and blue if she made a mistake, and even left with nothing to eat. This was especially the case when she was a little older and about to begin receiving guests: she was taught how to welcome guests and show them out, to act as their host and keep them company, in a manner similar to training to be an actor. If she neglected any of the guests, she would be scolded and even beaten. And Li was not the only prostitute, for at that time their number was legion.

As early as 1902 (the twenty-eighth year of the Guangxu emperor) after Russia had opened the Dong-Qing Railway, the industry and commerce of Harbin blossomed intact with the building of the town and the rapid increase in population. Because of the large-scale construction work, refugees escaping from famine swarmed to Harbin from all over China, the greatest number being single men from provinces such as Shandong and Hebei who had come to support themselves by the sweat of their brow. And so all walks of life in Harbin gradually prospered, and with the increase in the city's size small houses of prostitution began to appear everywhere, at that time scattered among the houses of ordinary citizens. At first it was often the case that husbands and wives or lovers went into the prostitution business as partners. Later some of them began increasingly to buy girls cheaply from traffickers and so start up brothels. Since the income was good the size of the brothels increased, as did the number of prostitutes, and a very rapid development took place. Beginning in 1910 (the second year of the Xuantong emperor), a steady stream of women and young girls came to

Harbin after being purchased in the south of China. On September 16, 1910, the *Far Eastern Reporter*, founded by the Dong-Qing Railway, published an article called "Traffickers in Humans Again Resurgent," in which it was written:

> In recent days the city has seen the arrival of women being brought up for sale from the south, with several arriving each day. They are mostly sold to bordellos in the area around Peach Blossom Alley, and it is also said that some are transported to Heihe and Sanxing. There are around four or five women on every steamship and their selling price is four to five hundred rubles per head. When they arrive in Harbin they stay in one of the many inns in Peach Blossom Alley; the traffickers live in other parts of the town and they leave one of their womenfolk there to watch over them. There are reports that there was another consignment of young boys and girls yesterday, and that they are now also staying in the inns, where new owners are being sought for them.

Cases of this type were by no means uncommon. For instance, on May 19, 1911, a Suzhou man Zhu Laomo abducted a married woman Xu, born Wu, from Xu village, lying ten *li* to the west of Changzhou. He sold her to a low-class brothel, but as she was not willing to work as a prostitute, she ran away on the night of June 24 that same year and was taken to the "Institution for the Promotion of Decency." Similarly, in June 1911 Wen Xian, a prostitute in the "Two Winds Mansion" brothel on Tongfa Street in Fujiadian, was forced by the brothel madam and the pimp Li Guilin to kneel for a long period of time on a wooden plank, whereupon she was scolded and beaten over and over again with iron implements until the skin was ripped off both her knees and she was swimming in blood. Yu Hong, a prostitute at the "Double Pleasing Team" brothel, was regularly scolded and beaten by the procuress in a savage manner as she could not attract enough customers and therefore did not make much money. There was also the case of a prostitute called Yin Fu, who was sixteen years old; she had been sold to a brothel as a child, where she learned to sing and play music. She was later sold to a brothel in Tianjin as a prostitute and from there to the "Three Joys Team" brothel in Harbin. She was subsequently bought by a customer by the name of Lin from Ningbo, and after traveling around with him for a few months, she was finally sold to the "Rising Happiness Team" in Peach Blossom Alley. Yin Fu was young and pretty, and in this low-class brothel she was forced to receive no fewer than seven or eight clients a day. She was several months' pregnant at the time and could not bear to receive guests so often. Unable to get any rest, she asked that she be given fewer customers, but the pimp Wang Haishan refused and continued to force her to take customers every day. Finally, unable to stand it any longer, she escaped to the "Institution for the Promotion of Decency." Finally, there was the instance of Yu Ru, a prostitute at a low-class brothel in the Peach Blossom Alley area, who being older in years did not receive many customers and so was cruelly tormented by the madam. Unable to bear it any more, she also absconded to "Institution for the Promotion of Decency."

Seeing the rapid increase in the prostitution business, the Japanese also got in on the act and began starting up brothels. By the end of 1911 there were already fifteen Japanese brothels in operation, which exclusively employed Japanese prostitutes and accepted customers of all nationalities. Each brothel made more than a thousand rubles a month and sometimes many hundred rubles more than that. By the spring of 1916 (the fifth year of the Republic) a survey showed that out of the Japanese population of Fujiadian there were twenty-one families who ran brothels. By August of the same year, the number of brothel keepers had risen to twenty-eight and there were 198 prostitutes: an increase of 30 percent in the space of just six months. There was also a large increase in the number of brothels opened by Chinese, these being situated among the homes of the general population. The fact that brothels were lying side by side with the homes of decent families was seen as a problem, and so in 1911 (the third year of the Xuantong emperor) the subprefect of the Binjiang government office, Lin Xiaoting, decided to copy the methods that had been applied in Fengtian (now Shenyang) and asked the provincial governor for money to set up the Pingkangli brothel district. In December 1916 (the fifth year of the Republic), it was decided to locate the district in Dongsijiazi (now an area to the east of South Sixteenth Street in Daowai); public land was set aside especially for the purpose and preparations were made for the construction to begin. Because the public funds forthcoming were insufficient, however, the Binjiang county magistrate Li called a meeting of local gentry and merchants to investigate methods for the design and construction of the brothel district and make estimates as to its cost. It was decided to construct twelve buildings, and the cost of more than 200,000 yuan was to be covered by holding back the revenue from the lands sale and spending it locally. But when the money raised in this way was still found to be insufficient to cover the costs, it was agreed to adopt the method of raising money by different parties buying shares in the project, with each share selling for one thousand rubles. The capitalists saw this as a good opportunity to make a profit, and many of them invested in the construction project. Work on the Pingkangli neighborhood began in the spring of 1917 (the sixth year of the Republic). More brothel areas, divided according to class, were later built in this fashion, with the construction being funded through private investment and the buildings then being rented out. The phenomenon of brothels and citizens coexisting side by side was in this way gradually eliminated and prostitution came to be concentrated in certain centers.

In 1910 (the second year of the Xuantong emperor), the Binjiang government office looked into the matter of prostitution and found that prostitutes were being badly treated and that there were more and more of them running away and lodging complaints, so that the situation was getting out of hand. They therefore decided to set up the "Binjiang Institution for the Promotion of Decency," whose sole purpose was to admit unwilling prostitutes who had absconded from their brothels. The women were then provided with alternative occupations. It was stipulated at the time that the brothels had no right to demand the return of any of those who sought refuge in the "Institution for the Promotion of Decency," and so there were pimps (commonly known as "big teapots") standing guard at the brothels and "inns" (the lodgings where the prostitutes, madams, and pimps ate and slept); if the prostitutes went out they were always accompanied by a pimp or a madam to prevent them from escaping.

All those in power in the old society viewed prostitution as an indispensable means of maintaining their domination through the weakening of the people's health. The system of prostitution greatly affected the physical well-being of the population and its reproductive capability. The prostitute registration figures for 1939 (sixth year of the puppet Kangde emperor) show that there was a total of 1,971 prostitutes, which was an increase of 10.4 percent over 1938. In an examination of 41,665 people over a period of time, it was found that 2,935 were suffering from venereal diseases, an incidence rate of 7.1 percent. The rate among Chinese prostitutes was 10.2 percent. It can be seen from this that prostitutes were the main medium of the transmission of venereal diseases. The incidence rate was higher among Chinese prostitutes than it was among foreign ones; one in five was a carrier of the diseases.

After Liberation, the Harbin Municipal People's Government adopted measures appropriate to dealing with the situation. In November 1949 the prostitutes were sorted into different groups: those with homes to go to were sent home, those who were ill were given treatment, and there were also more than two thousand prostitutes sent to work for an honest living in the gold mines and the Hegang and other coal mines. Then the more than twenty brothel neighborhoods scattered throughout the city were totally cleared away, and thereby the conditions that favored the transmission of venereal diseases were thoroughly eradicated.

1. Archaeologists unearthing one of the thirteen Jin Dynasty tombs found in Xiangfang District, Harbin, in 1982. Richer finds have been done in the old Jin capital in Acheng, but the Xiangfang graves prove Nüzhen activity inside the present city limits. From *Harbin Looking Ahead* (Hong Kong: The Red Flag Publishing House, 1987), p. 309.

2. The Harbin Railway Station was the heart of the city, and a crossroad for international travel between Europe and East Asia. By courtesy of the Royal Danish Library.

3. Chinese immigrants, squeezed together like cattle, on their way to Harbin. By courtesy of the Royal Danish Library.

4. In the early 1920s, when this photo was taken, Harbin was already a modern metropolis. From *Manchuria. Land of Opportunities* (New York: The South Manchuria Railway Company, 1924), p. 53.

5. A view of Harbin from the early 1930s, focusing on the Russian cathedral. From Lucien Gibert, *Dictionnaire Historique et Geographique de la Mandchourie* (Hong Kong: La Société des Missions-Étrangères, 1934), p. 215.

6. The main street of Fujiadian, Harbin's "Chinatown," from the early 1930s. From Lucien Gibert, *Dictionnaire Historique et Geographique de la Mandchourie* (Hong Kong: La Société des Missions-Étrangères, 1934), p. 215.

7. The Harbin waterfront, around 1935. The Songhua River has played a crucial role in Harbin's economic life throughout the century, particularly as a means of transportation for the bulk commodities of the region, such as soybeans and wheat. From *Fifth Report on Progress in Manchuria to 1936* (Dairen: The South Manchuria Railway Company, 1936), p. 72.

8. The Hotel Moderne. Its owner in the early 1930s, Josef Kaspé, was an extremely wealthy Jewish businessman, whose son was kidnapped and killed by Russian fascists in 1933. The Moderne, now the Madier (in Chinese), was for many years the city's finest hotel, and housed, among other prominent guests, the League of Nations Commission when it came to Harbin in 1932 to investigate the "Manchurian Affair." From *Harbin Scenery* (Hong Kong: Haerbin Renmin Zhengfu Bangongting, 1983), p. 37.

9. In 1932, shortly after the Japanese had occupied Harbin, a serious flood hit North Manchuria. More than 100,000 people were made homeless by the 1932 flood. The picture shows a Russian *droshky* struggling with the water in one of the main streets of the city. By courtesy of Kai Ibsen, author of *Den kinesiske traad. En dansk familiekroenike* [The Chinese Thread: A Danish Family Chronicle] (Copenhagen: Woeldike, 1981), p. 118.

10. During the 1932 flood, even the new Japanese masters had to resort temporarily to more humble means of transportation. By courtesy of Kai Ibsen, author of *Den kinesiske traad. En dansk familiekroenike* [The Chinese Thread: A Danish Family Chronicle] (Copenhagen: Woeldike, 1981), p. 118.

11. To the left is the small Russian-style building that housed the CCP Manchurian Committee in 1933–34. In 1988 this building was reconstructed in a more impressive shape and inaugurated as a Memory Hall *(right)*. From *Longjiang dangshi,* no. 6, 1988, p. 1.

12. Street venders. Many Russians in Harbin were extremely poor, and in the early 1930s the streets were reported to be crowded with Russian beggars, earning for the city yet another name: The grave of the white man's prestige. From James A.B. Scherer, *Manchukuo: A Bird's-eye View* (Tokyo: The Hokuseido Press, 1933), after p. 76.

13. The Harbin Polytechnical Institute, established in 1920 primarily to train technicians for the CER, is the oldest and most prestigious of the city's universities. From *Harbin* (Harbin: The Office of Foreign Affairs of People's Government of Harbin City, 1985), p. 77.

14. On 27 February 1950, Mao Zedong visited the Harbin Railway Car Factory on the way home from his stay in Moscow in the winter of 1949–50. In a 1988 publication the event is—still—pictured in a 1960s fashion. From *Haerbin Cheliang Gongchang jianchang jiushizhounian jinian, 1898–1988* (Harbin: Haerbin Cheliang Gongchang, 1988), p. 2.

15. Harbin has always been deeply affected by changes in Sino-Russian/ Soviet relations. This picture is from a 1969 demonstration in connection with clashes on the Ussuri River. The banner says: "A Strong Protest Against the Soviet Revisionists' Encroachment of the Territory of Our Country." From *China Pictorial*, no. 5, 1969, p. 21.

16. Present-day Harbin from the air. On the riverbank are the Stalin Park and the monument for the 1957 struggle against a threatening flood. From *Harbin* (Harbin: The Office of Foreign Affairs of People's Government of Harbin City, 1985), p. 12.

17. Early June 1989. Pro-democracy demonstrators on Central Avenue. Photograph by Søren Clausen.

3

Japanese Occupation: 1932–1945

An Outline History

The Defense of Harbin

On September 18, 1931, officers of the Japanese Guandong Army engineered the Mukden incident by blowing up the South Manchurian Railway line north of Mukden (Shenyang) and blaming the explosion on the Chinese. When the Guandong Army under this pretext moved into South Manchuria it met no opposition from Zhang Xueliang, who in full understanding with Chiang Kai-shek and the Guomindang government in Nanjing immediately ordered his troops to follow a policy of nonresistance (see Coble 1991, pp. 11–55, for a discussion of the nonresistance policy). Within a few days the Japanese were in control of the major South Manchurian cities.

While intramural China felt paralyzed and humiliated by Zhang Xueliang's surrender, some of his commanders in North Manchuria defied his orders and turned against the invaders. This was the case in the Harbin area, where the military situation soon grew highly complicated. At this time the city was administratively divided in four parts under various Chinese authorities, and the military situation reflected this fact with local troops being under different lines of command (for an overview of the troops and their shifting loyalties after the Mukden incident see Wang Xiliang 1987 and Jing Nan 1985). The Japanese preferred to conquer Harbin through Chinese collaborationist (or "puppet") forces because of the intricate international situation in the city, and this strategy initially seemed to work. The head of the Eastern Provinces Special Zone, Zhang Jinghui, cooperated closely with the Japanese, and so did Xi Qia, who was acting governor of Jilin Province. Other commanders did not agree with the policy of nonresistance, however, and the armed forces in North Manchuria soon split into collaborationist and nationalist factions. By January 1932 commanders such as Li Du and Feng Zhanhai were prepared to defend Harbin against the Guandong Army and their Chinese puppet troops (Wang Xiliang 1987, pp. 2–7). Inside the city the situation was getting tense. Qiqihar had fallen already on November 18, and Harbin was now the last obstacle to total Japanese control over Manchuria. The Japanese had instigated a series of fires and explosions in the city to prove the need for law and order, and rumors circulated that the Red Army would soon intervene in Manchuria to protect Soviet interests (Wang Xiliang 1987, pp. 2–4; Stephan 1978, p. 63). The Soviet Union was not interested in fighting the Japanese alone, however, and Harbin was left to its fate.

On January 25 anti-Japanese soldiers under the command of Li Du moved into Harbin and took control of the city. Together with other local commanders Li established the Jilin Provincial Self-Defense Army General Headquarters counting over 15,000 men, and the puppet army, which had reached the southern suburbs of Harbin a few days earlier, suffered a serious defeat in its first encounter with these forces (Jing Nan 1985, pp. 34–38). In early February the Japanese army took over and, supported by tanks, heavy artillery, and aircraft, it completed its invasion of Harbin on February 5 after heavy fighting (Wang Xiliang 1987). The Japanese were enthusiastically welcomed by the White Russian population, but for the Chinese citizens their entrance marked the beginning of thirteen years under new foreign masters (Stephan 1978, p. 63). Fighting in the area continued, and anti-Japanese forces even attempted to recapture Harbin between April and June, but the Japanese control of the city was never seriously threatened (Wang Xiliang 1987, pp. 12–16; Liu Hua'nan 1987, pp. 44–49).

Inside and outside China, Ma Zhanshan, the hero of the Nonni River Battle in November 1931, became the main symbol of patriotic resistance to the Japanese invasion of the Northeast (Coble 1991, pp. 14–15). In a special issue of *Text Materials on Harbin History* from 1987, the Harbin historians show that the Defense of Harbin, in which Ma also played an important role, equaled, if not surpassed, the Nonni River episode in importance ("Haerbin kang-Ri baoweizhan" [The Anti-Japanese Defense War of Harbin], *Haerbin wenshi ziliao*, no. 11, 1987). The number of Japanese killed in the battles around Harbin is given at over 1,100, a high figure compared with the Japanese claim in March 1932 that only 378 military personnel had been killed in Manchuria (Wang Xiliang 1987, pp. 16–17; Coble 1991, p. 14). The issue consists mostly of vivid accounts from participants and eyewitnesses, who reflect the complicated, even confused, military and political situation at the time. The introduction brings home the message that Harbin's name through this battle is closely associated not only with patriotism but also with the Communist Party. The connection is established by pointing to the fact that those areas where the anti-Japanese forces were most active in 1932–33 later became centers of CCP guerrilla activity:

> In a certain sense, the anti-Japanese guerrilla struggle led by the CCP in northern Manchuria is inseparably bound up with the anti-Japanese activities carried out by the Jilin Self-Defense Army and the National Salvation Army in order to protect and recapture Harbin. If the first one is like a vast ocean of a mass nature, then the latter is like the first stream contributing to that ocean. (Wang Xiliang 1987, p. 18)

It has been shown by Chong-Sik Lee that the CCP was facing serious difficulties in Manchuria around this time, not least so in Harbin, and the party's active role in the Defense of Harbin must have been limited (Lee 1983, particularly pp. 127–57). The Harbin historians do not try to magnify the party's importance for the resistance, but rather present the patriotic movement as *pointing forward* toward the coming of the party.

Japanese Administration

After the entry of the Japanese troops, Harbin became part of Manzhouguo (Manchukuo), which was established by the Japanese on March 1, 1932. Changchun, renamed Xinjing, became capital of this puppet state formally headed by Pu Yi, who was given the title of emperor in March 1934.

In July 1933 the separate sections of Harbin were merged to form Harbin Special Municipality (*Haerbin tebie shi*), which was placed directly under the Manzhouguo government. The Special Municipality, which also included areas formerly under the counties of Acheng and Hulan, covered 925 square kilometers and had a population of over 500,000.[1] A Self-Government Committee was set up with twenty-one members (thirteen Chinese, three Japanese, three Russians, and two other foreigners) (*Manchoukuo: Handbook of Information* 1933, p. 118). The city mayor and most city government officials were Chinese collaborators, while the positions of vice mayor and other key posts were held by Japanese. Japanese control over the formerly cosmopolitan city was further strengthened in March 1935, when the Soviet Union sold the Chinese Eastern Railway (from this time called the North Manchuria Railway), formally to Manzhouguo, but in fact to the Japanese, who, as part of the deal, took care of the transfer back to the Soviet Union of over 20,000 Soviet railway employees and their relatives; more than 13,000 of them had been based in Harbin (*Fifth Report on Progress in Manchuria*, pp. 58–65). The Japanese considered Harbin the natural center of North Manchuria, and several administrative organs, first of the North Manchuria Special District and from 1934 of Binjiang Province, were set up here. In 1937 Harbin's status as a Special Municipality was abolished, and instead it became the capital of Binjiang, one of the sixteen provinces into which Manzhouguo had been divided by that time. In January 1938 the Self-Government Committee was replaced by a Consultative Council (ziyihui), and in 1941 the administration of the city was in reality put into the hands of the Concordia Society (xiehehui; Jap., kyuwakai), a fascist organization with the official aim of promoting the harmonious coexistence of the different peoples of the Northeast (for a Chinese discussion of the Concordia society see Jiang et al. 1991, pp. 226–42). With each of these changes the Japanese monopoly of power in the city became ever more thinly masked.

Economic Development

The Japanese occupation deeply influenced the economy of Manchuria. A unified currency, the Manzhouguo yuan, was introduced in 1932 to replace the different Chinese and foreign currencies in circulation in the area at that time, and in 1935 its value became linked to the Japanese yen. Also, public finances and tax administration were centralized (for developments in currency and finance in Manchuria after 1931, see Jones 1949, pp. 123–39). The railroad net was extended with several new lines, and modern roads and airfields were built. These investments in infrastructure paved the way for an exploitation of Manchuria's rich natural resources of coal, iron, and other minerals and for an expansion of industrial production, particularly in heavy industry.

The industrial development of Manchuria was not left to chance. "Special companies" under the control of the Japanese state through the South Manchuria Railway Company monopolized all those branches of mining and manufacturing that were said to be vital for national defense. Gradually, and particularly after 1938, Japanese control over the supply of raw materials, prices, and so on, was extended to all major industries, even the production of vegetable oil, flour, and liquor, branches that traditionally were strong in Harbin (Sun 1969, pp. 75–79; Jiang et al. 1991, pp. 325–31). Japanese investments in Manchuria during the occupation were massive, 10,400 million yen up to 1944, equivalent to almost U.S. $2,500 million by 1941 exchange rates (Beasley 1987, pp. 214–15). This led to a rapid industrial development of the region. Kungtu C. Sun's calculations show that industrial production in Manchuria grew rather slowly in the late 1920s, dropped slightly just after the invasion, but rose dramatically after 1934, so that it almost trebled between 1933 and 1942 (Sun 1969, p. 102). Such figures have generally convinced Western historians that the Manzhouguo era was characterized by considerable economic progress. F. C. Jones, one of the first to analyze this period, concluded that "the Japanese had built up in Manchuria an industrial potential which was far ahead of anything which existed elsewhere in Eastern Asia, exclusive of Japan herself and of the Soviet Far East," although he added that Manchuria had a war economy that was too closely linked to that of Japan (Jones 1949, pp. 164–65). Kang Chao, in another influential study, found that "the Japanese left behind them a most important economic legacy when they surrendered in Manchuria in 1945. They left a much more developed region than they acquired."[2] In his study of Japanese imperialism, W. G. Beasley also emphasizes the difference between purely exploitative imperialist behavior and the Japanese policy toward Manchuria, which included the development of industry, the provision of an infrastructure and the training of a work force (Beasley 1987, pp. 255–58). Chinese historians of the 1980s sharply disagree with the view that the Japanese occupation should have promoted the economic development of the Northeast. They generally base their work on the same sources as the above authors, that is, primarily Manzhouguo and Japanese surveys and statistics from that time, but their conclusions are different. They tend to emphasize the exploitation of the Manchurian work force, the plundering of natural resources, the unbalanced growth geared to the needs of the Japanese war machine, the one-sided dependency on Japan, the liquidation of the Chinese national bourgeoisie, which could have sustained a more "natural" capitalist development, and the stagnation in the agricultural sector. They therefore judge that the Japanese regime was of a clearly colonial nature and that the post-1949 industrial development of the Northeast took place not because but in spite of what happened under the Japanese.[3]

Regardless of the situation in the region as a whole, Harbin did not experience an industrial expansion on a scale similar to that of the urban centers in South Manchuria, where Japanese investments were most concentrated. The soybean processing industry never fully recovered after the Great Depression, and its markets inside and outside China were further weakened in the 1930s. To make matters worse the Japanese decided to concentrate soybean processing in Dalian, so that the number of oil mills in Harbin dropped from 39 in 1927 to only 17 by 1935 (Jiang et al. 1991, pp. 319–22). As described in Text 2D the wheat milling industry was hit by a similar crisis. Much of the city's transit trade moved to ports in Korea and South Manchuria, and the total trade of the city dropped dramatically from 105.1 million yuan in 1930 to just 5.2 million in 1936 (Sun 1969, pp. 97–98; Jones 1949, p. 212, based on *Contemporary Manchuria*, vol. 2, no.

5 [September 1938], p. 84). The exodus of the Soviet citizens after the sale of the railway added to the depression, and many foreign companies chose to move out when they were forced to accept Japanese "advisers" and were in other ways harassed by the occupation authorities, who put more and more restrictions on their business activities (for an example of Japanese pressure on a foreign company in Harbin see Ibsen 1981, pp. 112–52). On top of this came natural disasters, when the Songhua River flooded the city in 1932 and 1934. On the first occasion, which was also the most serious, the main disaster area was Fujiadian, where the Chinese population lived, but the streets of Daoli were also flooded. Around 100,000 people had to flee their homes, the city's infrastructure broke down, and epidemic diseases followed (Zheng Yingshuang 1988).

In spite of such difficulties, Harbin still saw a relative flourishing of small- and medium-scale enterprises in service and industry during the first years of occupation. According to a survey carried out by the Manzhouguo Central Bank, Harbin had 456 such enterprises by 1937, half of which had been opened after 1931. Two-thirds of them had capital of less than 5,000 yuan, and a similar proportion employed between six and thirty workers.[4] The capital normally came from one or two people who had moved to Manchuria from Shandong or Hebei, so many Chinese must still have seen the business climate in Harbin as at least tolerable. Later, however, Japanese control over all business activities made it almost impossible to make any profits, and many had to close down.

As for the economic history of this period, the main focus of the Harbin historians has been on the fate of the Chinese national bourgeoisie. Two leading figures in the flour milling industry, Zhang Tingge, whose biography is translated in Text 2C, and Shao Yueqian, who tells his family's story in Text 2D, can serve as examples. In both texts the emphasis is on the harm inflicted on the native capitalists by the Japanese occupation authorities. What these texts also illustrate, however, is that intense transactions took place between the Chinese businessmen and the Japanese, not least in the form of bribery. This was to be expected in a situation where the Japanese set the rules, and no Chinese company could probably survive without it, but it is remarkable that this coexistence and adaption to political realities is in no way denounced by the historians. Likewise, the relationship between the national bourgeoisie and the workers is portrayed as non-antagonistic. Where exploitation and poor work conditions are described, the scene is set in foreign-owned enterprises, as in Text 2B. This could be described as a United Front tactic applied to the field of historical writing: the fact that the Harbin capitalists were allies in the struggle against the Japanese exempts them from blame in other contexts.

Life in the City

The population of Harbin grew during the Japanese occupation, from around 400,000 in 1932 to 500,000 in 1938–39 and then to around 700,000 in the early 1940s. By 1947, when population figures are again available, Harbin had 800,000 citizens, a doubling in fifteen years (Li Shuxiao 1986). This development partly reflected the immigration policies of the Japanese who immediately after the invasion encouraged Japanese and Korean rather than Chinese settlement in Manchuria. They therefore set up restrictions on Chinese immigration, the effect of which was strengthened by Chinese reluctance to live in the occupied areas. After 1937, however, the need for manpower grew with the industrial development. This led to a more active immigration policy culminating after the start of the Pacific War, when the Japanese even started to force Chinese workers to relocate to Manchuria. The main sources for immigration were still the provinces of Shandong and Hebei (Li and Shi 1987, pp. 89–106; Jones 1949, pp. 167–69). The rapid growth of the Chinese population probably reflected the fact that economic opportunities in Harbin were better than in the villages from which the new immigrants came.[5] Still, wages were low, housing conditions in the crammed slums of Fujiadian and Taiping districts were miserable, and unemployment, hunger, and cold were constant problems. In 1938 the average daily wage was only 0.8 Manchurian yuan for an ordinary Harbin workman and 1.7 yuan for a bricklayer. The wages of the Japanese workers in Harbin were three to four times higher (Jones 1949, p. 216, based on *The Far East Yearbook, 1941*, pp. 852–53). Crime was rampant in the city, and even more so in the surrounding countryside, where the *hong huzi* (bandits or "redbeards") ruled. In 1935, more than 90 percent of the Chinese immigrants coming to Manchuria were male, and in 1937 the proportion of males to females in Harbin was almost two to one (Li and Shi 1987, p. 102; Li Shuxiao 1986, p. 259. The exact figures were 289,470 males and 168,510 females). This was one of the reasons behind the boom in prostitution described in Text 2G. The "Opium Law" promulgated by the Japanese in 1932 had the official aim of controlling the traffic in drugs, but in reality it only helped the Japanese to monopolize the opium market. By 1936 Harbin had 65 official opium dens and 194 opium shops. Some years later the number of opium dens had gone up to 120 (Tian Deshen 1988, p. 26). The fact that much of the immigration to Harbin was only temporary, with many people traveling back and forth to their homes in intramural China, added to the social confusion of the city.

The living conditions of the Chinese population receive relatively little attention from local historians, except for general statements about poverty and hardships. Although apparently no systematic research has been done in this field, the memoir literature typical of the *Historical Text Materials* (cf. Chapter 5) offers occasional insights, mostly as by-products of political history, particularly party history, like in Texts 3A and 3B.

The Japanese occupation changed the ethnic composition of Harbin's population, but only gradually. In 1930 the foreign population of Harbin consisted of 3,910 Japanese, 1,422 Koreans, and 69,987 from other nationalities, mainly "white" and "red" Russians. The Chinese population numbered 309,253 (*Manchuria Year Book 1931*, p. 7). By the end of 1939, when the Chinese population had grown to 433,234, the number of Japanese and Koreans had risen to 38,197 and 6,330 respectively, while the number of citizens of other nationalities had dropped to 39,366, out of which 28,103 were white Russians. In other words, half the Russian and European population had left and been replaced by Japanese and Koreans (Fochler-Hauke 1941, p. 223, obviously drawing on official Japanese statistics). According to one source, there were still 38,134 foreign nationals in Harbin in 1947, but the composition of this group is not given (Li Shuxiao, p. 342). Westerners who lived in or traveled to Harbin during the 1930s described the city as a worn-out, decadent, almost desperate, but somehow still charming beauty, clinging to her reputation as the Paris of the Far East, but step by step being taken over by the new Japanese masters. These writers mainly identified with the Russian refugees from the Bolshevik revolution, whose social déroute they saw as tragic but more picturesque than the abject poverty of the Chinese majority (see for example Cordes 1936, pp. 39–55). In the early 1930s the Russian population was still almost equally divided between "reds," with Soviet passports, and "white" émigrés, but after the Chinese Eastern Railway was sold in 1935, most of the reds returned to the Soviet Union. The situation of the whites, who had welcomed the Japanese occupation forces in 1932, became still more critical as business opportunities narrowed in step with Manzhouguo's international isolation and the expanding Japanese control over the city's economy. The frustrations of the once wealthy immigrants made Harbin a fruitful breeding ground for the Russian fascist movement, for which Harbin became the main international center due to the nature of the Harbin Russian community, which remained for decades a miniature replica of prerevolutionary Russia. In addition to their political activities, Russian fascists also organized kidnappings of wealthy Jewish citizens, such as Semion (or Simon) Kaspé, son of the owner of the fashionable Hotel Moderne.[6] A considerable exodus of white Russians took place during the 1940s to cities like Shenyang, Tianjin, and Shanghai, but at the time of the

Japanese surrender Harbin still had a considerable Russian community (Du Que 1985, p. 40).

The strong Jewish community that existed in Harbin in the 1920s was decimated during the following years, when the Kaspé affair and other anti-Jewish incidents convinced most of the Manchurian Jews that they would be safer in the international settlement in Shanghai or in other Chinese cities. One source says that 70 percent of Harbin's Jews had fled by the mid-1930s.[7] Many businessmen from European countries also moved their activities to intramural China, while several missionaries remained in the city.

The Japanese domination was visible in the streets of Harbin. A Danish businessman who returned to Harbin in 1939 for the first time since the Japanese occupation described the changes in the following way:

> On our way from the railway station we went through Uchaskovaja, a business street in the center of town. The street was swarming with ladies in kimonos tripping along respectfully behind their masters in their wooden sandals. Here and there you could see people smiling and bowing to each other, or little groups carrying out the traditional Japanese greeting ceremony. The ladies always made the deepest bows. And then there were the many Japanese soldiers in their bright yellow-beige uniforms, maybe on leave from the war in China or from the more indefinite front in the Northwest. The stores in Uchaskovaja were almost all Japanese, and even the big department stores from Tokio had opened branches here. The white flag with the big red sun in the center was waving everywhere. The clicking sound of wooden sandals was unmistakable. Well, this part of town we call "Little Tokio," my father said. (Ibsen 1981, p. 120)

Like the Russians before them, the Japanese were modeling Harbin in their own image, but not without Chinese opposition. Chinese, and particularly Communist, resistance to the occupation is a major theme of historical writing in Harbin.

Resistance and Suppression

While the CCP had faced severe difficulties in Manchuria already in the 1920s, the division of Harbin into zones under different police authorities had still left some room for oppositional activities. The Japanese occupation led to an even more efficient persecution of the party members, and the memoirs of veterans of the 1930s show how staying alive and maintaining the most rudimentary contacts with the party organization were their primary concerns. The Japanese counterintelligence (*tewu;* Jap., *tokumu*) was well informed about party affairs, and callously and repeatedly cracked down on all traces of opposition (Lee 1983, passim). In January 1932, the CCP Manchurian Provisional Committee headed by Luo Dengxian moved from Mukden to Harbin, which was at that time still considered safer, and that same month Yang Jingyu, who later in the 1930s became one of the main anti-Japanese guerrilla leaders in Manchuria, was made secretary of the city party committee (Lee 1983, particularly pp. 287–93; Li Shuxiao 1986, p. 203). Under his leadership the CCP apparently made some headway, but in October and November 1932 the Japanese raided party printing offices in Harbin, and new arrests followed in 1933 (Lee 1983, pp. 153, 198). In April 1934 the Japanese again directed a major blow against CCP and Communist Youth League (CYL) cadres in Harbin, and according to a Japanese source there were only 100 CCP members and 75 members of the CYL left in the city by October 1934 (Lee 1983, p. 227). One of the reasons why the party was repeatedly rolled up by the Japanese was its work style. Party members distributed leaflets, painted slogans on public monuments, and organized brief, unannounced "flying meetings" (*feixing jihui*) in the streets, thereby making themselves highly visible to the Japanese without really accomplishing much organizationally.[8] After each wave of arrests new cadres were sent in, however, among them Han Shoukui, who plays an important role in Text 3A. Han had been trained in Moscow, and he arrived in Harbin in 1936 with the task of reorganizing the party organization and implementing a new popular front strategy, which should appeal more to the anti-Japanese sentiments of the population. As described in detail in Text 3A, Han was arrested in April 1937 and later executed. On the same occasion 156 party members were arrested in Harbin and vicinity, and 42 of them were executed (Lee 1983, pp. 250–54, gives a detailed account of Han's work in Harbin and of the arrests). This amounted to a near-total annihilation of the CCP in Harbin. Zhang Ruilin, then head of the organization department of the Harbin Special Committee, and author of Text 3A, suggestively titled the chapter of his memoirs dealing with the period from the summer of 1937 to 1940 "Searching Everywhere for the Party." After five years of Japanese occupation, the few and scattered remains of the party organization were driven more effectively underground than ever, and Zhang Ruilin, significantly, ended up leaving the city to join one of the guerrilla groups operating in the countryside (Zhang Ruilin 1981, pp. 41–49). Cultural opposition to the Japanese occupation was expressed by a small group of Harbin writers active in the early 1930s. The most famous of them today is probably Xiao Hong, who was born in neighboring Hulan County. She went to middle school in Harbin from 1928, and lived in the city with her lover, the writer Xiao Jun, until 1934. On this basis she is considered a local celebrity, and small studies of her life and career have turned up in Harbin historical journals. Those of her works that are set in Harbin offer, besides their psychological insights, evocative pictures of the lives of poverty-stricken, freezing, and hungry Harbin intellectuals and workers of the early 1930s.[9] While Xiao Hong felt so intimidated by the Japanese authorities that she moved south in 1934, some intellectuals remained in the city even after the suppression became tougher. One of them, Guan Monan, describes in Text 3B how political and literary activities were merged in a closely knit circle of left-wing writers and other intellectuals during the 1930s. The group survived several rounds of arrest, but in the end its members also had to flee the Japanese. Some of them were later killed in CCP-controlled areas by suspicious party cadres of peasant stock, who fundamentally distrusted such urban intellectuals.

Texts 3A and 3B are typical for autobiographical writings on party history of this period in their insistence on allotting just measures of praise and blame to the participants in party underground activities. Giving information to the Japanese, even under torture, was treason and cannot be excused even today. True patriots, on the other hand, who were falsely accused during earlier periods of PRC history, should be rehabilitated. Nowhere in the historical writings is the current interpretation of historical events of such crucial importance for the destiny of living people as in Guan's story of the stigmatized victims of the "Harbin left-wing literature incident."

Most writings on this period are memoirs of party veterans, while works of professional historians are few. As Chong-Sik Lee has shown, the relationship between the central CCP authorities and the Manchurian branch was problematic during the early 1930s, and although some orders from the center could be explained as "left-wing deviations" that were later corrected, an analysis of the party's failure to organize the urban population in general and the workers in particular against the Japanese would easily lead to a questioning of the wisdom of several central-level decisions (Lee 1983, passim). The CCP veterans are generally able to circumvent such questions by sticking closely to their own personal actions and observations supplemented by standard interpretations of party history.

War Crimes of Unit 731

Japanese atrocities and Chinese victimization are major themes in local writings on the history of the occupation, and the most powerful symbol of these issues is the Japanese Army Unit 731, whose former camp site in Pingfang, some twenty kilometers south of Harbin's center, is now the Exhibition Hall for Evidence of the Crimes of Unit 731 of the Japanese Invasion Army in China.

The brain behind the outrageous experiments carried out by Japanese military and medical personnel in and around Harbin was the microbiologist Ishii Shiroo, who was sent to Harbin in 1932. In 1933 he set up a laboratory in Nangang District and a bacteriological factory in Beiyinhe, Wuchang County. In 1938 he and his unit moved to a new and much larger complex closely sealed off from the world in a military zone in Pingfang, complete with its own airstrip, railway line, power plant, and so on, and with a total staff of 3,000 people (Han Xiao 1985, pp. 1–2). Ishii's Pingfang camp became the center for Japanese biological warfare research, and methods for disseminating infectious diseases such as the plague and typhoid were developed and tested there. Furthermore, unimaginable cruelties like vivisection and pressure and dehydration experiments were carried out on live human beings (see in particular Williams and Wallace 1989, pp. 31–50). According to Chinese sources more than 3,000 people were killed in Pingfang during such experiments in the period from 1940 to 1945 alone (Han Xiao 1985, p. 2). Ishii's misdeeds have received surprisingly little international attention compared to those of the German Nazi doctors with which they are directly comparable. The wall of silence was broken in 1981, when the Japanese Communist daily *Akahata* (Red Flag) carried a series of articles on the subject written by Morimura Sei'ichi. Morimura's work was later published in three volumes under the title *The Devil's Gluttony*, and led to a heated debate in Japan, where the occupation of China is still an extremely sensitive issue, as reflected in the recent debate about the coverage of this period in school history textbooks. (The book was later revised; see Morimura 1983a.)

In Britain Peter Williams and David Wallace produced a documentary for Television South called *Unit 731—Did the Emperor Know?*, which was later supplemented with new evidence and published in 1989 as a book titled *Unit 731—The Japanese Army's Secret of Secrets* (Williams and Wallace 1989). Their carefully researched work, which also included the findings of Morimura, raised considerable debate in the West, because it presented convincing evidence not only of the atrocities committed in Pingfang and other places, but also of international cover-up activities after the war. One of their main points was that the American government had made a deal with Ishii, guaranteeing that he and his colleagues would not be prosecuted as war criminals if they gave full information about the results of their experiments on live human beings. (Harris 1991 reaches the same conclusion.) Ishii and his accomplices were, in fact, never punished and were even allowed to pursue their professional careers after the war. Williams and Wallace further showed that if it is true, as claimed by the Chinese and the North Koreans, that the American forces used biological weapons during the Korean War, then it is very likely that they did so in cooperation with senior scientists from the former Unit 731. Hence the history of the Unit 731 camp in Pingfang has far-reaching consequences for China's relations with Japan and the United States, and it is, perhaps, the single event in Harbin's history to attract international attention during the 1980s.

Harbin historians have played an important role in making the atrocities of Unit 731 known to the Chinese public and to the world. Guan Chenghe and Xu Mingxun translated Morimura's book into Chinese, and published it in Harbin in 1983–84 (Morimura 1983b, 1984a, b), and when a revised edition appeared in Japanese they translated it as a special issue of *Harbin History and Gazetteer* in 1987 (Morimura 1987). When Morimura visited Harbin and Pingfang in 1982, Han Xiao, director of the Exhibition Hall and author of Text 3C, and members of the Local History Association served as his hosts and helped him check a number of details (Morimura 1984b, pp. 37–41). In their own writings, of which Text 3C is a typical example, the Harbin historians deal exclusively with what actually happened in Pingfang without elaborating on the wider ramifications (besides Text 3C see also Han and Zou 1983). Besides going through the archives, Han Xiao has interviewed over 170 Chinese who worked or lived in Pingfang at the time, and though all the prisoners of Unit 731 were systematically murdered before the retreat of the Guandong Army in August 1945, Han found interviewees who could shed new light on, for example, the plague epidemic caused by infected rats from the Pingfang camp, which killed more than a hundred people in nearby villages during the autumn of 1946 (Han Xiao 1985, p. 1, 32–35; William and Wallace 1989, pp. 81–88; Levine 1987, p. 148). The articles we have seen are written in a matter-of-fact style without the emotional outbursts that the subject could easily provoke. None of them mentions Ishii's postwar fate, or the possible connection to the Korean War. This may simply reflect the sources to which the local historians have access, but it also shows their general inclination to confine their field of work rather narrowly to local events.

The Harbin historians appear to have worked and published steadily on Unit 731 up through the 1980s. In an interesting article on the historiography of Manzhouguo, Gavan McCormack mentions the activities of Unit 731 as "a past which the Chinese authorities tend alternately to reconstruct and to forget, at will, in cycles as the vagaries of the Japan-China relationship of today requires more or less pressure to be applied" (McCormack 1991, p. 123). While this is probably true at the national level, the work of the local historians has not gone through similar fluctuations. The production of ammunition for the struggle of historical interpretation has been proceeding steadily, while it has been up to the higher levels to decide when to fire the bullets.

Local Historical Research

The fourteen years of Japanese occupation of Manchuria have received relatively little attention from PRC historians. In his postscript to the revised edition of *A History of Puppet Manzhouguo*, maybe the first major PRC attempt at subjecting this era to a sober historical analysis, Yu Ciyun describes the prevailing attitude among his colleagues to Manzhouguo history as follows:

> Because of the influence of "leftist" ideology it has always been felt that [this period] was "false" [or "puppet," *wei*], so there was no need to write about it. Why glorify the colonial puppet regime by writing its historical records? "We don't recognize it at all!"[10]

During the 1980s this attitude gradually changed, partly as a response to the growing volume of Japanese literature on the subject, some of which was seen as coming out in defense of the aggressors (Jiang et al. 1991, pp. 664–65; for examples of direct critique of Japanese works, see Wang Chengli 1988, pp. 315–27 and 328–38). An Editorial Committee for the History of the Northeast during the Fourteen Years of Occupation was formed in 1986 to promote work in the field, and it held its first academic conference in 1987 attended by 117 Chinese scholars (Wang Chengli 1988, p. 339). In 1991, a new comprehensive history of the period was published (Wang Chengli 1991). In spite of the growing interest in Manzhouguo history at the regional level, however, we found significantly fewer articles on Harbin in the 1930s than in the 1920s, and practically nothing on the Pacific War period. The heroic sides of Harbin's history, particularly the defense of the city in 1932, underground party activities, and other types of active opposition to the Japanese have been covered rather intensively, as have the atrocities committed by the Japanese occupiers, while works on social and economic history are harder to find.

Notes

1. Information on the Japanese administration of Harbin is based on Zhang Chunlin 1987 unless otherwise indicated.
2. Chao 1982, p. 21. According to Gillin and Myers 1989, p. 21, the economy of Manchuria actually constituted the world's fourth-largest industrial complex by August 1945.
3. This point of view is found in Wang Chengli 1988, a collection of papers from a

1987 conference with more than a hundred participants on the Northeast under Japanese occupation. Wang Xiliang 1988 is a representative example.

4. Jiang et al. 1991, pp. 326–29. The latter two figures are for Shenyang, Harbin, and Changchun together. At this time, Harbin was still largely a commercial city. A 1934 Japanese survey showed that almost 43 percent of the gainfully occupied men were in commerce or transportation, compared to only 26 percent in manufacturing (Taeuber 1974, p. 381).

5. Gottschang 1987, pp. 480–81, presents evidence that real wages were higher in Manchuria than in North China and that peasants' decisions about emigration were based mainly on economic calculations.

6. For a history of the Russian fascists, including a wealth of details about the Russian community in Harbin, see Stephan 1978. See also Melnikov 1991.

7. Tokayer and Swartz 1979, p. 55. This book tells, in a fiction-documentary form, the remarkable story of a Japanese plan, which eventually failed, to offer Harbin (and, later, other places in East Asia) as a haven for Jews persecuted in Europe. The aim was to make use of their commercial and technical skills in the development of a Far East controlled by Japan.

8. This was true of Manchuria as a whole, cf. Lee 1983, pp. 309–10, and has also been recognized as a major problem by Harbin veterans; see Zhong Ziyun 1986, p. 2.

9. Many of Xiao Hong's autobiographical essays (*sanwen*) portray the life of her and her friends in Harbin; see Xiao Feng 1982. For an English translation, see Xiao Hong 1986. Chapter 14 of Xiao Hong's most famous novel, *The Field of Life and Death* (Sheng si chang), describes a peasant woman's meeting with Harbin's decadent and cynical life-style, see Xiao Hong 1991, pp. 126–36; the English translation is in Xiao Hong 1979, pp. 88–100.

10. Jiang et al. 1991, p. 664. The first edition of this book came out in 1980. McCormack 1991, p. 106, gives a similar evaluation of Chinese writings on Manzhouguo history.

Texts

CCP Underground Activities and Japanese War Crimes

A major topic in historical writings about the 1932–45 period is the extremely dangerous life of Harbin Communists. The city's party organization was repeatedly unraveled, many members were arrested and executed, and the general atmosphere was one of secrecy and even paranoia. The memoirs of party veterans, the main type of historical writing about this period, are full of clandestine meetings, false identities, and constant doubts about whether comrades could have turned into traitors.

Text 3A describes one of several successful Japanese offensives against the Chinese Communist Party (CCP) in Harbin, the "April 15 incident" in 1937. The author, Zhang Ruilin, had been fighting under the famous guerrilla leader Yang Jingyu and built up a CCP branch in Sanchahe township, before the party sent him to Harbin in 1936. In June he was put under the command of "Mr. Wang," alias Han Shoukui, who had just returned from training in Moscow. Han had come to reorganize party work in Harbin, and he put Zhang in charge of the organization department of the Harbin Special Committee responsible for all underground work in the city. In his memoirs, Zhang places all responsibility for the disaster in April on Han and other comrades who ignored the party's security rules. Political questions are not discussed in the text.

The author of Text 3B, Guan Monan, was born in Jilin in 1919, but went to school in Harbin, where he started a career as a writer and came into contact with the CCP's underground organization. The main theme of this selection from his memoirs is the "Harbin left-wing literature incident," which had tragic results for most of the participants. A group of youthful Harbin writers and party activists interested in literature and propaganda work tried to escape the suppression of the Japanese by moving to areas in Shandong controlled by the CCP. There they were suspected of being Japanese agents, and many of them were killed.

The first two sections translated here deal with the group's activities in Harbin in the late 1930s. The last two describe their later fate in Shandong and their rehabilitation in the 1980s. In the description of the process of rehabilitation we notice the name of Liu Binyan, famous for his investigative journalism in the early 1980s and pioneer of the dissident movement of the late 1980s; Liu Binyan participated in the activities of Harbin left-wing intellectuals in the late 1930s and joined the group led by Guan Monan in 1939. The text shows how historical writings can be a matter of life and death. Members of the Harbin group were persecuted during the Cultural Revolution because of "historical questions," and even their descendants were discriminated against. This case was not unique, and rehabilitation is a major objective in writing autobiographical literature.

The other principle topic of the historians is Japanese atrocities during the occupation, of which none surpasses those described in Text 3C: the biological and medical experiments carried out on live human beings in the Pingfang prison camp run by Unit 731. The author, Han Xiao, is head of the "Exhibition Hall for Evidence of the Crimes of Unit 731 of the Japanese Invasion Army in China" situated on the premises of the old camp. Keeping alive the memory of Japanese war crimes during the occupation is the cardinal task of this institution.

3A. In the Endless Night—Remembering the Cruel Years of Underground Struggle in Harbin (Excerpts)

Zhang Ruilin

The April 15 Incident: Harbin's Underground Party Suffers Great Destruction

In October 1936, the international communication line was destroyed; the Harbin Special Committee was cut off from its source of funds, making it impossible to pay the living allowance to several unemployed comrades as well as the return travel expenses for comrades from other parts of the country. In the social conditions that prevailed at the time, a lack of money made life impossible—how could this not have an affect on our revolutionary work? Even though the problem could be solved for a short period of time by having comrades club together and help one another, in the long run this would not be enough, and it was a situation of great concern to everyone.

In the latter part of November "Wang" told me: "Don't worry, we have borrowed some money. Go and get Liu Yongshan to take a look at the Yonghechang mirror shop, there's a registered letter there for him, which he should pick up and give to you. Tell him that it was posted to you by a friend of yours."

I was a little taken aback upon hearing this. I wondered to myself how it could be that someone in his position could be so heedless when it came to keeping secrets? Yonghechang was our No. 1 top-secret stronghold, and to use it blithely as a place for a message drop was violating every rule of secrecy. If something were to happen to the person sending the letter, we could easily be uncovered. It also led me to think about the times when I met with "Wang" in my lodgings. We had a rule that he should always arrive between nine and ten in the morning. The arranged signal was that I would tear off that day from the calendar and paste it onto the northern doorpost of the outside door. If there was no slip of paper, it meant that there was something else happening at home or else that I had gone out, and

Zhang Ruilin, "Zai manman chang ye zhong—ji Haerbin dixia douzheng de jianku suiyue," *Heilongjiang wenshi ziliao* [Heilongjiang Historical Text Materials], vol. 2 [1981], pp. 18–49.

in such cases it was then agreed that we should meet at seven that evening in Daoli at a point just beyond the righthand side of the Hotel Moderne (now the Harbin travel agency) and in front of the entrance to the Palace cinema. But sometimes he didn't come at the time we had agreed, not arriving until after ten at night. And on other occasions he came straight into my room even though the signal paper had not been pasted up. This kind of behavior, ignoring the rules the party had laid down for clandestine work, was impermissible, and I had previously criticized him for it. Thinking about all of this, I told him sternly, "How can you use the shop just as a message drop point? If that place were to get found out, there's a good chance that the party's entire underground organization would be wrecked."

He explained at once, "The man sending the letter is Fu Yingxun, who came back with me from the Soviet Union and is now head of the propaganda unit at the Fangzheng County party committee east of Harbin. He is politically reliable, nothing can possibly go wrong with him and I'm not going to tell anyone else about the place afterward." As it turned out, it was precisely this letter that brought great destruction on the underground municipal party committee, the Special Committee, and even all the other party organizations in the major cities of the Northeast, and which led to the party's suffering irreparable losses.

Liu Yongshan had a client relationship with the Yonghechang store and he was very well acquainted with it. He ran a carpenter's workshop producing mirror frames, Buddhist shrines, palace lanterns, and so forth, all of which were supplied to the Yonghechang mirror shop to sell. Not two days after "Wang" had told me about the registered letter, Liu Yongshan picked up a letter from the Yonghechang store; luckily there were no instructions at the top of the letter telling him to pass the letter on to Zhang Zhiheng [the author's cover name at this time], for if this had been the case I would never have been able to make my final escape. As soon as I got the letter, I immediately passed it on to "Wang." I later learned from enemy records that when Fu Yingxun came to Harbin to meet with "Wang," he was arrested on the way back to Fangzheng County, turned traitor, and revealed to the enemy the location of his contact point with the Harbin Special Committee. The enemy forces subsequently used the Yonghechang mirror shop as a thread in their unraveling and total destruction of the municipal party committee and the Special Committee. Because Fu Yingxun had "rendered great service," he was put into the employment of the enemy and sent as a special agent to the Xiguitu Banner. After Liberation he was executed by our government.

One day at the beginning of April the following year (1937), Liu Yongshan was told by the shopkeeper Nan at Yonghechang that there had been two men claiming to be from the Tongfalong store in Daoli and asking where Liu lived: they said that Tongfalong had received a registered letter for him and that he should come and collect it. That evening Liu Yongshan asked me, "Has your friend posted a registered letter to you at Tongfalong as well?" I replied, "No, he hasn't. Whatever you do, don't go and pick it up." On April 11, Liu Yongshan came to Yonghechang on business, and shopkeeper Nan said to him again, "There have been more people from Tongfalong in Daoli asking after your address, since you haven't picked up the registered letter, and so they're going to deliver it to you when they happen to pass by." Nan had not understood what the visitors were really after and had given them the number of Liu's house. Shortly after, on the next day (April 12), two strangers knocked on the door of our house and asked, "Does Liu Yongshan live here?" Liu was working at home at the time and he opened the door saying, "I'm Liu Yongshan." The two men looked at Liu and in the end just replied, "Sorry, we've mistaken you for someone else," and left. In the evening Liu reported what had happened; I thought it was very strange, and my apprehension increased. On April 13, "Wang" came and I gave him a report on the situation. The two of us worked out that the enemy must have tracked us down from the registered letter, and they were trying to follow the trail through Liu Yongshan as far as they could and smash the party's underground groups. The situation was critical, so we had to act swiftly and put our contingency measures into effect. "Wang" said to me, "You had better find new lodgings as quickly as you can. This time you should live on your own and you had best not let Liu Yongshan or your brother-in-law know your new address."

On April 14, I rushed around the whole day, but was nevertheless unable to find suitable lodgings. At dawn on the 15th, I heard people calling outside for the door to be opened. Liu went to open the door and a group of people entered, asking him roughly, "Are you Liu Yongshan?" Without an explanation, they manhandled him out of the door and then a car engine could be heard starting up. Liu did not return, indicating that he must have been taken away in the car. The men who were left began to ransack the place, turning out the drawers and cupboards and going over the room from top to bottom. My small room was connected to the main room by a door next to the *kang*, so there was no way for me to get out. While they were searching outside, I got dressed and sorted through my pockets and the things in the small room. Not finding anything that could be suspicious, I sat down on the *kang* and waited. When they had finished searching the larger room, they began to go through the small room. They ordered Liu's apprentice, Yin Yongcai, and me into the main room, and after giving us a body search, they subjected us to a detailed interrogation, asking our names, ages, occupations, and so forth, questions that I answered according to the entry in the residence register. They then tried to dig into my relationship with Liu Yongshan, and I told them that we were fellow carpenters, that we were living together because I could find nowhere else to stay, that we each got on with our own work, and that there were no economic relations of any sort between the two of us. When they wanted me to write down a résumé, I was afraid to reveal my handwriting and therefore refused, saying that I had never been educated and was illiterate, but that my brother-in-law could write it down for me. In actual fact, my brother-in-law had had even less education than me. After he had written the résumé, the men looked at it and then folded it away in a pocket. Their search had been very rigorous, and even the record player that "Wang" had brought me had been taken apart; they had looked inside it with a flashlight and examined all the records one by one. Finding nothing, they eventually left.

No sooner had they gone than I was also on my way. I told those in the room that I was going out to get my record player repaired as I had to give it back to someone soon. As I went out of the door, my sister quietly asked me when I would be coming back and I replied, "I will not be coming back, don't bother waiting for me at dinner." I added that she should tell my brother-in-law to meet me at noon in the small park in front of the Tongfa-long store in Daoli and that it was important he be punctual.

I left carrying the record player and wondered where to go. Feng Cean lived on Anguo Street in Zhengyanghe at the house of a resident Soviet man. He could always keep secrets from others, and I decided that I should go there as it would be relatively safe. When I arrived, I peered in from outside the courtyard and saw that the prearranged contact signal had not been changed. I entered the courtyard, but found that the door was locked. Imagining that they had gone to a small restaurant for lunch, I strolled around for a while, but when I returned the door was still locked. I saw that they had a paper in their newspaper box, and so I took it out; it was the *Great Northern News* and not knowing what else to do I sat down on my record player and began to read it. Feng's Soviet landlord then turned up. Speaking Chinese with a fair sprinkling of Russian and accompanied by hand gestures he explained to me that both Feng Cean and Ai Fenglin had been arrested. I peered into their room through a chink in the window and saw that indeed their things lay scattered all about, on the bed and all over the floor, confirming what the landlord had said. I told the old man, "They were both good men. I shall go and get them released." I then picked up the record player and hurriedly left.

Lugging the record player around was extremely inconvenient, so I went to a pawn shop on Central Avenue and pawned it for 30 yuan. I bought a pair of rubber-soled shoes with the money, changed into them, and pawned the leather ones that I had been wearing. After this, I went to a food stall for a bite to eat and then to the barber's to get my long hair cut. Seeing that it would soon be twelve o'clock, I returned again to a point near the small park in front of the Tongfalong store and waited for my brother-in-law.

At first I strolled around, staying at a little distance and watching to see whether anyone was shadowing my brother-in-law. When he arrived at the park, I moved swiftly in his direction, allowing him to catch sight of me, and then walked toward a back street with him following behind. When he came up, I asked him whether there had been any new developments at home and he told me, "Not long after you left, a dozen or so agents rushed in and demanded to know where you had gone and when you were coming back. I told them that you had left without a word, so I didn't know where you had gone or when you would be back. They didn't believe what they were told, and they ranted and raved for a considerable time. I managed to slip away, but the agents will still be there waiting for you!" I thought that it was possible that the enemy had used torture on Liu Yongshan and found out that the registered letter had been passed on to me and what my real identity was. They had obviously come back to get me. I said to my brother-in-law, "You shouldn't go back either, returning now would be too dangerous, they would certainly arrest you. I'll give you some money so that you can quickly leave Harbin and hide somewhere in the countryside; you can work as a hired laborer for the time being, but you shouldn't go back to Sanchahe or Jingxing County either." He then said, "If I run off what will happen to your sister?" And I replied, "At least one getting away is better than none. My sister is a woman and besides she hasn't done anything; the enemy won't be able to touch her at all." He refused to listen to my advice, saying that neither had he done anything against the law and so the enemy wouldn't be able to do anything to him. I saw that he was bent on returning and there was nothing I could do to stop him. When we parted, I told him first to go to the cotton-fluffing plant on Fifteenth Street in Daowai and inform Zhu Shaozhen that he should wait for me at eight in front of the Lopato cigarette factory. He passed on the message, and that evening Zhu Shaozhen and I met as planned. I gave him a brief rundown of the situation and made arrangements for him to leave Harbin immediately; he went along with my decision, seeing it as his only escape from imminent peril.

Since my brother-in-law had never taken part in any party or mass orga-nizations, he had not developed any wariness of the enemy. Even as he was returning home full of his innocent and well-meaning ideas, the enemy was already lying in wait for him, and as soon as he entered the house he was dragged away. Right up until his arrest, he was unaware of the fact that April 15 was to be a day soaked in blood, a day when the enemy forces would with planning and deliberation carry out the savage destruction of the Harbin underground party. I too had not imagined that that parting was to be our last one. In November, I gathered some money together for travel expenses and sent Chang Zuochen, disguised as a fortune-teller, to visit my family in Sanchahe and find out what had happened. When Chang Zuochen returned he told me that after my brother-in-law was arrested, the enemy used the most cruel tortures on him, but could not find any evidence against him or get any useful information out of him. After being incarcerated for about half a year he was broken so badly that he lost his reason, and after this he was set free. Upon his release he was not able even to look after himself, and he died a miserable and wretched death.

On April 15, I stayed the night at Chang Zuochen's house. His family lived on South Eighteenth Street in Daowai, and no one knew of this but myself. The next morning I told Chang that the enemy had wrecked the place where I was living and that I needed to find someone to go and see if their agents had left yet. The two of us agreed that the old Mrs. Chang should make a trip there on the pretext of buying soybean residue. When the old lady arrived she was surrounded by waiting secret agents, searched and then interrogated, and she managed to extricate herself from the situation only with great difficulty.

Even though I had escaped the danger for the time being, something kept nagging away and worrying me. I had originally agreed to meet with "Wang" at my lodgings at nine on the morning of the 17th. If he were unaware of what had happened, he might, as previously, fail to heed our prearranged signals, blunder right into the room, and be arrested by the secret agents. What we had learned by sending Mrs. Chang as a scout only added to my concern. If anything should happen to "Wang," it would jeopardize the party leadership and the party's underground organizations over the whole of the Northeast. What was I to do? I thought about going down to Twenty-first Street myself on the morning of the 17th and intercepting "Wang," but then again, I thought, this would not work. On the day they had come to arrest Liu Yongshan, the agents had already seen the scar on my face, and if I went out there was a good chance that I would be discovered. And so I changed my plan; on the evening of the 16th I would call on Kong Fuxiang and tell him to go to the southern corner of South Eleventh Street and Nanxun Street on the morning of the 17th disguised as a shoe repairman and intercept "Wang" there. Early on the morning of the 17th, I also directed Chang Zuochen to try to intercept him, this time on the Northern corner of South Eleventh and Fengrun Streets. I gave them both a detailed description of "Wang's" clothing, appearance, and characteristic features. I told them that if they saw him they were to address him as "Mr. Wang" and tell him that Mr. Zhang had guests at home, which meant that he should not go there, but instead meet him later at the other rendezvous. I also told them that they should wait only until eleven and then leave. I then went to Lan Ziyuan's younger sister's house.

At around twelve, Lan's sister came back for lunch and said to me, "Brother Zhang, the agents caught a man on South Eleventh Street who they say is a bandit. The man was really formidable; as he ran away he was hitting out with bricks at the agents chasing him. In the end, the agents opened fire and shot him in the leg and then they arrested him." As I listened to her I realized that it must have been "Wang" who had been arrested. Analyzing the events at the time I assumed that his arrest might have been the result of his ignoring the arranged meeting times and signals. After Liberation, my sister said that at around noon on the 17th, "Wang" hurried into the room and was immediately encircled by enemy agents. As they were examining his clothes, he seized his chance, flung his large padded overcoat at them, and fled. After being wounded by the enemy agents, they carried him back to the room, where he lost a great deal of blood, and then they drove him away in a car.

I did not know anything about what happened to "Wang" after he was arrested. At the end of 1937, I read in the puppet regime's *Binjiang Daily* an article relating the course of events behind the savage crushing of Harbin's underground party organization in the "April 15 incident." There were also photographs of the executions of Han Shoukui (i.e., "Wang") and Feng Cean. It was later learned that after his capture, Han Shoukui was unable to withstand the tortures, extortion, and lures of the enemy, and he shamefully turned traitor, although his final fate was in any case to be execution at their hands. . . .

(edited by Zhang Jing)

3B. Remembering the Harbin Left-Wing Literature Incident (Excerpts)

Guan Monan

. . .

6. Footprints on Sunshine Island

. . .

After the outbreak of the war of resistance against Japan in the Lugouqiao incident on July 7 [1937], Wang Zhongsheng's[1] home district, Shen County in Hebei, had become an area of guerrilla warfare visited by both the enemy and our own forces. Wang returned home once a year on a visit. Apart from seeing his family, he also took part in some local military work, and if his visit coincided with enemy activity he would fight for several days as a guerrilla. Every time he went home he would report on the situation in Harbin to the local revolutionary groups, and upon returning he would give us information about the war of resistance in the areas outside the Northeast. In those days enemy control of the Northeast was extremely harsh and reactionary; a ration system was being introduced for basic commodities, and Chinese were generally not allowed wheat flour or rice to eat. The common people were lacking in both food and clothes, and in the winter many of them froze to death on the streets. There was also enforced conscription into the army, and workers were pressganged into hard labor; many of those sent out to repair the border defenses died in the process. Police agents were everywhere, and one wrong word or book would result in ones being arrested as a "dangerous-thought offender" and sometimes subsequently tortured to death. All young people have a thirst for freedom and light, but we were trapped in a life as black as night, which oppressed the spirit and never allowed us to breathe easily. Under Wang Zhongsheng's dim lamp we would often look up at his calm face with its inflexible will and listen to his tales of the fierce anti-Japanese struggle waged by the people of our motherland. The flames of revolution would rise up in our

---

Guan Monan, "Yi Haerbin zuoyi wenxue shijian," *Heilongjiang wenshi ziliao* [Heilongjiang Historical Text Materials], vol. 20 (1986), pp. 124–75.

hearts, the will to resist and to fight would surge through us, ardent companions that we were, and the news of our country's resistance would spur us on and give us hope and faith in the future of China.

Among the members of the "Harbin Marxist Literature Study Group," Kong Guangkun and his wife, Zhu Jianqiu, had already left the Northeast for the Chinese heartland. Bian Hui (Shi Ning) and Liu Xin were shop assistants and could not take part in all the activities because they were so busy with their work. Guan Jie carefully avoided enemy surveillance and together with Tong Xingyu strengthened the leadership of our group. Because Guan Jie's husband, whose surname was Zuo, had developed a negative attitude toward the revolution, and because he sold opium and "white powder" (i.e., narcotics), Guan Jie divorced him, and a romantic relationship slowly grew between her and Tong Xingyu. Before long Su Xueliang returned home to Shandong, and no news was heard of her again. I saw Ai Xun (Wen Chengjun) almost every day and was often together with him; I also saw Tong Xingyu to a lesser extent and Liu Huanzhang (Sha Yu, Zhu Fan) sometimes visited me as well.

Ai Xun's father was a Harbin railway worker, and his family lived in Jingwei Ninth Road in Daoli. After graduating from the Shuidao Road Middle School in Daoli he sold stamps in the post office in Daowai. He was a year younger than me, a little taller, with a long oval face; he was rather quiet and gentle by nature and talked humorously with a slightly sarcastic tone. His family circumstances were a little better than my own. Every month when he got his wages he could buy several books. Besides those written by Chinese authors, he bought the works of writers such as Gorky, Flaubert, or Anatole France, and we often went together to choose them in the bookshops in Daoli and Daowai. Using the pen name Wei Wei he wrote many prose pieces for the *International Cooperation Reporter*. Later, taking as his subject matter the lowest levels of the Harbin proletariat and vagabond children, under the name Ai Dun he wrote a short story called "The Two Hay Cutters" for the *Binjiang Daily* and one titled "The Children Who Stole Firewood" for the *Great Northern News*.

Liu Huanzhang wrote under the pseudonym Sha Yu. Several of his short poems, full of the deep meditation characteristic of the epoch, appeared in Harbin newspapers and the *New Youth* magazine published in Fengtian.

The grocer's shop run by my family closed down in 1938 as it was losing money, and the whole family moved to 92 Jingcha Street. With my father unemployed, life for my family became even more difficult. After returning home from the Hailaer post office I spent all my time looking for work. In those days I and my family believed that the enemy's puppet organizations existed solely to serve the enemy and that to work for them would be a betrayal of the motherland. The postal service, however, preserved links with all countries in the world and was not quite so unclean. I decided therefore that I should take the postal service entrance examination. They had a rule at that time, however, that they could not take on people whom they had previously employed, and so I was forced to change my original name, Guan Dongyan, to Guan Yan and again take the examinations for the Harbin postal administration office. At that time there was a man called Xu Zelin working in the Harbin central post office; he was about forty years of age, knew foreign languages after having studied in France, and was the director of the international office. He wrote stories under the name Xu Yi and had edited the literature and art pages of the *International Cooperation Reporter*. He was, however, a believer in art for art's sake and had published a long novel "The River Collection," which dealt solely with love and women. Ding Ning and Ai Dun knew him and asked him to help by putting in a word for me with the post office administration. I passed the examination once more, and on January 1, 1938, entered the general affairs section in the general affairs department of the Harbin postal administration office. I started off as a basic employee with wages of 17 yuan a month and after a year was promoted to an office worker and my wages increased to 20 yuan. Our whole family of six had to survive on these 20 yuan a month. Later it was simply not enough to support them, and the family's second son, Guan Zhongyan, had to give up studying at middle school and go to work as an apprentice at a motor transport company. He toiled day and night there covered in oil and grime, earning first 3 and later 4 yuan a month to help the family.

In the general affairs section I filled out name cards for postal employees from the whole province, as well as filling in employee identification cards and badges that were sent to post offices throughout the province. I was also in charge of attendance record books. I worked for eight hours every day and was not allowed to arrive late or leave early. In the same office, apart from the Japanese section head and two Japanese subordinates, there were also two Chinese subordinates with the surnames Liu and Song. I had the impression that they were very loyal to the Japanese and was therefore cautious in my dealings with them. During this period there was an employee called Zhang Zidong and a young man with the surname Du, both of whom came under my influence to a certain extent; and not long afterward the young Du escaped to the Chinese heartland.

The atmosphere in the staff common room was gloomy, with several of the employees appearing to be dead to the world. When there was a suitable occasion, such as a transfer to or from the office or some other excuse, they would go out to a restaurant, get dead drunk, and together with their Japanese colleagues sing "The Girl from Manchuria."

I continued to devote all my energies to reading books and writing articles. In order to save the bus fare I would walk home from work, using the same route I took in the morning, going from Nangang over the Jihong bridge, down Xiewen Street and Central Avenue all the way down to my family's house by the river. In the evenings I would eat a little cooked millet and pickled vegetables. Bent over the family's one and only table I would work deep into the night. I never considered my life to be hard, however; my heart was given over to literature and to our common cause. . . .

Every Sunday in the summertime we would gather together on Sunshine Island, some of us going over in motorboats and others in small rowing boats. Our youth furnished us with a never-ending supply of vital energy, and we would splash about in the river, scamper about the beach under the burning sun, or stroll in the thick shade; Sunshine Island was criss-crossed with our footprints. But all this was actually just a cover, something we did to avoid the ears and eyes of the enemy. And it was our ideals and literature that made us different from other young people in that we did not regret having to stop our play. We wanted to discover and explore, we wanted to use even more of our time on studying and on our creative work. Each time, after bathing, we would go to our small lodge and hold a secret meeting.

At a group meeting one Sunday in 1939 the subject of discussion was my story writing, and I gained a great deal of insight and enlightenment. We ate bread in the small plank lodge, sitting in the gentle breeze blowing in from the open window, and made reports on our own creative activity. I talked about the story I was planning to write, "A Certain Town, A Certain Night," a tale of a mine workers' representative who fought against the mine owner.

Ai Dun said, "The plot certainly has a strong general appeal . . ."

However, Guan Jie asked me with a smile, "From our point of view can it be right that you get him to kill the capitalist? Can that really solve the problem?"

Tong Xingyu tried on the one hand to defend my position and on the other hand criticized me, saying, "Monan understands that we don't advocate the use of such methods, but this tendency has revealed itself more and more in his recent works as a way of finding something strange and bizarre for the plot . . ."

He looked at me and said in a serious and emphatic tone of voice, "You must not sacrifice ideology just for that reason. In my view you were following the correct path in the collection 'Wasting Time'; you have to start out from real life and then begin to dig deeply . . ."

Whereupon the discussion was taken up by all the others.

We were comrades, a militant collective group, and there was proletarian-style criticism and self-criticism. Here everybody accepted the bright light of the sun and the falling rain, and they absorbed the nourishing milk that allowed them to grow and develop.

How would I ever be able to forget the red evening sun reflecting on the river as we journeyed over in the small boats to the southern bank, the inspiring gaze of my comrades-in-arms and their hearty handshakes as we parted. All this made us think about the age we lived in, about humanity, about life with ideals and with a meaning! We went forward with firmness and resolution, just like the footprints we left on Sunshine Island! . . .

9. From Harbin to the Hebei-Shandong Border Area

. . .

[The protagonists of this section, Kong Mofei and Zhu Hong, another name for Zhu Jianqiu, mentioned above, were a married couple, who were both members of the Harbin literature group. They had been the first to leave Harbin for the CCP bases in the Hebei-Shandong border area. On the way they had left their young son, Wang Xinsheng, with a friend, Wang Zhizhen, in Tianjin, while taking Wang Zhizhen's daughter, Wang Yun, with them.]

Not long after their arrival in Ningjin [in the Hebei-Shandong base area], Kong Mofei and Zhu Hong came under suspicion: they came from Harbin in the Northeast, were dressed in a peculiar manner, and they even knew a lot about Marxism-Leninism—that all seemed very strange. It was as if Marxism-Leninism was something that cadres could not learn and therefore was something that they been taught by the Japanese. And so both husband and wife were transferred to Leling County for observation. It was later felt that the couple had to be separated, and so Kong Mofei was again transferred, this time to Ling County. The secretary of the county party committee, whose surname was Guan, had people search through his room and his possessions, and it was found that he had two Western suits and money from the enemy areas: things that Kong Mofei used in carrying out secret operations inside enemy-occupied territory. However, it seemed to them that they had found evidence and an order was immediately made for Kong's arrest, after which party secretary Guan personally conducted the interrogation. They found in Kong Mofei's coat pocket a mimeographed copy of a party committee working document. This was a paper that Kong, being a secretary of the county office, had to be familiar with in connection with his work, and it was also something that he had to take with him when he was transferred, given the current situation where the enemy often came on mopping-up operations. Kong Mofei was interrogated just for a single night. The next morning he was taken out and shot.

No matter how Kong tried to explain matters, saying that he was their own comrade, it was to no avail. He died wrongfully in a pool of blood, shouting the slogan "long live the Chinese Communist Party!"

After Kong had been executed by Secretary Guan, Zhu Hong, who was working in the Leling County women's federation, met a newspaper correspondent who had been together with Kong, and it was only after she put a pen of her husband's into the coat pocket of this man that she discovered the news. She knew better than anyone her husband's loyalty to the revolution, and she naturally cried and sobbed herself hoarse. Later the leader of Zhu Hong's unit said, "Now that she has heard she may try to escape, so it would be best if we simply buried her alive . . ."

All of Zhu Hong's desperate pleading was also in vain; she was pushed into a hole in the ground and shovelfuls of yellow earth rained down on her head. She was only heard to say: "I could never have imagined . . ."

As to the fate of their daughter, Kong Zhaozhao, and Wang Zhizhen's daughter, Wang Yun, who lived together with them, there were people who even proposed, "We can't let these two special agent whelps survive, if you're weeding out you have to dig up the roots . . ."

If they really had gone this far it would have been unbearably tragic. Ding Xuefeng, who in 1982 was dean of studies at the Shandong Administrative Cadre School, was in 1940 head of the organizational group in Ling County and did not support the execution of people when there was no evidence against them.

Thanks to obstruction by comrades like him, Kong Zhaozhao and Wang Yun did not share Zhu Hong's terrible fate of being buried alive, and two young lives were spared. At that time many of the cadres being executed had children, and the remaining orphans had to be given over to the charge of revolutionary comrades. Yang Yichen and his wife, Xiao Sai, who in the 1980s served as the Heilongjiang provincial party secretary and chief procurator of the Supreme People's Procuratorate respectively, were at this time in the same region, and the child they were assigned to look after was Kong Zhaozhao, the daughter of Kong Mofei and Zhu Hong.

Zhaozhao grew up during the war, and when Yang Yichen and Xiao Sai received orders to go to the South it was decided that it would be too difficult to take Zhaozhao on the train, so she was handed over to the Shanxi-Hebei-Shandong-Henan No. 2 Cultural Troupe, and she changed her name from Kong Zhaozhao to Kong Luoping. Later the troupe was renamed the Chengdu-Chongqing Railroad Cultural Troupe and Luoping was married to the troupe's manager, Wei. On April 15, 1980, Wei was transferred to the Beijing Film Production Plant as a director, and Luoping also came to Beijing and worked in the Beijing Experimental Drama Theater.

Since she was older, Wang Zhizhen's daughter, Wang Yun, who had lived with Zhu Hong, was under greater suspicion than Zhaozhao, and she was held by the Ningjin County government. The county center contacted Wang Zhizhen in Tianjin and told him that he should send a reliable witness to come and collect her. The head of Ningjin County, Li Shaolan, acted as a guarantor and since Wang Zhizhen had been working for the cause for many years, Wang Yun was released.

At roughly the same time that Kong Mofei and Zhu Hong were executed, Chen Zi was also brought into custody on the grounds that it had been discovered that she had been suspiciously writing letters with medicine late at night and had kept in contact with the Northeast. What they did not know was that Chen had been writing to Harbin to tell Tong Xingyu and others to come and join the revolutionary forces as soon as they could. After a lengthy interrogation, it was decided that because of the great length of her revolutionary experience and because no one could confirm the charges, she could not be dealt with immediately; she was therefore sent for investigation to the Hebei-Shandong Border Union of Writers for a short period. Tong Xingyu, Qin Zhanya, and others were sent to the Southern Hebei administrative office for observation, all of them coming to live in Nangong County. Wang Guangti was sent to the youth newspaper office as an editor, and Song Zhen (Song Min) worked temporarily for the county women's federation. The only exception was Wang Zishu (Wang Zhongsheng), who at this time was transferred to the Linyi County government as an administrative section member.

Wang Guangti had just been married and was still passionately in love when he left Harbin and arrived in the Hebei-Shandong border area, where life was indescribably harsh. Seeing how Kong Mofei and Zhu Hong had been executed had been a great shock for Wang, and he could not help but long to return home. He did not realize that he was under observation and from time to time would hum songs such as "Song of the Four Seasons," which had been sung by the Shanghai film actress Zhou Xuan. Someone reported this, and the leader of the newspaper office mentioned in a speech to the cadres' meeting that "It seems likely that we have one of the enemy in our midst who is disseminating pornographic materials and trying to corrode our fighting morale. Everyone should sharpen their vigilance . . ."

Wang Guangti was at the meeting and, realizing that it was he the leader was talking about, he became extremely frightened. That night he ran away, leaving a note on his table that read, "You people are too cruel, I simply cannot live together with you!"

When it was discovered that he had escaped, soldiers were sent to capture him. Wang had no choice but to head for the blockade line, and with his pursuers firing after him he ran inside an enemy blockhouse. Relying on his excellent Japanese he explained that he was a businessman who had run into the Eighth Route Army on the road and had come there to find sanctuary. The enemy troops had themselves witnessed the Eighth Route soldiers firing after him and so they eventually released him.

Wang Guangti's running away at this time was a matter of no small import; the note he left behind and the fact that he entered an enemy blockhouse were concrete evidence that led some people to conclude that the group from Harbin were all enemy agents.

Thereupon, certain leading cadres in the Southern Hebei administrative district's party committee, rejecting all dissenting opinions, issued orders that Chen Zi, Tong Xingyu, Qin Zhanya, and Song Min be executed on the spot. The explanations and pleas offered by the four condemned were in vain. Like Kong Mofei, Tong Xingyu and Qin Zhanya were shot standing up; Chen Zi and Song Min suffered the same fate as Zhu Hong—they were pushed into a pit and buried alive with earth, spade by spade. The circumstances and the surrounding atmosphere were exactly as if they had been genuine enemy agents. This all took place in the summer of 1940, in Nangong County in the Hebei-Shandong border area. . . .

Wang Xinsheng [the son of Kong Mofei and Zhu Hong, whom they had left with Wang Zhizhen in Tianjin] worked as a doctor and assistant director of the surgical department at the Zaozhuang Municipal People's Hospital in Shandong. Over a period of twenty years he appealed fourteen times for an audience with the central authorities and made countless appeals to the provincial authorities. Because Kong Mofei and Zhu Hong had this direct descendant to apply on their behalf, on March 25, 1982, the Shandong civil administration office, on the basis of instructions from the provincial party committee and the provincial government, posthumously conferred on Kong Mofei and Zhu Hong the title of revolutionary martyrs in its Document No. 61 of 1982. For the others, who lacked direct relations to apply for them, the only thing that could be done was to clear their cases up and reach a verdict that they had been wrongfully killed. On May 11, 1983, the Zaozhuang municipal civil administration office also sent letters to the work units of others involved in this affair, including Guan Monan [i.e., the author himself], Shi Ning, Wang Zhongsheng, and Liu Xin, informing them that this period of history had now been clarified.

On May 13, 1984, with the support of the leaders of the Zaozhuang civil administration office and the Zaozhuang municipal party committee, the leading comrade of the municipal People's Political Consultative Conference announced to an assembly that "the martyrs' earlier comrades-in-arms Liu Binyan, Guan Monan, Wang Zhongsheng, Shi Ning, and Zhang Rui, together with relatives of the martyrs Zhu Baoyuan, Zhu Baotai, and others, had rushed from Beijing, Shenyang, and Harbin to take part in the ceremony of the laying of the ashes of the martyrs Kong Mofei and Zhu Hong in the Taierzhuang cemetery for revolutionary martyrs." The *Zaozhuang Daily* reported on May 16 that "the two revolutionary martyrs, Kong and Zhu, had in the early days taken part in the struggle of resistance led by the Chinese Communist Party in the Northeast against the Manzhouguo puppet regime and the Japanese. In 1939 they entered the Hebei-Shandong border region and made great contributions to the armed struggle against the Japanese and to the construction of political power.". . .

Note

[1. Wang Zhongsheng was the owner of a small secondhand book store. He was one of the key organizational figures in the Harbin literature group, and the one who recruited Guan Monan.]

3C. A Compilation of the Fascist Atrocities Committed by Unit 731 of the Japanese Army (Excerpts)

Han Xiao

. . .

3. Germ Experimentation on Living Human Subjects in "the Square Building"

The square building inside Unit 731 was the center for germ research, production, and experimentation. In the building were located all of Unit 731's research teams, along with the general affairs section, clinic, dissection room, and cremation oven; it was also equipped with two secret prisons. This was where the butchers of Unit 731 carried out their acts of unparalleled savagery: germ experiments on living human subjects.

a) Collective Homicidal Mania

We have found in historical documents[1] the testimony of Yamada Toyoki, who was once on the staff of Unit 731. He states that it is generally thought that using living persons as subjects of experiments with infectious germs was the task of Section One. This was not in fact true; this was also done by Section Four, which was the section responsible for germ production, and personnel from Section Three and the clinic were also involved. When it came to outdoor experiments, the spread of the personnel taking part was even wider, with practically the entire staff of the unit having the opportunity to take part. It can truly be said that the whole of Unit 731 was a devil's nest of germ-warfare murderers.

Before any of the research teams carried out a particular experiment it would first make an appointment with the "Special Team." The Special Team would write down registration numbers of those to be experimented on, based on the age, sex, race, and state of health proposed by the research team. After this they were assigned their subjects. Sometimes the research team was able to make its way directly into the prison block and personally

---

Han Xiao, "Rijun qisanyao budui faxisi baoxing jilu," *Heilongjiang wenshi ziliao* [Heilongjiang Historical Text Materials], vol. 19 (1985), pp. 1–35.

point out the subjects it wanted through a barred window. The personnel present when the germs were being administered were from Sections One, Three, and Four, the clinic, from the Special Team itself, and from the military police. Force was used against the experimentees if necessary, and all resistance was futile; once they had been escorted into the experiment room they were at the mercy of the experimenters. Anyone putting up strong resistance would be shot dead on the spot by the military police; sometimes they were even killed with poison gas.

The testimony of Ueda Yotaroo[2] confirms that in February 1942 the prisoners on the first floor of Prison Block 7 resisted the germ experiments and were cruelly gassed to death. In April of the same year, when Ueda Yotaroo was walking along the central corridor to collect bacteria from research team No. 1 of Section Four, he suddenly ran into a smell of gas so strong that it made his eyes tear. He guessed that the gas was coming from Blocks 7 and 8. When he got back to the research room his colleague technician Kobayashi laughed, "So you got a taste of the security exercise as well, did you?" and added salaciously, "What about that girl in Block 8?" When technician Itoo, who was listening, said that she had been used on the previous exercise, Komori shamelessly replied, "That's a real pity, they've even killed my little girl." It so happened that before she died this girl had been subjected to Kobayashi's bestial violation.

Ueda Yotaroo also testifies[3] that in 1945 there was an insurrection on the second floor of Block 7 instigated by a Soviet prisoner. Somebody had reported that the prisoner had fallen ill, but when the guard entered the cell to investigate, he suddenly jumped up and knocked the guard unconscious with a swing of his handcuffs. He then took the revolver and the keys to open the cell. All the other cells responded to his call and began to rebel. In the end Ishii Shiroo ordered the use of poison gas, with the result that all the inmates of Block 7 were killed. Following this incident unit leader Ishii received a reprimand from the Guandong Army Command.

b) Experiments with Injections of Germ Cultures and with Forced Exposure to Germs

In January and February 1942, the Mitani Squad of the Kawashima Division carried out experiments on prisoners by infecting them with plague germs via the three methods of injection, emplacement under the skin, and ingestion. There were forty-five subjects chosen for the experiments on each occasion, with each method being employed on fifteen of them; then they were further divided into groups of five. The volume of plague culture injected varied between 0.1, 0.2, and 0.3 grams. This was the same for the amounts placed under the skin and ingested. The experiments showed that injections produced the highest transmission rates—those injected with the lowest volume of culture were all dead within a day. The second-highest results were obtained from the emplacement method while ingestion gave the lowest transmission rate, with the first subjects only dying after six days. For these reasons the butchers of Unit 731 concentrated their efforts on research into transmission by injection.

In the middle of January 1943, under the command of the head of Group One under Section Four, Major Suzuki Tetsuyuki, the technician Uno Makoto was charged with carrying out a germ culture injection experiment on two Chinese patriots. The aim of the experiment was to determine the toxic strength of the plague bacteria. These two men were particularly indomitable of spirit and they cursed their captors, calling them "animals in white coats." An employee of the Special Team called Wada helped to forcefully tie up the patriots, and the technician Uno Makoto gave each of them an injection of 1 cc of fluid containing 0.03 units of the germ culture. Three days later both men were seriously ill with plague, and they died shortly after.

It often happened in the experiments that the victims refused to go along with the oppression of the butchers and instead put up fierce resistance. On such occasions they were liable to be shot by the military police present. But it was not in the interests of the butchers for this to happen; they had to look after their "experimental material" and were not happy to see their victims die before they had reached their objectives. For this reason the butchers of Unit 731 often employed various types of deceit against their experimental subjects.

In October 1942, the technician Uno Makoto got Tamura Yoshio to assist him in a germ experiment. Five prisoners had earlier been deceived by being told that they were going to be given preventative inoculations. They first drew 5 cc of blood from each of the prisoners in order to determine the strength of their immunity. The next day four of the men were given injections containing different mixtures of vaccine, and a week later they were injected again. The fifth man was given no vaccine at all. In the middle of November they were tricked again by being told that to be immune from the disease they had to have a second set of injections, and they were even shown medicine bottles bearing the label "vaccine against all diseases." After again drawing blood from four of the patriots and determining the strength of immunity, the butchers actually injected all five of their subjects with 1 cc of fluid containing 0.05 units of baisidu [sic] bacteria. Three days later they had all fallen ill, and three of them died while still undergoing their period of isolation. Suzuki then carried out autopsies on the dead in the dissection room of Section One's Kasahara team.

The room for live experiments was located in the cellars of the prison. It was top secret, and ordinary members of Unit 731 were unaware of its existence; the room was strictly off limits to all those not directly involved with its operation. Only after a thorough screening were personnel given a special pass allowing them access to Prison Blocks 7 and 8.

According to the historical archives,[4] in April 1942, an employee by the name of Ueda Yotaroo, assistant to Sergeant-Major Eda Takeichi of Unit 731, went to Prison Block 7 to observe the condition of Chinese prisoners who had been used for germ experimentation. Ueda was in possession of a "germ experimentation assessment chart," which had a serial number at the top and columns for the recording of such things as body temperature, white blood cells, red blood cells, hemoglobin, erythrocyte sedimentation rate (ESR), blood pressure, and blood culture. Whether these charts were used or not, even if they had been incorrectly filled in and scrapped, they had to be handed back in when they were finished. Ueda accompanied Eda to a downstairs cell on the south side of Prison Block 7. Here there were five men being kept in isolation cells. They were all around thirty years old, but their illnesses had already turned them old and gray. The day before, they had been subjects of a plague injection experiment. Ueda called them to the examination window by number and examined them item-by-item according to the required headings, entering the figures in the chart. Ueda was subsequently ordered to take the body temperature of the experimental subjects twice a day, and once a day measure their white blood cells, red blood cells, hemoglobin, blood pressure, and so on. By the third day of his investigation one of the subjects had already died. He immediately informed the guards, who then brought the body to the dissection room. After this the dissected corpse was put into the incinerator. In order to fill in all the details on the chart, Ueda took part in the whole process, finally giving the observation chart to Sergeant-Major Eda.

At the beginning of May of the same year, Ueda received orders from technician Kobayashi Matsuzoo to make observations on prisoners in a downstairs cell-block on the north side of Prison Block 7, who had also been injected with plague bacteria. On the first day Ueda made a chemical analysis of blood samples taken from the subjects; by the second day one of them had already died. Ueda followed the corpse wagon to the dissection room and saw that on this occasion the body was divided into eight sections and bacterial samples were taken separately from the internal organs. Afterward, the empty shell of the body was incinerated. That afternoon another two of the experimental subjects died, one of whom was a man of over thirty who had just been captured and who had particularly slender fingers, suggesting that he was not an ordinary working man. The two remaining subjects luckily survived the experiment and were healthy again after a week although they were still in a rather weakened condition. But Ueda knew full well that the lives of these survivors would in any case only be short ones and that soon they would perish in this or in another experiment.

The technique for experiments with forced consumption of germ culture was different from normal treatment with oral medicine; the subjects had to be tied up and then liquid with baisidu, cholera, typhoid, or diphtheria bacteria was forcibly poured into their mouths.

In May 1943, Yamashita Masu was transferred from the medical section of the Guandong Army Command to Unit 731. When performing germ experiments he always used ten captives and sometimes even carried out two experiments in a single day. The experimental subjects used in the forced consumption tests were Chinese or Russian, and they included women. The death rate for infection with cholera was relatively high, most people dying within three to seven days. The effect achieved with plague infections through the stomach was not so marked, but a small number of the subjects died nevertheless. Yamashita Masu admitted that "while I was working as assistant in germ experimentation in just over one year we carried out consumption tests on well over one hundred anti-Japanese elements, the majority of whom died. Those who survived were used as subjects for other experiments."[5]

c) Frostbite Experimentation

After the Japanese imperialists staged the "September 18 incident," a large number of invading soldiers were plunged from the warm climes of Japan into the frozen Northeast of China and the Japanese were also preparing to launch an attack on the Soviet Union. The problem of how to adapt to a severely cold climate, and particularly that of how to prevent and treat frostbite, was therefore one that the Japanese army of invasion urgently needed to solve. Responsibility for carrying out this task was placed with Unit 731. The Yoshimura team in Section One specialized in research into frostbite.

Every year during the coldest weather, the Yoshimura team would take some Chinese and Russians from the prison and escort them to a closely guarded courtyard. The prisoners were then forced to expose their hands, feet, arms, or thighs and leave them open to the cold for varying amounts of time. In temperatures of thirty to forty degrees below zero they were generally left to freeze for periods of twenty minutes to an hour or more, often leading the prisoners to lose consciousness. The members of the Yoshimura team would hit the hands, feet, arms, and thighs of the experimental subjects with wooden sticks, and only when they heard the blows make a hard cracking sound would they haul them back inside.

After this, the Japanese would then take one group of subjects and pour cold water over them so that the parts of their bodies that had been exposed would immediately freeze over with a sheet of ice; the arms and legs of another group were plunged into warm or hot water so that the frozen parts would become red and swollen and in some cases the skin would peel off. Many people died in agony under this brutal torture. Some of the survivors were given no medical treatment so that their frostbitten areas would begin to fester, their bones would turn black, and finally they would have to have their arms or legs amputated. Some of those with less severe frostbite would be smeared with antifrostbite ointment, but would nevertheless often be left with fingers or toes missing. Even more barbarous was that the butchers sometimes smeared some of the victims' frozen areas with a bacterial cream, which quickly resulted in their deaths.

According to the testimony of one of Unit 731's former workers, Yamauchi Toyoki, in the winter of 1940 the Yoshimura team forced Chinese to run to and fro across the courtyard carrying heavy loads and wearing only thin, unlined clothes. The team leader, Yoshimura Jujin, personally supervised this experiment, ensuring that the subjects ran a fixed distance within a certain period of time. The experiment was repeated day after day for more than ten days. The originally strong and healthy experimental subjects became gradually thinner and weaker. They were forced to run for all they were worth to keep out the menacing cold. When they had used up all the energy in their bodies, they would collapse on the ground and would subsequently get frostbite. The experimental subjects were thus reduced day by day until eventually they had all been "lost in action."[6]

The Yoshimura team also set up a special frostbite experiment room. One day in April 1943 Ueda Yotaroo personally witnessed three guards wearing padded cotton clothes drag a Chinese man into the experiment room. They then forced the man to put his hands into a bowl of iced water. After a while he was made to take his hands out of the water and place them in the draft of a small electric fan. In the end the hands became frostbitten and the man collapsed on the floor in extreme agony. Not long afterward Ueda saw the man again in Prison Block 7; his fingers had been amputated, leaving just the palms of his hands remaining.

d) Experiment Group "A"

In the middle of May 1940 Unit 731's vaccine team formed an experiment group, under the code name Group "A," which carried out experiments comparing the performance of two different vaccines. The vaccines used by Watanabe and Yamauchi had been prepared using ultrasonic waves, while Captain Nakakura and the employee Hosoii used vaccines prepared using the methods of the Army Military Medical College. They chose twenty experimental subjects from the prison, all of them in their twenties and thirties. The experiments were carried out in rooms 7 and 8 of the Special Team. First of all Kobayashi told the technician Hosoii to carry out an inoculation. Eight of the subjects were injected with cholera vaccine made using ultrasonic waves, eight others received vaccine prepared by the Military Medical College method, and the four remaining subjects were given no preliminary inoculation at all.

Twenty days after the immunization treatment, the experimental team began its bodily infection experiments. Technicians Kawana and Chiba mixed cholera bacteria in milk and forced the experimental subjects to drink it. The lethal dose of this type of cholera bacteria was 0.001g and the amount used in the experiment was 0.002g: there was no chance that anyone would survive without immunization. The results of the experiment were that those who had been immunized with the vaccine produced with ultrasonic waves were by and large unaffected—only one of them had slight head and stomach pains, and he felt better after a day. However, most of the subjects immunized with the vaccine produced by the Military Medical College method contracted cholera, three of them were seriously ill, and one died. The four who had not been inoculated all fell ill and were dead after three days.

Later the experimental team conducted similar experiments with plague vaccine, and again confirmed that vaccine prepared using ultrasonic waves was the most effective. And so, on the basis of these results obtained at the cost of the lives of the experimental subjects, Ishii Shiroo ordered the vaccine team to manufacture large amounts of vaccine using the ultrasonic wave method. . . .

Notes

1. Extracted from files in the Central Archives.
2. Ibid.
3. Ibid.
4. Ibid.
5. Ibid.
6. Collated on the basis of files in the Central Archives.

4

Socialist Transformation: 1945–1989

Red Flagship: 1945–1949

The Political Framework

Early on the morning of August 17, 1945, veteran Communist prisoner Zhou Weibin was sweeping the yard of the Xiangfang Prison in Harbin, where he had spent six years, when he discovered that there were no guards on duty. News of the August 15 Japanese surrender had not been communicated inside the prison, which held more than a thousand political prisoners, but with the guards gone Zhou Weibin simply started to walk toward the center of Harbin. Soon others followed suit, and the famished ex-prisoners staggered into a city deep in the throes of chaos. Economic activity had come to a standstill, mass hunger threatened, and the only thing in abundant supply was armed bandits.

Zhou Weibin had worked for the Soviet intelligence network in Harbin in the 1930s. His first move was to try to contact his former employers, but the Soviet consulate was locked. The Soviet forces had not yet arrived, and some of the ex-prisoners huddled together in the homes of the very few comrades who had escaped arrest and survived in the city during the period of Japanese occupation. While struggling for physical survival they also immediately set to work restoring the party organization, and within two weeks they had established, with Soviet help, a headquarters, a dormitory, and a "Temporary North Manchuria Chinese Communist Party Committee." Their discipline and determination were a tribute to the CCP's organizational power, nevertheless the odds seemed impossible for this small and isolated group. Even the Communists themselves would have found it hard to believe at the time that they in fact represented the future of Harbin and that soon the city would become a flagship in the party's strategic move from the countryside to the modern cities.[1] As had happened before, events in Harbin were preconditioned by developments in the larger theater of big power politics. At the Yalta Conference Stalin gained U.S. and British acquiescence in a restoration of tsarist Russia's position in Manchuria, including a Sino-Soviet condominium of the Manchurian railways. On August 8, 1945, the Soviet Union declared war on Japan, and Soviet forces took control of Manchuria in the following weeks. Harbin was secured by the Soviet Red Army on August 18. The United States actively helped Chiang Kai-shek restore power in Japanese-occupied eastern China in a race against Chinese Communist forces struggling to expand into the territories being surrendered by the Japanese, but in the Northeast the Soviet takeover presented a unique strategic opportunity for the CCP. On August 11, CCP Commander-in-Chief Zhu De ordered his troops in the North China "border regions" to move into Manchuria, and on September 17, 1945, the CCP Central Committee adopted the new strategic line of "expanding toward the North while defending [positions held in] the South" (*xiang bei fazhan, xiang nan fangyu*). Around 100,000 Communist-led troops were redeployed to Manchuria in the autumn of 1945, approximately one-sixth of the party's military force, along with a large number of experienced cadres. The CCP's bold move into the Northeast eventually became the decisive element in the 1946–49 civil war, with Communist victory in Manchuria as the stepping stone to nationwide victory over the Guomindang.

Until early 1946 the U.S. government assigned rather low priority to the situation in Manchuria, hoping that Sino-Soviet cooperation could by itself stabilize the situation. This left Stalin with the possibility of pursuing a dual strategy, negotiating with Chiang Kai-shek for substantial economic concessions in Manchuria and a permanent Soviet stake in the region, while at the same time helping the Chinese Communists secure an important new base area.[2] During October and early November 1945 Chinese Communists assumed leading positions in several Soviet-occupied Manchurian cities, but in November Chiang Kai-shek managed to obtain a Soviet promise of withdrawal by February 1946 and Soviet cooperation in the Nationalist takeover of the Northeast. In late November the political representatives and military forces of the CCP were ordered to leave the cities in Manchuria, and representatives of the Guomindang regime were allowed to establish provincial and municipal administrations in the region. The Soviet Union maintained its military control, however, and new procrastination in evacuating the Red Army followed in the winter of 1945–46, leaving the CCP time to consolidate its positions in the Manchurian countryside. Mounting U.S. pressure eventually produced a Soviet turnaround, and the Red Army was pulled out during the months of March and April 1946 in what was essentially a conciliatory move to counter the emerging Western alliance against the Soviet Union. In Manchuria, however, the consequence was war.

The Communist military commander in Manchuria, Lin Biao, moved quickly to seize power in the wake of the departing Soviet troops. Changchun was occupied on April 18, 1946, and Harbin was taken on April 28 by 12,000 Communist troops led by the legendary 359th Regiment from Yan'an against an opposing force of 5,000 poorly organized Guomindang soldiers. But the tide of war soon turned. In May and early June the Nationalist Army inflicted a string of serious defeats on Lin Biao, who pulled his remaining troops northward across the Sungari. In early June the CCP forces were preparing for the evacuation of Harbin, the last major city under their control, as the Nationalist Army prepared for the assault less than twenty miles away. The Nationalist advance was halted by the Marshall truce of June 6, however, which in all probability saved the CCP's position in Harbin.[3] When fighting was resumed in the fall of 1946 the Nationalist Army, despite its military superiority at the time, refrained from attacking Harbin, reportedly because Chiang Kai-shek feared provoking Moscow by attacking a CCP stronghold so close to the Soviet borders (Levine 1987, p. 240). As the balance of power changed during 1947 and 1948 Harbin became ever more important for the CCP as its Manchurian war capital as well as a testing ground for the new stage of the Chinese revolution: control and transformation of the cities under CCP leadership.

The CCP's Approach to Power

Having established military control in Harbin, the Soviet occupation authorities decided to appoint the city's leading Chinese businessman, Zhang Tingge, to the post of acting mayor. Zhang had already served as a figurehead of municipal administration for long periods of time ever since the establishment of the Self-Administrative Council in 1926 (cf. Text 2C). In the autumn of 1945 municipal administration in Harbin was an empty shell, however. Its operations have been summarized with the following formula: "First of all, provide food for the employees, and only then strive to maintain administrative work. Everyone guard against difficulties on their own, and try to obtain money from many different sources. Act only when there is money, otherwise stop the activity. Uphold the old regulations and don't make any new rules" (Han Jing 1983, pp. 30–31). Funds were provided mainly by Zhang's own Shuanghesheng Company and by the Chamber of Commerce.

The Communist organization in the city drew on three different sources. The freed prisoners mentioned above were one element, but though their organizational instincts were intact, they had been completely cut off from the central party leadership for a decade and lacked political direction. Another group comprised the survivors of the Communist anti-Japanese guerrillas, who had retreated to the Soviet Union in 1941 after their final defeat by the Japanese; now they returned with the Soviet Red Army. In Harbin the leader of this group was Li Zhaolin, a former commander of the Third United Anti-Japanese Army in Manchuria with a legendary reputation. On August 23, 1945, he established the "Harbin Office of the United Anti-Japanese Army" but remained at a distance from the "Temporary North Manchuria CCP Committee" set up by the former prisoners on August 30. The third group consisted of cadres pouring in from Yan'an and the North China border regions after the middle of October. Cadres with experience from Manchuria were in precious short supply within the CCP (cf. Levine 1987, p. 106), but the Harbin group was led by Zhong Ziyun, who had lived in that city from 1928 to 1934 and joined the party during that time (an autobiographical account is found in Zhong Ziyun 1986, pp. 1–3). The Yan'an cadres immediately made contact with Li Zhaolin, and it was decided to dissolve the "Temporary Committee" and establish instead the "CCP Binjiang District Work Committee" with Zhong Ziyun as its secretary and including Li Zhaolin and the leading ex-prisoners. Zhong stayed on in the position of party secretary in Harbin for the duration of the civil war period. The party committee was under the leadership of the newly established Northeastern Bureau headed by Peng Zhen; Chen Yun was the leader of the North Manchurian Subbureau and served as the immediate superior of the Harbin party committee. He came to the city in mid-November 1945 but had to leave for the surrounding countryside soon afterward, as the Soviet authorities on November 20 ordered all CCP political and military personnel out with only three days' notice.

In the meanwhile a Sino-Soviet Friendship Society had been established in Harbin in mid-October. The Soviet authorities had tried out the idea in Chifeng and decided to apply it in Harbin in order to facilitate the work of the occupation forces (Loboda 1990, p. 216). Li Zhaolin was made chairman of the society, which served the multiple purposes of providing a means of communication between the Chinese and the occupation authorities, disseminating Soviet propaganda, and securing for the CCP a foothold from which to operate. The Soviet participants reported initial difficulties, particularly between the Yan'an cadres and the local gentry representatives invited by the Soviet representatives to join the board (Loboda 1990, pp. 216–17), but soon the Friendship Society became a useful front organization for the Harbin Party Committee during the period of Guomindang "takeover."

In the period of semi-illegality from late November 1945 to April 28, 1946, the Communists in Harbin opposed the Guomindang representatives through CCP strongholds in the media such as the *Harbin Daily* and the local radio station. Propaganda centered on the demand for democratic elections, and it appears that the Communists also managed to maintain a measure of influence within the local business community. From the outset they used their position in the Friendship Society to milk the local business elite for financial contributions to the CCP-controlled military forces in the area (Guo Jiyun 1986, p. 17). Two hundred new party members were trained in one-month crash courses organized by the CCP-controlled Student Federation (Wang Jiangfu 1988, p. 11). A CCP-led militia, the "Harbin Safety Protection Militia" (Haerbin baoan zongdui) had been established under Li Zhaolin's leadership in October 1945. A motley collection of former Manzhouguo puppet troops and unemployed workers was recruited around a nucleus of Communist veterans, and this militia grew to around 3,500 men by the time it was forced to leave Harbin on November 22 for the surrounding countryside. It was by no means a reliable unit, and during the winter of 1945–46 more than a thousand militia members turned against the CCP leadership, temporarily shaking the very foundation of CCP power in the Harbin area (Zhong Ziyun 1986, pp. 10–11). Only with the arrival of the 359th Regiment in late February 1946 did the rural areas around Harbin become firmly controlled by the party. Inside the city the widely popular Li Zhaolin, still operating under the protection of the Friendship Society, was murdered on March 9, 1946, presumably by Guomindang agents. The Friendship Society organized demonstrations and a mourning rally that attracted scores of thousands of participants and managed to transform Li's death into a political victory. The final showdown on April 28 was a pushover victory for the Communist forces; they entered the suburbs while the last Soviet units were still packing and encountered only minimal resistance from local troops loyal to the Guomindang.

After the takeover the CCP's hold on Harbin remained tenuous for several months. The fragility of CCP power is reflected in Text 4C, which describes an uprising in August 1946. The secret society behind the rebellion counted thousands of followers; they were defeated by a company of Korean Communist soldiers stationed in Harbin. Another destabilizing factor was the large Japanese population stranded in Harbin, around 100,000 people against a Chinese population of around 600,000. Veteran CCP leader Zhang Wentian was put in charge of the evacuation operation, and the Japanese were successfully returned home in the early fall of 1946, apparently without any incidents or loss of life (Liu Dazhi 1986, p. 59). Social order turned out to be a much more stubborn problem. At the time of the takeover in April 1946 the situation in Harbin was no better than it had been in the wake of the Japanese surrender. The city was teeming with demobilized puppet troops and Guomindang followers, and the general attitude of the Harbin population toward the new Communist masters was very negative. The CCP cadres had to draw on the entire inventory of party-led mass mobilization to turn the situation around. "Speak bitterness" meetings (*suku dahui*) were held in some factories, and a major victory was won with the execution of two leading "local tyrants" in July 1946, as described in Text 4B. A Harbin Worker Representatives' Congress was established in October 1946. Trade unions were set up for the different sectors of production, and by 1948 membership of these unions had grown to 58,000.

A first attempt to organize street committees in the summer of 1946 had to be given up because popular support was lacking, but in the winter of 1946–47 the municipal leadership managed to establish grass-roots organizations in the form of six districts and fifty-eight "street offices" (*jiegongsuo*) supported by "self-protection militia" (*ziweidui*) (Zhong Ziyun 1986, p. 19; Levine 1987, pp. 144–46). Still public order remained a stubborn problem. In February 1947 the mayor of Harbin, Liu Chengdong, complained that some citizens were committing robbery under the pretext that the revolution encouraged poor people to "liberate themselves" (*fanshen*), and even after twenty months of CCP rule in Harbin the Public Security Bureau reported widespread bandit activity in the city (Levine 1987, p. 146). Surveillance carried out by neighborhood watch groups was tightened up, and persons failing to report crimes were warned that they would be judged equally guilty with the criminals themselves (Levine 1987, p. 147). The CCP operated through its various front organizations while the party organization itself remained "underground" until July 1948, when membership stood at 2,710. By the autumn of 1948 this figure had risen to 4,013 (Zhong Ziyun 1986, p. 19).

Learning Economic Management

With the growth of Communist military strength during 1947 and 1948, Harbin assumed new strategic significance as a production center for military supplies. The management of industrial production became crucial, and there were considerable disagreements within the CCP in this new and unfamiliar field (see, for example, Liu Chengdong 1986, pp. 62–63). At the time of the April 1946 takeover production and commerce in Harbin had almost come to a standstill. The approximately twenty large oil and grain mills that had survived the Japanese occupation lacked raw materials and had ceased production. Electricity and water were in very short supply. The initial approach of the new administration was to confiscate the property of two pro-Japanese collaborators while supporting the remaining manufacturers. A "people's livelihood company" (minsheng gongsi) was organized under the authority of the CCP-appointed mayor in June 1946. The first task of this company was to sell to the urban population the grain and other commodities confiscated from collaborators and defeated Guomindang troops. The funds thus generated became the first working capital of the new administration, and the operations of the company soon expanded as it assumed a role in distributing the 1946 autumn harvest grain to the privately owned mills; this was the humble beginning of the system of "raw materials supplied by the government, private manufacturing, and products bought up by the government" (baoxiao, jiagong, dinghuo) first developed in Harbin and later adopted nationwide as a vehicle for the transformation of private industry. The "people's livelihood company" competed with the private grain merchants, establishing a network of distribution outlets as well as expanding supplies by setting up a number of producers' cooperatives. The company was reorganized in September 1947 into a Bureau of Production under municipal administration, while the grain trade was delegated to the government-run Dongxing Company (Liu Yizhong 1986, pp. 194–98). The continued struggle for public control of distribution in the food business is reflected in the final sections of Texts 2C and 2D as well as in Text 4A, which describes conditions in the Chicken and Duck Company during the 1945–48 period. A grain rationing system was introduced in the spring of 1947 to ensure low-priced grain to the city poor, but the system proved unworkable (Levine 1987, p. 180).

Throughout 1946 and 1947 Mayor Liu Chengdong on several occasions thundered against the "treacherous grain merchants" and "reactionaries" striving to undermine price stability (Liu Yizhong 1986, p. 196). A government-led bank, the Northeast Bank, set up shop in September 1946. There was at the time a profusion of competing currencies in the city, and inflation was rampant. During the following months Soviet, Manzhouguo, and Guomindang currencies were gradually replaced by the "Northeast currency notes" (Dongbei liutongjuan), but inflation remained a pernicious problem throughout the civil war period.

In 1947 the political and economic climate changed again. This was the period of "leftist excesses" in the Manchurian land reform drive, and the effects of land reform spilled over into Harbin as rural cadres entered the city to ferret out fugitive landlords in the "dig for hidden wealth" campaign (*kanwa yundong*). It was no simple matter to distinguish between the "exploitative" activities of landlords and the "legitimate" interests of city merchants and manufacturers, particularly in those cases where the two social categories met in the same person.[4] But there was also a pressure for more radical measures from below and from inside the party. By the spring of 1947 it was claimed that all public enterprises in Harbin were under worker management, and in private industry the traditional year-end bonus system was pushed in the direction of eliminating profits altogether (Levine 1987, p. 184). In the case of the Lopato Tobacco Company this was a direct threat to municipal finances, which depended largely on revenue from the sale of cigarettes. According to the city mayor, many grass-roots party members supported the workers' economic demands, and it required a major effort to stem the leftist swing in 1947 (Liu Chengdong 1986, pp. 70–71). The General Labor Union in Harbin began to confront these problems as early as October 1947, however, well in advance of the Anti-Leftist Campaign initiated by Mao Zedong in February 1948, and the Harbin press publicized cases of workers who "voluntarily" accepted lower wages (Pepper 1978, p. 354; Levine 1987, p. 184).

During the remainder of the civil war period Harbin became the testing ground for the implementation and perfection of *wage incentives* in an economic environment of public-private cooperation under government supervision (Pepper 1978, pp. 355–57; also see discussion of the experimentation with wage incentives in Harbin in Guo Linjun 1986). Harbin leaders learned to focus on "promoting production," turning the city into a major asset as supplier to the People's Liberation Army during the strategic counteroffensive in 1948. In May 1948 Harbin hosted the Sixth All-China Labor Congress, attended by 504 delegates from both CCP- and Guomindang-controlled areas, and the congress confirmed the new production-oriented line (Pepper 1978, pp. 361–64; for a Chinese account of the congress, see Zhu Xuefan 1986). A breakthrough was also achieved in organizing a housewives' home industry. By the end of 1948, 30,000 Harbin women were involved in home spinning and weaving (Ying and Jing 1986, p. 93). Impressive economic growth in Harbin was reported for the year 1948, but many problems remained. As late as the Spring Festival of 1948 the privately owned flour mills were still able to manipulate the price of flour through joint stockpiling (see Text 2D), and great difficulties in the introduction of "scientific management" were admitted to in the summer of 1948 (Pepper 1978, pp. 375–76). City administration was generally quite loose during the civil war period, and a centralized system was not instituted until mid-1949.[5]

Local History Research

There is an abundance of material on the 1945–49 period in the publications on Harbin local history. By far the greatest part is provided by the participants themselves, while there is little independent research by the historians, who serve primarily as editors of veteran cadre memoirs. Obviously, with the advent of the CCP in a leading role, Harbin local history becomes essentially the story of "implementation of the party line," and all other historical themes pale in comparison. But given this precondition, the material is fertile and provides many insights into the actual conditions of political work in Harbin during the period. On some issues the sources vary, but they are mostly uniform. For example, all accounts agree on the initial hostile reaction of Harbin's population toward the Communists. The stock phrase describing the mentality in Harbin during the years from 1945 to 1947 is "orthodoxy" (*zhengtong guandian*), a euphemism for Guomindang sympathies. The CCP activists sent to the city were clearly amazed to find the urban people, including the industrial working class, so hostile to Communist ideas. Dozens of sources describe the indifference or outright hostility of Harbiners toward the CCP in all spheres of life, and the indignation of the new leaders because this ungrateful reception has left a lasting mark in the pages of Harbin local history.

Other issues are uniformly left in the dark, such as the economic activities of the Soviet occupation authorities in Harbin. The Soviet forces dismantled many industrial enterprises in Manchuria during the occupation, transporting the equipment to the Soviet Union by rail. The damage to China was estimated by a U.S. representative at U.S. $895 million in direct damage or U.S. $2 billion in production loss and replacement costs (Levine 1987, p. 69). But judging from the Harbin local historical records no Soviet dismantling of industry took place in that city. This is very unlikely and probably reflects political guidelines on how to approach—or rather, avoid—this painful issue.[6] This does not imply, however, that Harbin local history is above criticism of the Soviet occupation forces. There are in fact several critical remarks, and in comparison only a few references to Soviet helpfulness; one looks in vain for descriptions of warmth in the relationship between the Soviet and Chinese comrades. Indignation shines through the account, in Text 4A, of the arrogant behavior on the part of Soviet representatives in trade relations. Far more serious was the case of veteran CCP cadre Lu Dongsheng, who was robbed and murdered by Soviet soldiers one evening in mid-November 1945 while carrying Chen Yun's luggage. Chen Yun at this time served as the top-ranking CCP representative in Harbin (for a detailed account of this incident, see Liu Chengdong

1986, pp. 47–49). The Soviet expulsion order to the CCP on November 20, 1945, also caused great anger among the Chinese Communists. The general tone of the various Chinese accounts toward the Soviet Union and Soviet representatives is one of resentment thinly covered by diplomatic restraint.

As for errors and stumblings in the process of working out suitable policies relevant to the urban environment, one finds considerable variation among the different sources. As a general rule, the more highly placed the source, the more room for self-criticism. For example, a general account of CCP policy in the city during the civil war period by a Harbin historian contains hardly a trace of negative comment or evidence of political immaturity (Lin Huanwen 1986), whereas the memoirs of the Harbin mayor during the civil war period provide many glimpses of the political difficulties of the time, even including a critical remark about one particular meeting of the Northeastern Bureau in 1948, which produced "only some general Marxist statements but failed to relate these to the contemporary reality of the cities in the Northeast" (Liu Chengdong 1986, p. 69).

The People's Republic: 1949–1989

The Construction of an Industrial Metropolis

In the 1950s Harbin became one of China's main centers for heavy industry. Its population expanded rapidly, and new industrial and residential areas were developed in the outskirts of the city.

Several factors lay behind Harbin's economic growth during this period. The CCP gained control over Manchuria earlier than over any other region, and Harbin was the first major city to be taken over by the new government, so the ground was well prepared for an economic reconstruction along the new planning principles; the city was close, geographically as well as culturally, to the Soviet Union, the main ally of the new People's Republic; it was the natural center for a large region rich in natural resources and with a rather developed infrastructure; and its position far inland gave it a strategic advantage over urban centers in the more vulnerable coastal region.

The first important stimulus to Harbin's economy had come during the Korean War, when sixteen major industrial enterprises from Liaoning, closer to the frontline, were relocated to Harbin. The real breakthrough, however, came during the First Five-Year Plan (1953–57), when many of the large-scale plants that still make up the backbone of Harbin's industry were constructed. Out of the 156 national key projects that were implemented with Soviet assistance during this period, thirteen were placed in Harbin, among them huge plants for power-generating equipment such as boilers, steam turbines, and electrical machinery. To an even higher degree than elsewhere in China, investments were concentrated in heavy industry, whose share of the value of industrial output rose from 18 percent in 1949 to 65 percent in 1957 (Haerbin nianjian bianjibu 1987, p. 34). On Harbin's Friendship Road (*Youyilu*), the Friendship Palace, a massive building complex originally built to house Soviet experts, bears witness to the considerable Soviet input to the city's industrial development, but the few historical articles we have found on Harbin under the First Five-Year Plan never touch on this topic.

During the first half of the 1950s Harbin maintained its role as test site and model for the new government's policies toward the national bourgeoisie. Major figures among the prerevolution national capitalists like Zhang Tingge and Wu Baixiang initially received high posts, although Zhang only grudgingly accepted the new rulers, and Wu was persecuted as a rightist in 1957 (Fang Shijun 1989b, pp. 29–32 and 64–67; see Zhang's biography in Text 2C). As reflected in Text 4D, the years before 1956 are now seen as a golden age for Harbin, and historical research is beginning to move into this period.

Under the Second Five-Year Plan (1958–62), Harbin experienced much less stable development. Not only did it suffer from the general economic crisis after the Great Leap Forward, but the departure of the Soviet experts in 1960 after the Sino-Soviet split must have dealt a particularly hard blow to a city with so many Soviet-aided projects. Just as the historians downplay the positive Soviet role, however, they also tend to ignore the problems arising from Soviet withdrawal. According to official statistics, the value of industrial production dropped by almost 70 percent from 1960 to 1962, but quickly recovered over the following few years (Haerbin nianjian bianjibu 1987, pp. 34–35).

Population and Urban Development

Harbin's population exploded during the first decade of the People's Republic. The number of inhabitants doubled between 1950 and 1958, when it reached 1.6 million. In 1960 the population passed the 2 million mark for the first time, and then stabilized at this level for around ten years (Fang Shijun 1989a). Part of the reason for the fast growth during the first eleven years was an average annual birth rate as high as 4.6 percent, but the principal factor was a net immigration of 647,000 people spurred by rapidly expanding job opportunities (Haerbin nianjian bianjibu 1987, p. 49). Among these immigrants were skilled workers, technicians, and cadres transferred from enterprises elsewhere in China who brought with them valuable technical and administrative skills. These "southerners" are still highly visible in Harbin's political and technical elite. Most immigrants, however, were unskilled laborers from rural areas. Actually, the gross immigration to Harbin came to almost 1.7 million, and in 1958–59 alone 130,000 peasants from other provinces flooded the city looking for jobs. By 1960 there were as many as 500–600 people coming in every day, and many of them ended up as street hawkers or manure collectors (Li and Shi 1987, pp. 254–58). This uncontrolled immigration led to a severe shortage of housing and an enormous pressure on all urban facilities. In 1949 the average housing area was 3.62 square meters per person, but it shrank to 2.6 square meters by 1965 and only reached the 1949 level again in 1983 (Haerbin nianjian bianjibu 1987, pp. 290–91). In response to these problems, the city organized several campaigns to send superfluous manpower back to the villages, and even in 1955, while the economy was still expanding, more than 53,000 people were sent off (Li and Shi 1987, p. 256). During the recession period after the Great Leap Forward this rerustication policy became an even more central concern, and between 1960 and 1963, 422,000 immigrants had to leave the city (Fang Shijun 1989a, p. 460). Even through such drastic measures the authorities managed to push the population figure down below the 2 million level for only a few years.

Harbin's non-Chinese population, on the other hand, emigrated in great numbers during the 1950s. Just after 1949 around 25,000 Russians were still left in Harbin, and their relatively high educational level gave them a key role in industrial production in the early 1950s. According to one source they were even able to "monopolize" the production of some types of technologically advanced equipment, for which they demanded high prices (Ren Tingxi 1988, pp. 23–24). The socialization of industry in the mid-1950s together with an active resettlement policy led to an exodus of Russians between 1955 and 1959. Some went back to the Soviet Union, but many preferred new destinations abroad, primarily Australia and Brazil (Li and Shi 1987, p. 189). By 1964 only 903 foreigners were left in Harbin, half of them Russians (Fang Shijun 1989a, p. 486). The population of the city was now, for the first time in its history, purely Chinese.

During its period of industrial expansion the city mushroomed in all directions. The huge plants for power-generating equipment and machine building were concentrated in the new Power District (*Dongliqu*) southeast of the center, while the chemical industry and the production of building materials were placed in Taiping District and Sankeshu in the northeast. Other industrial areas were laid out west of the city and in Xiangfang. Although Harbin today is a badly polluted area, the planning of the 1950s managed to save the city center from the grimmest consequences of industrialization by concentrating heavy industry in these specially designated areas. The major institutions for education and research, such as Heilongjiang University and Harbin Medical College, were placed to the south, along Xuefulu. After the summer of 1957, when the city escaped flooding only through a massive effort by local citizens, rural work brigades, and the army, the dikes along the Songhua River were reinforced, and recreation areas were laid out along its banks and on the Sunshine Island.

Administration and Politics

In 1949 Harbin stood as the unchallenged economic and cultural center of North Manchuria, and its industrial expansion substantially strengthened this position. In 1954, however, the Chinese government decided to merge the provinces of Songjiang and Heilongjiang, and at the same time place Harbin, which had been ruled directly by the center, under the new Heilongjiang Province (Fang Shijun 1989a, pp. 107–8). As the city grew to one of China's ten largest industrial centers it felt hampered by its subordination to a rather backward province, and in 1962 it applied for the same status as "independent planning unit" (*jihua danlie*) that had just been bestowed on Tianjin, Shenyang, Wuhan, Guangzhou, Chongqing, and Xi'an, and which meant direct communication with the center on all planning issues, and better control over incomes and investments. In its application the Harbin party committee mentioned the serious problems facing the city after more than a decade of industrial growth: run down and insufficient housing, public transport, schooling and other public facilities; a severe shortage of consumer goods caused by the strong bias toward heavy industry; and a low wage level, which did not take into account the extra living costs caused by the cold climate. The center agreed to the proposal, and Harbin got its independent line in the state plans after 1964, but this was suspended in 1967 because of the Cultural Revolution (Haerbinshi dang'anguan 1985). As can be seen from Text 4D, Harbin had its share of political campaigns in the 1950s and early 1960s. The top city leadership appears to have been rather stable, however, with Lü Qi'en as city mayor from 1952 to the outbreak of the Cultural Revolution. Lü seems to have taken a special interest in physical planning and urban construction, and he is mentioned with great reverence today. (See for example his biography in Fang Shijun 1989b, pp. 102–9.) The most dramatic case of a dethroned Harbin party leader during this period is that of Li Changqing, who fell from his post as city party secretary in 1955 as a victim of the Gao Gang affair. As reflected in Text 4D, the present interpretation is that he was wrongly accused, and though the Northeast was supposed to be Gao's principal base, no other city-level leaders were apparently brought down by the affair. (For a full account of the Gao Gang affair see Teiwes 1990.)

Harbin since 1966

The almost thirty years that have passed since the beginning of the Cultural Revolution have not yet been the subject of significant historical research in Harbin. As mentioned above, the historians are beginning to work their way into the 1950s and early 1960s, and the social scientists take over from 1978 with their analyses of the reform process, but the interlude, the "ten years of turmoil" between 1966 and 1976, is largely undescribed and probably also unresearched. We were told that members of the Harbin Party History Committee had begun working on the Cultural Revolution in the late 1980s, but few written materials had survived, and few people wanted to discuss their actions during that time.

Harbin and Heilongjiang actually played an important role during a crucial phase of the Cultural Revolution, because the "revolutionary committees" (*geming weiyuanhui*) that were to become the universal organs of power all over China after 1967 were first set up here. Compared to the Shanghai Commune with its radical ideas of direct elections, the revolutionary committees established at the provincial and city levels in Harbin during January and February 1967 were more "conservative." The power seizure in Harbin, which was highly praised in the national media as a model for the rest of the country, was closely controlled by the army and the provincial leadership, and it was followed by a rather quick reinstatement of most of the criticized cadres.[7] It is plausible that Heilongjiang's strategic importance as a border region induced the center to test a more moderate and less risky strategy here, but this "national first" has not inspired local historians to look more closely into the matter.

Since the beginning of the economic reforms in 1978 Harbin has had some problems readjusting to the new trends. The domination of large-scale, state-owned, heavy industry plants that propelled Harbin to the position of one of China's main industrial centers in the 1950s has hampered the city's development at a time when industrial growth has taken place primarily in small- and medium-scale enterprises in the consumer goods sector. The return of the educated youth and cadres who had been sent to settle in the countryside during the 1960s and early 1970s has created new pressure on urban facilities. In 1979 alone, 159,000 people immigrated to Harbin, most of them returnees, and in 1982 the population figure for Harbin's urban areas passed 2.5 million (Haerbin nianjian bianjibu 1987, pp. 49–50). As reflected in Text 4E, and as visible in Harbin streets, the small private enterprises are back on the scene, yet the private sector in Harbin pales in comparison with China's coastal cities, and in the early 1990s Harbin remains a city very much under the central government's control (cf. *Newsweek*, June 4, 1990, pp. 38–41).

The expansion of trade between China and Russia is apparently leading to a new commercial burgeoning in Harbin, as its "Russian connection" again works to its advantage. The linguistic and cultural competences are certainly still present in the city. But these issues of the 1990s belong to the realm of Harbin's social scientists rather than to its historians.

The establishment of the People's Republic of China on October 1, 1949, represents a distinct demarcation line for the Harbin historians. More research has apparently been done on the brief period of transition from 1946 to 1949 than on all the following fifty years together, and only a few aspects of the city's post-1949 history have been covered. The study of the historical development of the People's Republic, called "contemporary history" (*dangdaishi*), is a field that has only slowly started to develop in China in the 1980s, and most historians justly consider it a minefield of touchy questions related directly to ongoing power struggles. The decision about writing local gazetteers with a special emphasis on the post-1949 era (cf. Chapter 5) has put local historians under heavy pressure to do more work on the contemporary period, and the gazetteers are making much new material available, but true to the nature of the genre it normally takes the form of presentations of bare data rather than analytical writing.

Besides the political sensitivity of many post-1949 issues, several additional reasons exist for the conspicuous lack of research on this period in Harbin. Whereas the compilation of historical documents, the interviewing of significant personalities, and the collection of materials for new gazetteers first began in the 1950s in many other localities, Harbin had to start more or less from scratch in the early 1980s. By then time was quickly running out for interviewing the former actors on the Republican scene, and it was therefore natural that such work got top priority. This was clearly the case for the people collecting the *Historical Text Materials* (cf. Chapter 5), who in 1986 presented a detailed list of research topics, all relating to the pre-1949 period, adding only a note that "the framework for the post-1949 period has not yet been worked out" (*Haerbin wenshi ziliao*, no. 4 [1984], pp. 130–42). This was also true for the Party History Committee, whose office for post-1949 research was set up as late as 1988.

We also heard the viewpoint expressed that the historical individuality of the different cities disappeared after the whole country became united, so that history became "more or less the same all over the place," as one social scientist put it, and the writing of local history therefore less meaningful. The many national-level political campaigns have created a sense of homogeneity and uniformity, which tends to conceal local variations, such as the Soviet factor in the case of Harbin.

The few historical writings on Harbin after 1949 fall in three groups. The first type, which is either a preparation for future work in the field or part of the gazetteer project, consists of lists of dates, events, and so on without much interpretation. The most important example is the *Annals of Harbin History 1950–1965*, a day-to-day account of big and small events in the city as they were presented in the official sources of the time. Only rarely are these sources considered to be so much at odds with present-day interpretations that a modification is needed, as in the following entry on the anti-rightist campaign in 1957, where the word in brackets, of course, represents the later correction:

> *December:* According to statistics from the Rectification Office of the City Party Committee, 1,336 people have [wrongly] been reported to be rightists, and 125 of them have already been criticized in the newspapers. (Fang Shijun 1989a, p. 216)

The second type, represented by Text 4D, consists of life histories of deceased local political leaders or other prominent citizens who have suffered some kind of injustice, but have later been rehabilitated. Almost half the people portrayed in the first volume of *Harbin Biographies*, for example, were victims of the Cultural Revolution (Fang Shijun 1989b). While these texts show a striking concern about giving the persecuted justice, they show no attempts at identifying the local henchmen. The villains are either anonymous or long-condemned central level leaders, such as Chen Boda in Text 4D.

Finally, there are a few articles in the historical magazines that address current social problems, such as Text 4E. They are obviously written by social scientists, but have a historical dimension, and their inclusion in the *Harbin History and Gazetteer* reflects the aim of the gazetteer compilers to cover contemporary affairs. There is a distinct difference between these texts and those written by historians. Whereas the latter stick closely to their tradition of allotting praise and blame in just portions to individual historical agents according to moral-political criteria, the social scientists use the survey method to investigate issues of relevance for the political decision-makers, deal primarily with quantifiable mass-agents, and offer their advice on policy formulation and implementation. Still, both types of text may serve as comments on contemporary political issues.

Notes

1. The description of the Harbin Communist prisoners in the wake of the Japanese surrender is based on a collection of memoirs; Wang Shuqing 1986, passim.

2. Steven I. Levine has produced a superb analysis of the U.S.-Soviet-Chinese strategic triangle in relation to Manchuria (Levine 1987). For the Sino-Soviet economic negotiations, Gillin and Myers 1989 is a valuable source.

3. According to Gillin and Myers, "the Communists were elated and warmly welcomed Marshall's representative to Harbin"; Gillin and Myers 1989, p. 52.

4. In Levine's apt phrase, "[t]hat the self-same evil landlord could become magically transformed into a legitimate merchant or entrepreneur by merely passing through the city gates was an incomprehensible subtlety of Marxist class analysis, akin perhaps to the fox fairies of Chinese popular tales who disguised themselves as beautiful maidens to deceive the unwary"; Levine 1987, p. 145.

5. According to Levine, Harbin municipal administration after the establishment of districts and street offices in the winter of 1946–47 was essentially "a sort of holding company for the street offices"; Levine 1987, p. 144.

6. Not surprisingly, Soviet sources emphasize the economic help of the Soviet Union in Harbin, e.g. Borisov 1977, pp. 212–13.

7. For an analysis of the Cultural Revolution in Heilongjiang, see Sargent 1971. Though Sargent's focus is on the provincial level, the article also contains much information about events in Harbin.

Texts

―――――

From Liberation to the Reforms

In April 1946 Harbin became the first major city to be controlled by the CCP, and in the following three years many policies that would be implemented at the national level after October 1949 were first tested in Harbin. This period is therefore a major focus of local history research. Text 4A shows how the Chicken and Duck Company, which was also the topic of Text 2B, was turned into a Chinese enterprise. Text 4B then presents an account of the "struggle" against two local gangsters, who were put on public trial and later executed, and finally Text 4C offers a description of the quelling of a secret society rebellion against the Communists just after they seized power. These three texts show the gazetteer project at work at the enterprise and the city district levels, in this case, Taiping.

The last two texts both deal with the post-1949 period. Text 4D, a biography of the former secretary of the Harbin Municipal Party Committee, Li Changqing, is the only mention we have seen of implications for Harbin of the Gao Gang affair in 1954. Text 4E is of a more sociological nature, but it also makes use of historical experience from the People's Republic period to justify today's policies in the field of individual employment.

Both texts are typical in portraying the early 1950s as a golden age, but it is interesting that the first one also focuses on the more problematic aspects of those years, first of all the tendency to expand the scope of political campaigns beyond what is now seen as reasonable limits.

4A. The Chicken and Duck Company Just after the Liberation of Harbin (Excerpts)

Wu Dongsheng, Jiang Haozhi, and Han Yanqiu

On April 28, 1946, all the factories, shops, schools, and houses of Harbin were festooned with lanterns and colored streamers in an enthusiastic celebration of the city's liberation. The only exception was the Chicken and Duck Company, which had earlier been under British and Japanese control and had once been taken over by the Soviet Red Army. The main gate of its factory remained tightly shut, not a soul stirred inside, and by the northern gate a British flag was flying.[1] This state of affairs aroused the attention of the Jilin and Heilongjiang Military Districts' Enemy and Puppet Regime Property Management Office, which at once sent a group headed by assistant section chief Tong Qi to find out what was going on.

1. Effecting the Military Takeover

After the Japanese surrender on August 15, 1945, the Soviet Red Army took over the Chicken and Duck Company and entrusted its operation to employees of White Russian origin such as Larin and Sedalikov. After the Soviet Army pulled out, no one was left in charge of the plant and production ground to a halt. As they were no longer being paid, most of the workers left the company to find other ways of making a living, although a few workers stayed on to look after the factory's property, conscientiously organizing a factory guard.

When Tong Qi's group arrived at the Chicken and Duck Company it convened a meeting with factory workers, among them Chi Xiangming, Wang Yushu, Zhao Baoheng, Zhang Erxin, and the head guard chosen by the worker Wang Jiaxian; the group explained that Harbin had now been liberated and that the Chicken and Duck Company was now under control of the army, which would organize the workers to restore production and pay them wages. The group also asked that the British flag be taken down. The workers received the news warmly, but the White Russian employee Larin steadfastly opposed the move and suggested that before they could

---

Wu Dongsheng, Jiang Haozhi, and Han Yanqiu, "Haerbin jiefang chuqi de Ji-Ya Gongsi," *Haerbin shizhi* [Harbin History and Gazetteer], no. 2 (1984), pp. 40–43.

decide they should first send a telegram to London. Tong Qi immediately reported on the situation to Zhang Yongli, the general manager of the Northeast Administrative Committee's Northeast General Trading Company (he later became deputy departmental head of the commercial department).

On April 23, 1947, Ye Lizhuang, Zhang Yongli, Li Zhen, and Tong Qi arrived in a horsedrawn cart together with their security guards at the Chicken and Duck Company courtyard. They had decided on the military requisitioning of the company in the interest of producing products necessary to the army's liberation of the entire country. They were led around by the workers, among them Chi Xiangming and Wang Yushu, taken to inspect the machinery in the works buildings, and shown the refrigeration plant, the machine saw plant, and so forth. Chi Xiangming and the other workers took out the keys to the factory buildings and the refrigeration plant, which had long been kept safe, and they lowered the British flag. Larin protested against the military requisitioning, and he refused to hand over keys to the account books and the goods stockhouse. Zhang Yongli decided that Li Zhen and others should stay behind and carry out the takeover work, giving instructions that "We must use only gentle persuasion, not military coercion."

Li Zhen sought out Larin and warned him that if he did not hand over the keys to the stockhouse he would be punished for opposing the military takeover. Not knowing what to do, Larin for a while made no answer. Seeing the angry faces and clenched rifles of Li Zhen's security guards, however, he had no choice but to meekly hand over the warehouse keys. Shortly afterward, Li Zhen summoned Larin and told him that he was not going to be kept on and should find something else to do. After his dismissal, Larin would still come to the company every day and hang about the factory yard until he finally left in anger.

Ye Lizhuang and Zhang Yongli returned to the Northeast Administrative Committee and decided after some deliberation to change the name of the Chicken and Duck Company to the "Northeastern Chicken and Duck Company," and they appointed Li Zhen as manager. More than ten people were transferred to the company from units such as the Northeastern General Trading Company and the 359th Regiment Harbin liaison station. These included Ming Ke, a military cadre from Yan'an (later bureau head at the Ministry for Foreign Trade) and Wu Liting (later manager of the Tianjin branch of the Chinese International Shipping Company). At the same time a platoon of guards was also transferred and stationed at the factory. Li Zhen and others convened a meeting of the workers living on the factory grounds and called for the workers to return and take part in production again. The workers rushed off to spread the word and mustered around 300 people, including more than ten foreign nationals.[2] The cadres at the Northeastern Chicken and Duck Company were paid half their salary in kind; they wore military uniforms and carried pistols. . . .

In the beginning of May 1947, the Northeastern Chicken and Duck Company was thronged with carts and its courtyard was crowded like a marketplace. Many resident Russian and Muslim townspeople had come to sell their sheep and cattle, pig breeders from the city suburbs had driven their pigs there for sale, and middlemen dealing in live chickens and ducks had also come along to sell all that they had. The company's leaders came every day to direct affairs in person; two men with experience in the trade, Yu Changxin and the Japanese veterinarian Oota, were responsible for quality checking and purchasing, the price being fixed according to quality and weight. The transactions were fair, and they were flexible without being disorderly.

Between May and the end of 1947, the company purchased 11,565 head of cattle, 33,510 pigs, and 3,008 sheep.[3]

On May 21, 1947, the company's slaughterhouse was officially opened. At the time the price of grain fluctuated greatly, and the workers' wages were calculated according to a piecework workpoint system. Every month the monetary value of the total number of workpoints was calculated according to the value of a single point, and this was then paid to the workers in wages. The workers' enthusiasm for work was very high, and they genuinely considered themselves to have become their own masters. When slaughtering cattle, the workers on occasion found bezoar [a valued ingredient in Chinese medicine], and they would then on their own initiative hand it in to the company's leadership so that it could be turned over to the Northeastern Administrative Committee. The Northeastern Chicken and Duck Company's incentive scheme stipulated that anyone who found bezoar when slaughtering cattle and handed it in would be given in reward a certain quantity of millet (having a cash value equivalent to the market price of the bezoar).

The inspection of meat products for export was carried out by Russian women resident in Harbin who were recruited by the Soviet trade representative and entrusted to judge whether the products reached the required standard. In October 1948, Tong Qi visited the Soviet consulate in Harbin and requested that our own personnel be allowed to control the quality of export products, but at the time the Soviet representatives would not agree to this. On just grounds, Tong Qi argued strongly against their decision, and in the end a resolution was reached requiring joint inspection of the export products by personnel from both sides. The company thereby gained the initiative in the quality control and inspection of export products, and it could put a stop to the Russian women's doing the work perfunctorily or groundlessly finding problems, thereby leading to losses for the company. Tong Qi arranged for ten Chinese women workers to work together with the hired Russian women, and in this way trained up our own meat inspection staff. . . .

Notes

1. When the authors visited Ming Ke, Tong Qi, and others, they all laid special emphasis on this point.

2. All these foreign nationals were former employees of the original company.

3. According to files in the archives of the Harbin Joint Meat Products Processing Plant.

4B. The Retribution Struggle against the Major Local Tyrants Yao Xijiu and Li Jiupeng

Gong Shi

After our Northeastern United Democratic Army entered Harbin [in April 1946], the Municipal Party Committee immediately began to organize propaganda units to arouse the masses. Under the slogan "fight the traitors and settle accounts, rent and cultivate public land, repair and occupy the houses of officials," they gathered together their forces and started on the retribution campaign against traitors and local tyrants. In May and June the public security office sent cadres to investigate the situation, first of all in the Xinyang, Guxiang, Daowai, Xiangfang, and Sankeshu areas, mobilizing the masses to settle accounts with the puppets of Japan, the traitors to China, and the local tyrants. After suitable preparations they organized a citywide struggle against the two leading traitors and tyrants, Yao Xijiu and Li Jiupeng.

On the eve of the city's occupation by our army, the secretary of the Municipal Party Committee, comrade Zhong Ziyun, ordered that comrades carrying out intelligence work in Harbin should gather evidence on the two despots Yao and Li and wait for the army to arrive in the city. When the army arrived they would be openly dealt with, giving a big push to the drive to mobilize the masses. Investigations revealed that Yao Xijiu and Li Jiupeng had been responsible for terrible crimes for many years; they had played the part of running dogs and traitors to China from the era of the old warlords to that of tsarist Russian domination, and from the days when the city was controlled by the Japanese to the days of the Guomindang, and they had ridden roughshod over the people. After our army entered Harbin, Yao and Li went into hiding, fearing the wrath of the people. With the support of the masses, our public security organs tracked them down and captured them, one in a small Buddhist temple at No. 9 Postal Service Road and the other at the Jewish Hospital.

Yao Xijiu came from a gangster family, and he became a major local tyrant, wallowing in blood debts and guilty of countless crimes. He served as a labor contractor on the tsarist Russian construction of the Songhua River Bridge, ruthlessly exploiting the construction workers and illegally

---

Gong Shi, "Qingsuan douzheng da eba Yao Xijiu, Li Jiupeng," *Haerbin shizhi* [Harbin History and Gazetteer], No. 1 (1988), pp. 19–20.

skimming large sums of money for himself. On several occasions he showed particular cruelty by intentionally disconnecting a pipe on the water pump, thereby drowning the workers working under the water level; there was a 600 yuan compensation payment for each worker who died, and this would go to lining Yao's own pocket. He was licentious by nature, having seven wives and concubines at home and in addition often forcing his attentions on women from good families. There was no counting the number of women he had used or the number of happy families and loving married couples he had wrecked. During the period of the Manzhouguo puppet regime he threw in his lot with the Japanese invaders, holding such posts as head of the fifth office of the puppet regime's Binjiang Province police affairs department, head of the Binjiang Province peasants' association and trade association, head of the Confucian society, errand boy for the Japanese secret service, member of the committee to "guard against espionage," and puppet district mayor. He did his all to render service to the Japanese invaders, and, in order to ingratiate himself with them, he gave them as a present an eighteen-pound heavy pair of shackles to be used for the cruel ill treatment of anti-Japanese patriots and oppression of the masses of the people.

Li Jiupeng sold himself to the Japanese invaders after the "September 18 incident," becoming an agent for the military police and helping them with their slaughter of anti-Japanese patriots. On the celebration of the tenth anniversary of the Manzhouguo puppet state, in collaboration with the Japanese military police, he began operation of the city's only semi-official gambling house, situated at the Taiping Bridge, which had two bars with girls, twelve gambling rooms, fifteen rooms for *paijiu* (dominoes), as well as four ball courts. He even laid on a special bus running from the town center to the Taiping Bridge gambling house and arranged for a lot of hoodlums to hang around hotels, restaurants, the railway station, and harbor, hoaxing people into getting involved in gambling. Li made over 1 million yuan a day on these gambling tables and ruthlessly bled the masses dry. Every single person who entered his gambling house was plundered of every last penny. Many people lost their families and ruined their businesses through gambling. After leaving the gambling house, many had no way out but to commit suicide. It was brought to light by the masses that as many as one hundred people had committed suicide in the vicinity of the gambling house. Li presented much of the money he made to the Japanese to support their war of invasion and also used the gambling house as a center for espionage, gathering information there about our soldiers and citizens fighting the Japanese enemy. After the victory of the war of resistance, Li Jiupeng threw in his lot with the Guomindang, often giving financial aid to Guomindang agents and their army building funds and on one occasion donating 100,000 yuan to the "patriotic group for the elimination of traitors," which was organized by Guomindang agents.

In the campaign against local tyrants, the masses again and again demanded that Yao and Li be dealt with and that the injustices suffered by the people be redressed. On the basis of the evidence gathered by the public security organs and acting on the demands of the masses, on July 10, 1946, the Municipal Party Committee held a public trial presided over by the city government to lay bare the crimes of Yao and Li and galvanize the masses. The trial, held at the sportsfield of the Daowai District Second Middle School, was attended by more than 10,000 people, many of whom had suffered at the hands of the two tyrants, and with tears streaming down their cheeks they denounced their crimes and asked that the people's government execute them and that their blood debt be repaid. The chairman of the Songjiang Provincial Government, comrade Feng Zhongyun, on the basis of the demands of the broad masses, immediately pronounced death sentences on the two tyrants Li and Yao on behalf of the democratic government. The next day, the tyrants Li and Yao were shot dead in Daowai Park. After their execution, the broad masses of the people clapped their hands in joy as an expression of their enthusiastic support. After this, our public security organs, acting in cooperation with work units in each district, launched the antityrant campaign across the whole of the city; some units struggled against former police, military police, and secret agents from the puppet regime, others struggled against major labor contractors and fugitive landlords. In the Daowai district there was a public trial of the feudal labor contractor Wen Delong. According to statistics the total number of people taking part in the retribution campaign in all the districts was more than 153,500. In the course of the antityrant retribution campaign more than 1,000 firearms were captured, many people who had suffered had their wrongs righted, anger was vented, fear was brought to the enemies, and through education the masses were won over.

4C. The August 28 Insurrection

Li Xiaotao

According to the recollections of comrade Wang Yutang (Work Group Leader in the Taiping district in the early period after the Liberation and later head of the Civil Affairs Section of the District Government): On August 28, 1946, an insurrection that was to shake the whole of Harbin was launched in the district of Taiping by the Yellow Rifles Society. The rebellion was instigated by Li Mingxin, a leader in the Yiguandao secret society. On July 14 that year Li had gathered together his accomplices, among them Li Wanfa, Zhang Jinlong, and Xiang Dexing, at a restaurant in Daoli to draw up plans for the rebellion. Li had bawled out something like, "The time has come, we have got to settle with those devils once and for all." They agreed that Li Wanfa should buy yellow cloth to make large flags and secret society banners since he was exceedingly wealthy and had a great deal of gold at home. The next day (i.e., July 15), two of the bandits taking part in the insurrection, Yang Fengshun and Niu Guangjun (an army officer under the Manzhouguo puppet regime), schemed together at No. 21 China Seventh Street in Daoli, with Niu calculating the number of people who could be counted on to take part in the insurrection. At nine o'clock on the morning of the 17th, the ringleaders of the rebellion gathered again at the Guangfu restaurant, and provisionally pieced together the command system, organizing the so-called Eight Key Offices: the leader of the First and Second Offices was to be Niu Guangjun, leader of the Heavenly Treasure Office was Li Yunqi, the Army Communications Office was to be led by Pan Changyuan, the Power of Buddha Office by Zhang Decai, the Cure Pestilence Office by Liu Fushan, the Office of Magic by Dai Shizhao and Li Lanting, the leadership of the All-Embracing Office was yet to be decided, and the Arhat Office was to be led by Yan Rongchun. All of these so-called office leaders were people who had made their living as preachers for many years. They also arranged what they called the "Four Roads Headquarters": the chief of the Eastern Road was Sun Yanyou (a full-time preacher), the chief of the Western Road Ma Zhankui, the chief of the Southern Road Zhou Zhenggang, and the chief of the Northern Road Li

---

Li Xiaotao, " 'Baerba' baodong," *Haerbin shizhi* [Harbin History and Gazetteer], No. 1 (1984), pp. 72–74.

Zhenru (son of Li Wanfa and a railway policeman under the puppet regime). Li Mingxin proclaimed himself Great Dharma Master holding the post of commander-in-chief and, besides key members such as Li Yuanqi and Li Wanfa, his motley following was composed of no fewer than three thousand people. They also pretended that if the members were called by their real family names their guns would not fire. These desperadoes believed in Li Mingxin's "Buddha's light," which could turn people into celestial soldiers, as well as transforming grass and trees into an army. They thought that the guns of the United Democratic Army would not be able to fire and that their rebellion would thus be able to succeed. After plotting with other ringleaders at the home of Pan Changyuan, No. 70 Tianhe Road in Guxiangtun, Li declared himself to be a living Buddha, the true Dragon Emperor, and he made himself an emperor's robes and selected two "imperial concubines" (Li Huishen, the daughter of Li Wanfa, and Li Fengxiang, the daughter of Li Lanting). He also granted such titles as "Eight Great Court Officials" and a "Supreme Military Commander." After the rebellion succeeded he was to go to the Confucian temple and be enthroned as emperor.

The reason Li Mingxin dared to covet such lofty imperial aspirations was that he commanded more than 4,000 religious followers and had swindled the sum of 170,000 yuan for himself. He had, moreover, close links with county inspector Wang from the army of the puppet regime as well as the Japanese agent Gotoo, and it was these remnants of the puppet regime's army, police, military police, and secret service who made up the rebellion's backstage supporters.

Li Mingxin was also known as Li Zhongliang, and his sect name was Zhi Shengxuan [Wisdom Bears Choice]. He originated from Neiqiu County in Hebei Province, and his whole family were Buddhists. He was a follower of the master Wang Enzhen from the age of fourteen and worked as his apprentice for three years (Wang called himself a priest and did intelligence work for a certain Wang who was county inspector in Xingtai). In 1943, with his period of apprenticeship complete, Li also began doing intelligence work for county inspector Wang in Xingtai, as well as for a certain Wang who was the puppet head of Neiqiu County, the head of the puppet regime's Peace Preservation Corps Qiao Rong, Liu Shengfeng (Li's uncle), commander of the puppet army's Tie group Xu Tieying, and others. He went especially to the liberated areas to gather intelligence about our army as well as other confidential matters. He was active in such places as Neiqiu, Yaoshan, Longping, Xingtai, Yongnian, Zhangde, Lincheng, and Jiaoyi in Hebei Province and Jingle in Shanxi Province. In February 1945, Li went to Beiping to meet the Japanese agents Gotoo and Maekawa and together they plotted to set up chapters of the "United Wandao Society" in Baoding,

Shijiazhuang, and Handan and snare the ignorant section of the population into opposing the Eighth Route Army. For many years Li had operated under the cover of religion, and he had been gathering intelligence about our forces and slandering our troops by making them out to be demons. On July 9, 1946 [the Chinese text says 1945, but this must be a misprint], he prepared weapons with leaders of the Buddhist society, Niu Changjun, Xiao Yucheng, Zhou Gen'gang, Li Wanfa, Li Lanting, and others, and they sent other people out to meet separately with their home districts, all in an attempt to overturn the Democratic Government, wipe out the United Democratic Army, and have Li enthroned as emperor. On July 17, he also colluded with the Guomindang Army Commander Jiang Pengfei (director of the puppet regime's Eastern Hebei Administrative Office and commander in the puppet Seventh Army) and together they established a United Command Post. At half past twelve on the night of the first day of the eighth lunar month of 1946 [the text again has 1945], Li led the masses in the insurrection in Harbin.

My work unit was stationed in the Taiping district at the time, and we went to wipe out the bandits east of the river. Some remnants of the Guomindang who had been routed by our army in Changchun had also arrived in Harbin (they went under the name of the "ironstone" unit), and they colluded with the reactionary societies and Daoist sects in an attempt to launch a surprise attack in order to capture guns from our work unit and the public security office. A member of the Yellow Rifles Society, Liu Baochang, passed on to us the information that the society was planning an insurrection that evening. After Wang Yutang and others among our work unit's officers of the rear heard the news, they immediately reported to the Municipal Party Committee, who issued a directive to "wipe them out on the spot." They sent for this purpose the Korean Detachment (which had a strength of just over a company) to ambush them at the head of Taiping Bridge and at the railway crossing. Secret pass signals were also fixed for the evening: the other party should first clap his hands and then ask for the password. At the same time the work unit also got in touch with the Nangang Seventh Regiment and the Daowai Law Enforcement Unit. That night hundreds of rebels, wearing yellow robes and with their heads swathed in yellow cloth, gathered by Taiping Bridge. They carried banners and arrows in their hands and chanted, "neither knife nor gun can pierce us, neither water nor fire can do us harm." The crowd gradually increased in size until there were several thousand people; it then surged off in the direction of the Taiping Mass Campaign Work Unit and the Taiping public security office. (The Taiping district public security branch office was located in those days in the "August First" courtyard, which is now used for civilian residences.

Zhang Guangxin was the director of the public security office at that time). However, the crowd ran straight into heavy gunfire from rows of our Korean detachment, who were waiting in ambush. The rebel bandits fell one after another like flies, and the survivors fled in confusion. Our troops advanced bravely and pursued the bandits to the river, where they were forced to swim for their lives, many of them drowning in the attempt, and the remainder were taken prisoner by our army. At daybreak the soldiers began to clean up the battleground: more than twenty rebels had been killed, including one woman who was said to be one of the imperial concubines. Some of the dead were still tightly clutching onto their arrows and banners of command; several dozen spears lay scattered about the place together with arrows and banners of various colors, making it look for all the world like a scene from an opera. The rebel prisoners were divided among the Nangang Seventh Division and the public security office and led away like sheep. The municipal authorities issued a directive that a meeting was to be held to reassure the public. They also bought more than twenty coffins, which were placed at both ends of the Taiping Bridge, and they passed around a message for the families of the deceased to come forward and claim their dead, but no one did so. After waiting three days, they buried the bodies themselves.

Li Mingxin, a long-standing enemy of the people and the leading organizer of the rebellion, was also taken into lawful custody by our city's public security office. With this, the August 28 insurrection, which had shaken the whole city, was well and truly crushed.

4D. The Pine Tree Stands Ever Green— A Noble Man with High Ideals. In Fond Memory of Comrade Li Changqing (Excerpts)

Wang Huacheng, Zhang Ping, Yu Huafeng, Wu Tongfu, Feng Baokun, and Mu Qingsheng

In March of this year [1988] the First Conference on Party History was jointly organized by the Party History Committee of the Harbin Municipal Party Committee and the Harbin Party History Research Association. As the comrades present were diligently summing up the historical experience of the period in Harbin from the founding of the People's Republic to the First Five-Year Plan, they also fondly remembered Comrade Li Changqing, the first secretary of the Municipal Party Committee after the founding of the People's Republic.

In his youth Comrade Li Changqing took part in the revolutionary student movement in Yanji [in Jilin Province], in 1930 he was involved in revolutionary work at the Republican University in Beiping, and in 1931 he joined the Chinese Communist Party. In 1935 he held the joint posts of special envoy of the Hebei Provincial Party Committee and secretary of the Beiping Municipal Party Committee, and was one of the leaders of the January 29 Movement, which shook the country and the whole world. During the anti-Japanese resistance war he served as secretary of the Propaganda Committee of the Jin-Cha-Ji Border Region. After the victory in the War of Resistance in 1945, he served as head of the *Northeastern Daily News*, secretary-general of the Propaganda Department of the Northeastern Bureau under the Party Central Committee, and head of the Hejiang Provincial Party Committee Propaganda Department. From August 1950 to April 1955, Comrade Changqing directed work in the Harbin Municipal Party Committee. Sharing the joys and sorrows of all the city's people, he worked his heart out for the revolution and the construction of the city and made outstanding contributions.

Comrade Changqing directed work in the Harbin Municipal Party Committee for only four years, and this is now over thirty years ago. Neverthe-

Wang Huacheng et al., "Songbai changqing gaofeng liangjie—shenqie huainian Li Changqing tongzhi," *Longjiang Dangshi* [Heilongjiang Party History], no. 6 (1988), pp. 8–12.

less, when we recall his indomitable revolutionary spirit and lofty moral character today we come to revere him even more.

In August 1950, after Comrade Changqing had undergone an operation to remove his spleen in Moscow, he rushed back to Harbin while still recuperating in order to carry out work for the Municipal Party Committee. Although he was still weak and his face pale and gaunt, his rousing manner and lively bright eyes gave evidence of his abundant revolutionary fervor and his capable and experienced visionary breadth.

At that time the War of Liberation had just finished, and there was a multitude of neglected tasks that needed to be tackled. The entire party faced a strategic shift to a policy centered on economic construction in order to restore and develop the economy. At the same time the campaign to support the War to Resist America and Aid Korea was raging like a fire. The Movement to Suppress Counterrevolutionaries, the Campaign against the Three Evils [corruption, waste, and bureaucracy within official organizations], and the Campaign against the Five Evils [bribery, tax evasion, etc., by owners of private enterprises] then followed hard on one another's heels. There were countless things to do and in this complicated and complex situation, tasks had to be performed strictly on time and in accordance with policy. Harbin was the first large city to be liberated, so a lot of the work was of a pioneering nature: there were no precedents one could refer to or experience from other districts that could be relied on. Faced with this intricate situation, Comrade Changqing showed the bearing of a leader, maintaining unswerving courage and conviction and at the same time preserving an open-minded attitude that allowed him to study things afresh. He threw himself intensely into the thick of his work, devising strategies within his command tent, busy but never confused.

As gunpowder smoke billowed over the battlefields of the War to Resist America and Aid Korea, Harbin, situated in the rear, saw support for the war as its all-important overriding task, and without delay it supplied the front line with the arms, ammunition, troops, and logistics for which it had the greatest need. The government decided to pursue a policy of "moving factories from the south to the north" and transferred a large contingent of workers near the front line to Harbin, including the Harbin Electrical Machinery Factory and fifteen other large plants. These factories were transferred distances of thousands of miles, together with tens of thousands of employees and family dependents and a great deal of their installations and equipment, with all of this arriving in Harbin at practically the same time. The Harbin Municipal Party Committee, led by Comrade Changqing and bursting with ardor and enthusiasm, spared no effort in taking on this enormous, complicated, and critical responsibility, proposing loud and clear that "the whole city supports the moving of factories from the south to the north." The Municipal Party Committee and the city government established a "New Plants Working Committee," which worked day and night at finding factory sites, assigning cadres, organizing the installation of equipment, and making arrangements for the daily lives of the employees. Comrade Changqing personally encouraged leading cadres in the whole city to "regard the interests of the whole situation as most important, forget about your own units, your partial and local interests, and make way for the moving of factories from the south to the north." And he also took severe disciplinary measures against any comrade who did not pay attention to the overall situation. Comrade Changqing always kept the overall situation in mind, and he did all he could to coordinate the work. He made overall plans for everything from cadres to the staff and workers, from the factory sites to the installations, from production to living conditions. He took all factors into consideration, made comprehensive arrangements and worked outstandingly and extremely efficiently in building the new plants and starting them up in production. Working in this way he managed to get the new factories settled in and production resumed very quickly, turning them into Harbin's first batch of backbone enterprises and increasing the strength of its engineering industry.

Comrade Changqing loyally carried out the directives he received from above; he was adept at uniting the general and specific policies of the Central Committee with the actual conditions in Harbin, and he was a rigorous, reliable, practical, and realistic leader always seeking truth from facts. He treated directives and documents from the Central Committee and from the Northeastern Bureau seriously and conscientiously, always studying them again and again to find out whether there were any new formulations or new spirit, striving to gain a thorough grasp of its content. At the same time he thought a lot about the concrete situation in Harbin and worked out carefully considered implementation suggestions.

Beginning in 1950, the "Movement to Suppress Counterrevolutionaries," the "Campaign against the Three Evils," and the "Campaign against the Five Evils" followed one after the other. In the violent storms of the political movements Comrade Changqing kept a cool head, continuing to seek truth from facts and striving to effect the stabilization of policies. In the "Three Evils" campaign he emphasized acting with both determination and caution. In the middle period of the campaign, new "tiger-catching criteria" with very broad parameters were passed down, which, if implemented, were bound to lead to the catching of even more doubtful "tigers," whose guilt could not be established, and to the creation of even more wrongful charges. Comrade Changqing momentarily blocked this directive from being communicated to the lower levels, and he asked the Northeastern Bureau for further instructions in order to prevent the range of attack from becoming even broader. At the time one comrade urged him to quickly implement these "tiger-catching criteria," but he earnestly replied, "Can you not see how broad the range of attack is going to be!" Later the Northeastern Bureau temporarily deferred putting the policy into effect, and an even more serious exaggeration of the "Three Evils" campaign was avoided. When Comrade Changqing was later wrongly dealt with, this affair came to be the charge of "refusing to implement Central Committee directives."

In the beginning of the "Five Evils" campaign in 1952, Chen Boda came to Harbin to carry out an investigation. At the committee room at No. 1 Yiyuan Street, Chen Boda made the peremptory accusation that the "Five Evils" campaign in Harbin was proceeding at too leisurely a pace and with a lack of momentum. With no fear of power and influence or thought of avoiding danger, Comrade Changqing at once made a sober and just appeal, explaining that the Northeastern Bureau had a unified approach and that the city was in the course of mobilizing the masses and completing its preparations: if one rushed hastily into battle it could easily give rise to chaos. He had refuted Chen Boda to his face, so shocking the other comrades present that they broke out in a cold sweat and were breathless with anxiety. When he was later wrongfully charged, this became one of the pieces of evidence for "not respecting comrades from the Central Committee."

In the course of the "Three Evils" campaign, there arose the "Aviation School Large-Scale Corruption Case" in Harbin, which shook the whole city. The departments in charge planned to hold a public rally attended by 20,000 people in Zhaolin Park, which would pass sentence on many of the people and give a push to the city's "Three Evils" campaign. On the eve of the execution of those involved in this so-called large-scale corruption, the city court discovered in its final review that the case was lacking in evidence and judging it unsound it hurriedly asked for instructions from Comrade Changqing, who quickly came to the decision that "these people should be spared and the case verified before they can again be sentenced." After being reviewed, the case was found to be totally without foundation. As a consequence of this affair, Comrade Changqing gravely told Comrade Yu Huafeng [one of the authors of this text], then serving as both secretary of the Municipal Party Disciplinary Committee and head of the city court, "You are in charge of party discipline and the laws of the country; you have the power of life and death and the slightest mistake can have fatal consequences. You must show caution and then more caution!" And he also gave Comrade Huafeng the concrete ruling that from then on he was to personally review all cases involving sentences of more than five years.

In the Movement to Suppress Counterrevolutionaries, Comrade Luo Mingzhe, the former deputy head of the City Education Bureau, was on the verge of being suppressed. After the victory over Japan, Luo had once served as section head in the Guomindang "City Office for Party Affairs Commissioners." During the "Suppress the Counterrevolutionaries" campaign, the departments concerned wanted to arrest and suppress him, although he was an honest patriotic intellectual and an influential figure among the Harbin intellingentsia. After the victory over Japan, he had for a time held blindly orthodox [zhengtong, i.e., pro-Guomindang] views, but after a short period working in the "City Party Commissioners' Office," he had abandoned the Guomindang and in April 1947 joined the Chinese Communist Party. This period in his personal history had led others to make certain conclusions. After Comrade Changqing had found out what was happening from the City Education Bureau, he firmly resisted the suppression of Luo Mingzhe. Comrade Changqing bravely took responsibility, protecting cadres, helping cadres free themselves from such labels as "historically doubtful," and so winning their trust and encouraging them to work with enthusiasm.

How was Comrade Changqing able to stay so calm and unruffled during these political storms and able to maintain such resolute, practical, and realistic political nerve? Apart from his having a deep and splendid grounding in Marxist theory and rich work experience, the most important thing was his firm party spirit and lofty values. In his own heart, he truly placed the party's cause and the interests of the people in a sacred and inviolable position. He acted to maintain this ideal with no regard for his personal safety, in a manner that set him apart from ordinary people and which gained him the heartfelt admiration of all those who knew him.

The First Five-Year Plan began in 1953, and Harbin's economic construction strode boldly into a brand-new era. The government received 156 key engineering projects from the Soviet Union, arranging for nine factories and thirteen projects in all to go to Harbin, making it one of the cities with the most key projects in the entire country. The factories included the Harbin Electrical Machinery Plant, the Harbin Steam Turbine Plant, and the Northeast Light Alloy Processing Plant, with a total investment of 1.27 billion yuan.

In the face of this economic construction's unfolding on an epic scale, Comrade Changqing radiated a sincere revolutionary passion, and he charged headfirst into the burning struggle without heed for his personal safety. At an all-city cadres' meeting he said, "To launch our large-scale economic construction is the great task that the first generation of revolutionaries longed for day and night, and it is the key to the flourishing of the

nation. Our generation has the good fortune to be able to realize it ourselves, and it is indeed a rare honor." The broad masses of cadres from the
whole city were moved by Comrade Changqing's revolutionary fervor; they
rubbed their palms in eagerness and felt proud that they could sacrifice
themselves for this "large-scale construction," and this sparked a kind of
"large-scale" fever.

Comrade Changqing was adept at uniting the aspirations of the masses
on the basis of the demands of the task at hand, at coming out with a
resounding slogan at the right time and bringing together the unbounded
latent powers of the cadres and the masses, and applying them to economic
construction. He was the first to come up with the slogan "put basic construction first," and after approval from the Northeastern Bureau of the
Communist Party Central Committee, this came to be heard in every city in
the country. In order to strengthen the leadership over basic construction,
the Municipal Party Committee set up the Basic Construction Work Department, and the city government established a Basic Construction Committee,
selecting strong and able cadres to fill its posts. The Municipal Federation
of Trade Unions and the Communist Youth League Municipal Party Committee also set up Basic Construction Work Departments serving as assistants to the party and carrying out constructive work. The other departments
involved also established Cultural Service Teams, Daily Life Service
Teams, and Medical Treatment Groups under the call to "deliver to the
door," and these would often enliven the construction sites. It came to be
that the cadres and masses of the whole city had only one concern in their
heart, and their energies were concentrated on one spot; they were all pull-
ing on the same rope and all their powers were channeled to the "basic
construction."

One of Comrade Changqing's estimable qualities was that he could not
only grasp the broad outlines, come up with resonant slogans, draw up
detailed plans, and mobilize massive forces, but he would also lead his men
in the charge, galloping at the head of his troops, penetrating to the grass-
roots level, carrying out direct investigations and research, and coming to
grips with the evidence firsthand. He had always been rather weak in body,
but he would never allow himself any rest: his working style drove him to
spare no effort in the performance of his duty without regard for his own
well-being. After July 1952 he served as secretary of both the Songjiang
Provincial Party Committee and the Harbin Municipal Party Committee,
which meant that he was busy all day with such duties as attending meetings, reading and commenting on documents, receiving visitors, and holding discussions, while in the evenings he would usually go out to the
construction sites to hear the opinions of the masses of cadres, experts, and

workers, helping to solve problems in their work and putting into effect face-to-face leadership at the grass roots.

He never thought about his own illness, but his heart was full of concern for the hardships of the grass-roots cadres and workers. He was worried about the things the grass roots worried about, and that year, in order to solve the problems of marketing linen cloth produced by the flax factory, he personally wrote a letter to the National Planning Committee and the Northeastern Bureau, which is still kept in the city archives. He often went down to the grass roots to investigate the condition of the workers' dormitories, worksheds, and canteens. Did the roofs of the worksheds leak? Was it possible to eat one's fill on the meals provided? In this way he taught the grass-roots cadres to show concern for the living conditions of the employees. He often said that if the leaders increased their interest in the hardships of their employees by 10 percent, the drive and enthusiasm of the workforce would increase by 30 percent.

Comrade Changqing was very strict about demands for the quality of work, and in basic construction he regarded as fundamental that "in projects of lasting importance, quality comes first." He said that if quality were poor in the key industrial projects then it was swindling the nation, a sin against future generations and a directly criminal act. Each of the key engineering projects set up sound regulations for the operation of machinery and a system of investigation and checking before the acceptance of deliveries; the Municipal Party Committee propagated advanced experience in good time and circulated a notice of criticism to units that were not up to scratch. The thirteen key engineering projects all delivered high-quality results. Thirty years later, we can still see the results of these projects, and their quality can still be commended as excellent.

After a thousand days and nights of arduous labor, the thirteen engineering projects were ready to start up production and a qualitative change had been made in this aspect of our city; from a backward city in terms of production, we had in one leap become one of the major industrial cities in the whole country, making contributions to support the construction of the national economy and the national defense and possessing a solid foundation for the future development of Harbin. In the Three Years of Recovery [1949–52], the value of industrial production in the city had risen by an average of 57.6 percent per annum, and the total value of the industrial and agricultural output jumped for a time to the sixth highest in the whole country. In the period of the First Five-Year Plan [1953–57], the value of industrial production rose at an average annual rate of 16.4 percent. It can be said that this was one of the best periods in the history of Harbin's economic development.

At the same time as ushering in large-scale economic construction, a schedule was also prepared, under the direction of Comrade Changqing, for urban planning and construction in Harbin. In the first period after Liberation only the districts of Daowai, Daoli, and Nangang had taken shape. The boundaries of the city districts were made up of scattered vegetable fields and pastures, and the present sites of the three large plants for power generating equipment were then a racetrack. Faced with an old city, the Municipal Party Committee under the direction of Comrade Changqing looked far ahead into the future and drew up a grand Harbin city development plan. They planned and arranged so as to achieve a rationally distributed whole. They built the Dongli district with its three large plants for power-generating equipment as the backbone; the development of the Taiping district was chiefly given over to chemical industries; Pingfang had its backbone in the three large aviation industry plants; in the Nangang district Xuefu Road was constructed leading to Shamantun, and the minor district of Xuefu was built up with schools as its main element. Haping, Heping, Kang'an, and Zhinong roads were widened and developed; the Kangzhuang, Fuxing, and Jiancheng bridges were constructed; the main lines of communication to Dongli, Xiangfang, Taiping, Pingfang, and the main industrial districts were broadened. All these measures helped to establish a foundation for the construction of the city of Harbin.

At the same time, attention was conscientiously paid to the construction of public utilities in the city. More water sources were secured and water treatment plants were built, a new fleet of public buses was purchased, streetlights were added, and more dwellings were built for staff and workers. Advanced academic institutions such as the Military Engineering College as well as cultural and recreational facilities shot up everywhere, and the construction of the Songhua River embankment gradually took shape. The face of the city underwent a huge change, and the lives of the people underwent a corresponding improvement; social order was stable, and all work in the city, such as the establishment of political power organs, culture, education and hygiene, commerce and finance, mass organizations, and physical culture, flourished vigorously and presented a truly prospering and thriving picture. . . .

Comrade Changqing was honorable to the core; he was selfless and fearless; in defending the interests of the party he paid no attention to personal gains or losses; he never flattered or fawned on his superiors, neither did he act contrary to his convictions. At that time Gao Gang had a powerful position, being Li Changqing's immediate superior with power over his destiny, but Comrade Changqing still dared to oppose Gao Gang's mistakes. Gao Gang called Li Changqing "a tough old bone, an iron bar."

Although this description was disrespectful and disparaging, it was none-theless truthful, for Comrade Changqing really did have tough bones. He was completely disgusted with Gao Gang's life-style and put up determined resistance to it; he indeed hated evil, and his bones were made of steel. . . .

After June 1954, Comrade Changqing began to be groundlessly impli-cated in the "Gao Gang and Rao Shushi antiparty alliance," and he was the subject of repeated distorted investigations and critiques. His normal work-ing relations with Gao Gang were misrepresented as "factionalism," he was seen as a "trusted follower," and his honest and prudent style of work was described as that of "a sanctimonious hypocrite," "the behavior of a patri-arch," and so forth; mud and filth were poured on him from all sides. In December 1955 it was wrongfully maintained that "the serious political mistakes he had made in the matter of the Gao Gang antiparty question were antiparty and anti–Central Committee in character," and it was de-cided to relieve him of the post of secretary of the Harbin Municipal Party Committee.

In January 1957 he was demoted to be the assistant chief of the Higher Education and Teacher Training Department of the Education Bureau, and not long after this the antirightist campaign started up. Generally speaking, when faced with new political storms, people who had fallen out of favor would go along with the wave, striving only not to make any mistakes and so create more trouble for themselves. But Comrade Changqing was no ordinary man, and he still possessed the true party spirit of a Communist Party member; he resolutely stood up to be counted with no concern for his personal safety, and his sense of justice demanded that he speak out on behalf of a person who was wrongfully labeled a "rightist." Because of this affair, he was the victim of a second injustice and in September 1958, on the grounds of "shielding rightists and continuing to oppose the party," he was branded an "out-and-out antiparty element." He was also expelled from the party, sacked from his job, and demoted with a pay cut to be a lecturer at the Inner Mongolian Teacher Training College. In August 1960, he was killed in a traffic accident while riding his bicycle to work. He was just fifty-six years old.

It is now thirty-three years since Comrade Changqing left Harbin and twenty-seven years since he departed this world. All his life, with an un-swerving loyalty and adherence to party principles, he fought hard and illustriously for the cause of the party, yet over a long period he repeatedly received unjust treatment that led to his own death and the destruction of his family; practically all his relatives had doubts cast on them, and for a long period they lived a miserable existence. Fortunately, the Third Plenary Ses-sion of the Eleventh Party Central Committee corrected injustices and the

Central Committee completely exonerated Comrade Changqing, restoring him to his true place in history and ensuring that his besmirched figure once again shone radiantly.

He remained "ever green"[1] like the pine and spruce—in the blizzards of darkest winter they stand up proudly in the teeth of the wind and do not change their true color; in the life-giving spring breezes and rain, they are even more luxuriant and brimming with vitality.

Note

[1. The literal meaning of *Changqing* is "ever green."]

4E. An Important Avenue in Resolving the Problem of Urban Employment— An Investigation of Individual Employment (*geti jiuye*) in Harbin (Excerpts)

Tian Jie, Bo Huiru, and Zhao Pu

The question of obtaining employment is an important problem for both socialist and capitalist societies, but it has a radically different character in the two types of society. In capitalist societies it is an unresolvable contradiction, while in socialist societies the problem can gradually be resolved in tandem with the development of production.

After the smashing of the "Gang of Four," work done on finding employment in Harbin has shown outstanding results. The number of young people seeking employment in Harbin is relatively large, the accumulative total from 1978 to the present is more than 480,000. In the space of three short years up until November 1981, the number of young people given permanent jobs was 385,633, which was 80.3 percent of those waiting for work [*daiye*], and in addition more than 50,000 were found temporary jobs. The long-standing problem of large numbers of young people waiting for employment, which was created under the influence of "leftist" mistakes, has now basically been solved. However, looking at the relationship between the supply and demand of labor in Harbin, demand for jobs still exceeds supply. In the coming years, the city will still have an annual average of around 100,000 young people waiting for employment, and the Labor Department can only deal with a portion of these. For this reason, finding employment is still going to be a conspicuous social problem for quite a long time to come, and the task of arranging jobs for young people is going to remain an arduous one.

In 1980, the Central Committee came up with a three-in-one employment policy. Because the national economy was in a period of readjustment, state-owned enterprises could not absorb more labor. To put this policy of the Central Committee into effect demands stressing collective employment

Tian Jie, Bo Huiru, and Zhao Pu, "Jiejue chengzhen laodong jiuye wenti de yige zhongyao tujing," *Haerbin shizhi* [Harbin History and Gazetteer], no. 1 (1983), pp. 34–46.

and individual employment. As was pointed out in Central Committee Document No. 42 (1981): "From now on, as we readjust production structures, it is necessary at the same time to emphasize the opening of new channels of employment in the collective and individual economies." However, recognition and opening of these channels for individual employment have up until now been beset by a number of problems, and some people have even directly contradicted this employment policy put forward by the Central Committee. It is therefore of great importance to analyze correctly and resolve the contradictions arising from individual employment. This will be significant for opening the channels and widening the doors leading to individual employment.

I. A Review of the History of Individual Employment in Harbin since Liberation

After the Liberation of the whole country, Harbin transformed itself from a city of consumption to one of industrial production, making it now the political, economic, and cultural center of Heilongjiang Province and one of the most important cities in the Northeast. Huge developments were achieved in both industry and commerce.

In the past thirty years, the history of the development of the individual economy and individual employment can be broadly divided into five periods.

1. 1949–1954: The Three Years of Economic Recovery and the Initial Period of the First Five-Year Plan

The city of Harbin was liberated in 1946. After Liberation, the party and the government devoted all their efforts to heal the wounds of the war, and there was in consequence a large development in economic and cultural facilities and excellent conditions for solving the problem of finding employment.

The government adopted relatively flexible policies for tackling the employment problem, and it followed a policy that combined allowing both state-arranged job allocation and the unemployed to find their own employment opportunities. This created room for the coexistence of different economic components, as well as, with certain limitations, the free recruitment of labor.

The city of Harbin implemented the policies of the Central Committee, and in this period the individual economy developed relatively quickly and the number of people employed was relatively high. In 1949, out of a total population of 780,000, there were 42,078 individual industrial and commercial enterprises employing 109,637 people, for an average density of 51.6

individual enterprises for every 1,000 inhabitants. By 1953, the population of the city had increased to 1,160,000 and the number of individual enterprises had reached 45,413, employing a total of 74,212 people, an average of 39 enterprises for every 1,000 people. This was the best era in our history.

In this period, the urban population was low, there was a high density of individual enterprises and a large number of service employees, the city markets were flourishing, and it was very convenient for the masses to obtain food, buy products, get repairs done, and purchase replacement parts. The masses commended these years, saying: "You could eat anything you wanted, and buy anything you wanted; you didn't have to worry about food or drink living in Harbin."

2. 1955–1959: The Central Years of the First and Second Five-Year Plans

From the time of "Three Great Transformations" to that of the "Great Leap Forward," we committed "leftist" mistakes in two areas: firstly, in directing the growth of industrial and agricultural production and, secondly, in the reform of production relations. Industrial and agricultural production in Harbin suffered greatly. Following the impetuous and rash advances in industrial and agricultural production, even larger leaps were made in the reform of the system of ownership; guided by the slogan "large in size and collective in nature," no effort was spared to effect a "transformation despite poverty," which almost totally wiped out the individual economy. With a total city population of 1,610,000 in 1958, Harbin had 169 individual industrial and commercial enterprises; included in that number were only eight remaining commercial enterprises employing eleven people and only seven catering enterprises employing a total of seven people; there was an average density of 0.1 individual enterprises per 1,000 people. Under these conditions, the difficulties involved in obtaining meals, having clothes made, getting repairs done, getting haircuts, and buying vegetables became more and more serious.

3. 1960–1965: The Final Years of the Second Five-Year Plan and the Period of the Readjustment of the National Economy

In order to relieve the problems in the development of the national economy and the people's livelihood caused by the "Great Leap Forward," the party Central Committee in 1960 introduced the timely policy of "readjustment, consolidation, replenishment and improvement." During the three years of readjustment in Harbin, the value of industrial and agricultural output began to increase once again on a large scale, the employment policy gained more flexibility, trade in the city's markets was lively, and there was new growth in the individual economy. In 1961, the city had a population of 1,940,000, and the number of individual industrial and commercial enterprises had grown dramatically from a figure of 104 in 1958 to 12,618, employing 12,618 people and giving a density of seven enterprises per thousand people. The markets started to show evidence of a revival, and there was a day-by-day improvement in the supply of everyday products, such as grain, fish, meat, and eggs. The living standards of the people also showed a large improvement compared to the period of the hardships, and the masses were keen supporters of the economic policies of the party and government.

4. 1966–1976: The Period of the Great Cultural Revolution

In the ten years of the "Great Cultural Revolution," the interference and destruction instigated by Lin Biao and the "Gang of Four" brought the national economy to the brink of collapse and the value of Harbin's industrial and agricultural output fell rapidly. In the area of employment policy, a system of complete monopoly control of the work force came into being, which did not allow individuals to find work for themselves, which put forward such slogans as "cut off the tails of capitalism," "sweep away ox-devils and snake-demons," and "suppress the feudal, capitalist and revisionist trash." People who ran small enterprises were paraded through the streets and "struggled against," the flower, bird, and fish market was wrecked, and the individual economy was on the verge of extinction. The population of the city in 1975 was 2,120,000, and there were at this time only 804 individual industrial and commercial enterprises, employing 804 people and giving a density of only 0.38 enterprises for every thousand inhabitants. In these years, the markets were stagnant, the methods of management were uniform, the people suffered great inconveniences in their daily lives, and complaints were rife among the masses.

5. 1976–1981: The Period after the Smashing of the "Gang of Four" and the Third Plenary Session of the Eleventh Central Committee

After the smashing of the "Gang of Four," and after the Third Plenary Session of the Eleventh Central Committee in particular, the people of the whole country, under the leadership of the Central Committee, stabilized public order, revived the national economy, and put into effect the building of the "Four Modernizations." These achievements created favorable condi-

Table 4

Attitude of Young People toward Self-Employment

	Category 1	Category 2	Category 3	Total
No. of people (% of sample)	62 (31%)	80 (40%)	58 (29%)	200 (100%)

tions for finding employment. The labor administration policy was also changed, leading to large growth in the individual economy and a daily rise in the number of those employed in individual enterprises. By December 1981, the total population of the city was 2,420,000, and the number of individual industrial and commercial enterprises had grown to 12,347, employing 14,497 people and giving an average density of five enterprises per one thousand people. The relatively rapid growth in the individual economy played a definite role in the revival of the markets and the invigoration of the national economy, and it was warmly welcomed by the masses. . . .

III. Some Problems That Urgently Need to Be Readressed in Order to Open Up New Channels for Employment in Individual Enterprises

There is a great need to mold public opinion, to give the individual economy a "good name," and so draw young people waiting for work into taking the road to individual employment.

In the course of opening up channels for creating employment in the individual economy, the greatest obstacle is the question of perception.

The great majority of the young people who are now self-employed were at first uncertain in their minds, harboring great doubts and only unwillingly taking the road of individual employment.

In six of Harbin's districts, Daoli, Daowai, Nangang, Xiangfang, Dongli, and Taiping, a survey of 200 self-employed young people was carried out using a method of random sampling at different levels. The results of the survey can be seen in Table 4.

Category 1. Wanted to continue being self-employed for a long period of time. There were sixty-two in this category, comprising 31 percent of the total. Many of these were people who were slightly older than the rest and unskilled. Their reasons for wanting to continue in this work for a long time were, first, that they had no special abilities and would be unable to change profession and do other work; second, that if they went to state-run or collective units, they would face a drop in income and would not have enough to support their families. They were therefore relatively content with being self-employed.

Category 2. Not wanting to be self-employed, but doing so to get by. There were eighty in this category, making up 40 percent of the total sample. Those with this attitude were for the most part relatively younger and their ideal employment would be in a state-run "iron rice bowl" job. They had various opinions about individual employment, but basically they did not want to be in this line of employment. As they had been without jobs, however, and had no money to spend, they had decided that keeping busy and earning money was better than just loafing around. They have therefore adopted a make-do attitude, looking on individual employment as a make-shift measure and waiting for an opportunity to transfer to a state-run unit.

Category 3. Wait and see. Fifty-eight people, comprising 29 percent of the total, were in this category. People with this attitude possessed a self-contradictory state of mind with regard to individual employment. On the one hand they wanted to continue in their jobs, but they feared that changes might occur that would destroy their "rice bowl" and they felt that their livelihoods were insecure. On the other hand, if they were not self-employed they would have no money and be unable to make a living, so they had no alternative. Therefore they have adopted a wait-and-see attitude toward individual employment: if the situation looked promising and the road ahead were clear, they would keep on working as self-employed; on the other hand, if they ran into difficulties, they would "rein in their horses at the edge of the cliff" and try to find another way to make a living.

It can be seen from the three categories described above that only a minority of the young people surveyed were really content with being self-employed and nearly 70 percent were discontent.

Why have these three attitudes taken shape? According to our survey of 200 young people, the main reason was that they harbored misgivings about individual employment that gave rise to a negative feeling about their work. This manifested itself concretely in the "five fears." These misgivings were shared to varying extents by all categories in the survey. (See Table 5.)

1. Fear of a change in policy was shared by 144 people, comprising 72 percent of the sample. They thought that the party's policies changed too quickly and if the policy were to be changed or ended, their livelihoods would be ruined. One of them said, "I do not fear the Communist Party's materialism, I fear dialectics."

Table 5

An Analysis of Misgivings about Self-Employment among the Different Categories of Young People

Category	Number	Fear of policy change		Fear of lack of security		Fear of discrimination		Fear of hardship		Fear of political stigmatization (daimao)	
		Number	%	Number	%	Number	%	Number	%	Number	%
First	62	48	24	3	1.5	8	4	9	4.5	5	2.5
Second	80	56	28	64	32	29	14.5	20	10	7	3.5
Third	58	40	20	44	22	21	10.5	12	6	8	4
Total	200	144	72	111	55.5	58	29	41	20.5	20	10

Table 6

Attitudes of Cadres toward Opening Channels for Self-Employment

	Attitude 1	Attitude 2	Attitude 3	Total
Number	12	18	10	40
% of Total	30	45	25	100

2. Fear that their livelihoods lacked security was shared by 111 people, 55.5 percent of the sample. They did not view running an individual enterprise as finding employment or having a proper job, as it lacked job security. They therefore did not feel that their lives had any real security, and they lacked peace of mind.

3. Fear of social discrimination was shared by fifty-eight people, 29 percent of the sample. They considered running an individual enterprise the lowest occupation in society and thought that their line of business was not respected by anyone. They worried about being mocked by their friends and relatives, having a hard time in finding a spouse, and having no prospects from a political point of view.

4. Fear of hardship was shared by forty-one people, 20.5 percent of the sample. In their opinion individual employment was too hard a way of life, with long working hours, a multitude of tasks to do, and the arduous job of managing their business. State-run enterprises on the other hand were "iron rice bowls" where one would still get paid even if one did no work and where one could find "comfort" and "leisure." They therefore did not plan to run their individual enterprises on a long-term basis.

5. Fear of "receiving a label" or being called "a reactionary tail that needs cutting" was shared by twenty people, 10 percent of the sample. They considered that individual enterprises were basically "going it alone," and therefore incompatible with socialism, as they were working in opposite directions. They were concerned about being one day labeled as "petty proprietors" or "capitalists," about having poor class status, and that in the event of another political campaign, they would be the ones to suffer.

Apart from this, a substantial number of cadres are confused about opening channels for individual employment, with some having a negative attitude toward it and others even being directly opposed.

Using various methods, we questioned forty cadres who have direct links with the individual enterprises, and they demonstrated three broad attitudes with respect to the opening of channels for individual employment. (See Table 6.)

The first attitude was one of enthusiastic support, and was held by twelve cadres, 30 percent of the total. From an ideological standpoint, they had clearly seen the necessity of opening channels to individual employment. They therefore supported self-employed enterprises and created good conditions for them to the limits of their functions and powers.

The second attitude was one of perfunctoriness and indifference. It was shared by eighteen of the cadres, 45 percent of the sample. They considered that there was "no great necessity" for opening channels to individual employment, and that having dealings with self-employed enterprises was "a lot of bother." However, as they had received a clear policy from above, they could not ignore them and therefore adopted an attitude of indifference.

The third attitude was one of opposition. This encompassed ten cadres, 25 percent of the sample. These people did not openly say that they were opposed to the policy, but from their enumeration of the many "crimes" committed by self-employed enterprises, it could be seen that they were in essence opposed to opening up channels to individual employment.

The three different attitudes among the cadres are related to unclear perceptions of the nature, position, and function of the individual economy.

There were a number of cadres who connected the individual economy with capitalism. They were of the opinion that in developing individual enterprises, one was developing the system of private ownership, and this was not compatible with socialism. They thought that it was going against the "laws of development," was "a step backward," and should not be supported.

Some of the cadres considered that developing the individual economy would not have a positive effect on socialism. According to them, individual enterprise was about making money for individuals, which would then go straight into their purses, whereas state-run enterprises made money for the country, which went into the national treasury! If one supported individual enterprises, what would happen to one's own position? Some cadres thought that it would not only fail to have a positive effect, but that it would have many negative side effects such as leading young people along the road to selfishness and a profit-before-everything mentality, and that it could give rise to evils such as profiteering and speculation.

It is clear that if the above-mentioned ideological problems are not resolved, it will be impossible for individual enterprises to consolidate and develop. Therefore solving the problem of perception is at present the key task to be tackled before channels can be opened for employment in the individual economy. If a proper grip is taken on this central contradiction the remaining problems will be easy to solve.

How should we tackle this perception problem?

The most basic way is to mold deeply public opinion, giving the individual economy a "good name" and raising the social position of the self-employed workers.

It is not accidental that there is a tendency to discriminate against the self-employed and look down on commercial and service occupations, for there is a historical background to this attitude. The remnants of feudal society, which lasted for over two thousand years, as well as the baneful influence of Lin Biao and the "Gang of Four," have led to its still being deeply rooted in sections of the cadres and masses. If public opinion is not substantially molded, we will never reverse these mistaken perceptions. . . .

5

The Harbin Historians

The Harbin historians function inside a centrally organized and carefully stratified nationwide multistringed structure, where they generally work on assigned tasks, not unlike those governing industrial production in the heyday of the planned economy. This is, perhaps, the most striking feature of local history writing in China, and it serves to explain why history is still being written at all in a country where the profession has brought so much trouble to its practitioners. As can be seen from some of the translated texts, the bureaucratic framework does not prevent the historians from being strongly, or even passionately, engaged in their research, but it puts narrow constraints on their work, ideologically as well as with respect to subject matter and style of presentation. This chapter first briefly discusses the Marxist historiographical legacy and the more recent national trends that have influenced the work of the Harbin historians during the post-Mao period and then turns to the institutional framework inside which their research is carried out.

Chinese Historiography and Marxism

The adaptation of Chinese historiography to the new framework of Marxism-Leninism appeared for many years as a generally smooth and successful process. The time-honored tradition of using history in a static way as a *moral mirror* for contemporary rulers had lost its appeal, and a Chinese Marxist historiography, which established itself in the 1920s and 1930s, offered a much-needed new dynamic perspective. Soviet-inspired historical materialism enabled Chinese intellectuals to see history as *development*, and they learned to look for the "forces"—productive and social—to be harnessed and employed by the Communist leadership in the service of progress and nation-building. But with the freezing of China's intellectual life in the wake of the 1957 Anti-Rightist Campaign, politicization of historical research escalated. After a more objectivist interlude in the early

1960s, when some historians tried to evade the role of political mouth-pieces, this politicization culminated during the Cultural Revolution in a simplistic approach to history as an eternal struggle between "revolutionaries" and "reactionaries." Historical studies were never entirely shelved during this period, as were so many other fields of social science and humanistic studies, but throughout the 1970s historiography was closely linked to political conflicts at the top level, serving as a toolbox for "insinuation through history" (*yingshe shixue*). It was only natural that the science of history also became a central stage for the eclipse of Maoist orthodoxy with the 1979 debates on "the criterion of truth" and the reappraisal of economic development relative to class struggle.

The changes of the late 1970s are hailed by some Chinese historians as "the return of spring to the world, with orioles singing and swallows darting, and historical studies bustling with vitality" (Wang and Yao 1989, p. 1). Others hold a less euphoric view, however. In the words of Dai Qing, dissident journalist and self-made historian, contemporary Chinese historical writings are like "other products of the ideological sphere: they're either specialized to the point of absurdity, or just a vast skein of lies" (Barmé 1991, p. 144). Evaluations by Western scholars also differ widely, although there is a general consensus that the ranges of permissibility are much wider than before, and that historical studies have indeed matured. Internal debates, as well as disagreement with the political leadership, are now tolerated within certain limits, and the doors to inspiration from the outside world—including non-Marxist historiography—have been opened.[1]

Despite obvious changes, Chinese historiography still ranks as a pillar of orthodoxy among the social and humanistic sciences. The tradition of defining the role of history writing primarily in moral-political terms is intact, and the impact of foreign contacts has been limited. While some new fields of study, such as political science and sociology, draw heavily on methods and models imported from the West and thereby confront orthodoxy by their very existence, historical studies have strong Marxist roots in China and are not irresistibly challenged by some powerful new paradigm from the outside. Thus the historians, with a few exceptions, were not a rebellious lot during the 1980s. As Jonathan Unger puts it, "[w]hen the ship of state under Deng's helmsmanship cast off from its prior ideological moorings, historians were aboard as ever-obedient oarsmen, awaiting orders" (Unger 1993, p. 6). Their quandary is, however, that orders have become increasingly vague and self-contradictory. The Maoist principle of "using the past to serve the present" is still in force, but what *is* the present? The growing reluctance among the historians of the 1980s to fit their results into universal Marxist categories seemed less a product of ideological revolt than precisely of their desire to "serve"—under conditions where Marxist orthodoxy was almost entirely inapplicable to economic and social realities.

Symptomatic of this problem, grand debates in the early 1980s on historical periodization, on the relationship between the development of the productive forces and class conflicts, and on the "objective historical laws" gave way in the mid-1980s to a "historiographical crisis" (*shixue weiji*) and a trend toward narrowly empirical research uncommitted to a specific interpretation. The conceptual dichotomy of "historical facts" (*shi*) versus "historical interpretation" (*lun*), which emerged in the late 1950s as a way to discuss the relationship between "pure empirical research" and the guidance of theory, contributed to this facts-only trend of the 1980s, wherein a meaningful political frame of interpretation has become increasingly difficult to identify.[2] During the late 1980s a number of historians in fact endeavored to produce new interpretative approaches. Jin Guantao and Liu Qingfeng, both scientists-turned-historians, applied the theories of cybernetics to construct a framework entirely divorced from Marxism; they had to pay for their daring with condemnation and exile after the 1989 democracy movement. Other historians have struggled to reformulate Marxist historiography by purging it of Leninist and Stalinist influence. But the mainstream historians tend to accept the framework of Marxism–Leninism–Mao Zedong Thought, albeit in a very vague sense, while concentrating on the nonideological technicalities of their specific research topics.

In contrast, the subjective angle is the hallmark of the "mass media historians" (borrowing Geremie Barmé's expression) that jumped to the forefront during the 1980s. Although the most famous work from this group, who generally are not historians by profession, is the macro-historical TV series *River Elegy* (Heshang), "historical journalism" (*lishi jishi*) focusing on individual life stories from modern and contemporary history has been their preferred domain. The huge amount of autobiographical material produced by retired Chinese Communist Party (CCP) leaders during the 1980s constituted a steady source of fuel for this genre. Oral history featuring the experiences of "ordinary people" during crucial historical periods was another popular style in the mid-1980s, practiced mostly by journalists and writers of fiction. Many of the most prominent "mass media historians," including Su Xiaokang, Yan Jiaqi, and Dai Qing, suffered punishment or exile in the wake of the 1989 democracy movement, but the fascination with the subjective dimension of history, which the fact-oriented professionals do not satisfy, has survived the repression of 1989 and 1990 and is manifest even in party-sponsored eulogies of deceased leaders such as the large number of Mao Zedong biographies published in connection with Mao's centenary in 1993.

Trends and Institutions in Harbin Historiography

All in all, a local history community of more than fifty full-time professional employees, and a further affiliated body of several hundred cadres and grass-roots activists were working on the history of Harbin during the 1980s. The general trends in Chinese historiography post-Mao were also reflected in their research, but local historiography has distinct features stemming from its purpose and organizational setup. At the most general level one could say that local historiography is, on the one hand, more cautious and "conservative" than historical research at the national level because of the lower status of local historians and their proximity to watchful local political authorities; on the other hand, however, local historiography by the nature of its purpose ventures into the study of events and phenomena for which no norms have been established because of their local character.

The Harbin historians faced this paradox of caution and boldness inside a bureaucratic structure and under ever-present political supervision. Bureaucratic, in the sense of nonacademic, organs play a far larger role in historical research at the local level than at the national level, as exemplified by the gazetteer project. The following outline of Harbin's local history community is not exhaustive, but it presents the most prominent actors on the stage.

The Harbin Gazetteer

The *Harbin Gazetteer* represents the local level of a nationwide bureaucratic effort to resurrect and modernize the age-old tradition of writing local gazetteers (*difangzhi*), and it is by far the largest and most influential branch of local history work.[3] The gazetteers are at the same time local histories and descriptions of the contemporary state of affairs in a certain locality, typically a province, a city, or a county. The traditional gazetteers, the *fangzhi*, were compiled under gentry direction and were considered an independent genre with its own distinctive functions and merits already by the time of the Song dynasty (960–1279). During Ming (1368–1644) and Qing (1648–1912) times, thousands of local gazetteers were compiled covering most of China. This work continued during the Republican era, and around 1956 the CCP decided to place high priority on the writing of a new set of gazetteers in the socialist spirit. As a result, some rural counties published gazetteers in the early 1960s, but the effort proved unsuccessful in the cities, and little was done in Harbin at that time. During the Cultural Revolution decade, the gazetteer work was brought to a halt and attention was shifted to the writing of workplace and family histories, genres better suited to the dominant theme of class struggle than the dry and rather bloodless gazetteers.

Like many other disciplines in the humanities and social sciences, the *fangzhi* tradition was revived in the late 1970s and early 1980s. A major breakthrough occurred in April 1980, when Hu Qiaomu, member of the CCP Politburo, warmly recommended the compilation of new gazetteers. In January 1981, the first issue of a national journal for local history and gazetteers was published, and in July the "Chinese Association for Local History and Gazetteers" was established.[4] Parallel to this academic structure, editorial committees containing a majority of nonspecialist bureaucrats from various sectors were set up. They were to have the final say over the form and content of the new gazetteers and guarantee their official status. By 1981 an editorial committee for the new city gazetteer had been established by the Harbin city government.

In April 1983, state control over the project was tightened when the secretariat of the party Central Committee appointed a Guiding Group (zhidao xiaozu), with academic heavyweights, mainly historians and geographers, among its thirteen members (names of the members are listed in *Zhongguo difangzhi zonglan*, p. 27). The group was placed as a separate unit under the Chinese Academy of Social Sciences (CASS) and was authorized to guide and supervise gazetteer work in all localities (*Zhongguo difangzhi zonglan*, p. 1). In the spring of 1985, the Guiding Group was expanded to seventeen members and given more independence; it was stressed that it should be in charge of the project politically as well as professionally and should report directly to the Central Committee and the State Council (*Zhongguo difangzhi zonglan*, pp. 3–4). The establishment of this group can be seen as an attempt to weaken the position of the local bureaucrats by placing the final authority in the hands of professionals with a genuine interest in academic quality. However, the Guiding Group obviously lacks an organizational framework for carrying out its control function, and it is our impression from interviews in Harbin that its actual power is limited.

National standards for the organization of the gazetteer work, as well as for the form and content of the final products, were laid down in a set of "Temporary Provisions for the Compilation of New Gazetteers," which was issued by the Guiding Group in April 1985 (rendered in *Zhongguo difangzhi zonglan*, pp. 5–7). These "Provisions" define the purpose of the gazetteers as (1) to provide the local leaders with scientific information so that they can make correct decisions; (2) to serve as reservoirs of information for local cadres in all trades by preserving important documents and other materials; and (3) to inculcate patriotic, Communist, and revolutionary values (§1). The new gazetteers should cover the period up to 1985. No specific starting date is fixed, but it is emphasized that they should concentrate on the immediate past and the present situation (§3).

As for the content, the new gazetteers should "describe the natural and social history and present situation of the region" (§1) and "reflect the special characteristics of the region" (§3). There should be no wavering in political attitude: the editors are told to "keep in step with the Central Committee" and "use the 'Resolution on CCP History (1949–81)' and 'Decision of the Central Committee on Reform of the Economic System' as their guidelines" (§2). When it comes to the coverage of "important political events" after 1949, "it is better to write sketchily than in great detail" (*yi cu, bu yi xi*) (§11). Attention should be paid to the regulations on state secrets, particularly in matters concerning border areas or relations to foreign countries (§6). This rule has special significance in Harbin because of the heavy foreign involvement in the city's history. All entries on politically sensitive issues should be submitted to the local party committee for approval (§22).

The "Provisions" leave the impression of a carefully supervised project under intense bureaucratic and political control. In spite of the formal authority of the Guiding Group, the real power over the project seems to rest in the hands of the local bureaucracy rather than at the central level, and the quality of the gazetteers therefore depends largely on the attitude of local leaders.

The Compilation of Gazetteers in Harbin

In the early phase, the compilation of materials for the Harbin gazetteers resembled a mass movement. Until 1983 all important work units established writing groups. Similar organs were set up in each of the city's districts as well as in the sector administrations, and an impressive number of people, more than a thousand, became involved in the collection of materials, as each sector administration delegated the task of compilation down to the basic level: the individual workshop, theater, hospital ward, and so on. The data gathered in this way were, of course, often of inferior quality and so numerous and detailed that the editorial organs were incapable of handling them.

The gazetteer project, however, never developed into a "find your roots" movement. The gazetteers were primarily intended to be tools in the hands of the bureaucracy, and the initial public enthusiasm for the new gazetteers appears to have waned rather quickly. The leaders of the gazetteer office in Harbin talked about a crisis in 1984–85, which they tried to solve through professionalizing the work. A veteran expert, Guan Chenghe, was put in charge, and more than 400 participants in the project were sent to training courses, some of them to other cities, in order to raise the professional quality of the work. By 1989, the gazetteer project had lost most of its "mass movement" character.

It is the Harbin Editorial Committee for Local History and Gazetteers (Haerbin difang shizhi bianzuan weiyuanhui) under the city government that is formally in charge of the project. The bureaucrats hold a solid majority in this committee, which in 1986 had only five professional intellectuals among its twenty-five members. Most of the others were either vice-directors of bureaus in the city administration or cadres of the local party apparatus. The deputy secretary of the Municipal Party Committee headed the editorial committee during most of the 1980s. It did not meet often, but it guaranteed bureaucratic backup for and ultimate control over the project.

The daily work is headed by the Harbin City Government Gazetteer Editorial Office (Haerbin renmin zhengfu difangzhi bianzuan bangongshi). Since 1986 this organ has ranked at the bureau (*ju*) level. It is run by professional academics (mostly historians) and has a staff of twenty-five people. When completed, the new Harbin gazetteer will consist of around fifty volumes with descriptions at two levels: At the higher level will be a "city gazetteer" (*shizhi*), which in only a couple of volumes will describe the city's history and present situation. The office has the sole responsibility for this gazetteer, which, in spite of its moderate size, is the most difficult to write, because it demands an independent analysis of the structural changes in the city over the last hundred years. The outline (*pianmu*) for the city gazetteer has therefore been under constant discussion since 1982. Thousands of work-hours have been spent on it, and proposals have circulated at all levels of the bureaucratic system. In 1989 the fourteenth proposed outline was under discussion.

At the next level there will be seventy-seven "special gazetteers" (*zhuanzhi*) on different sectors and aspects of the city's life, and seven "district gazetteers" (*quzhi*), one for each administrative district of the city. An important part of the office's work is to guide and supervise the writing groups responsible for these volumes. The writing groups, and thereby the framework of the whole gazetteer publication, are organized according to the vertical, sectoral administrative structure of the city. The groups are established and staffed by the city government bureaus, or by large enterprises that dominate their respective sectors, and the titles of the special gazetteers resemble a directory of the city administration. The district gazetteers also cover the various sectors inside their own area, but at a much more general level. In this respect the organization of the gazetteer work perfectly reflects the vertical and horizontal (*tiaotiao-kuaikuai*) structure of Chinese urban administration. Where no relevant bureau exists, editorial responsibility is handed over to professionals, as in the case of the volume on geography, which was written on a contract basis by teachers from one of the city's universities.

The office is also responsible for training the members of the writing groups, who in 1989 numbered around 400 people. The typical basic-level gazetteer workers are elderly, maybe even retired, middle-level cadres with a long career in the sector they cover. This means that while most writers are very familiar with the topic they write about, they generally know little about historical methods. The training courses therefore focus on the general history of the city, the nature of gazetteers, as well as on a number of the relevant academic disciplines, including new (in a Chinese context) branches of the social sciences, like urban sociology. Many of the instructors are highly esteemed intellectuals from other cities. According to the leaders of the gazetteer project, the most frustrating aspect of these training programs is that many trainees are transferred to other work shortly after they complete the course. We were told that by 1986 the majority of the people trained in Harbin in the first half of the 1980s had already been moved to other jobs. It seemed that the implementation of the urban economic reforms provided the main reason for this drain of qualified manpower. As enterprises and organizations were forced to be more conscious of their costs, many directors felt tempted to move staff from unprofitable gazetteer work to other jobs more closely related to production.

The office is also actively involved in the endorsement procedure for the special gazetteers. In the beginning the sector bureaucrats practically had a right of veto over all information published in "their" gazetteer. As part of the gradual professionalization of the gazetteer work in the late 1980s, however, the cadres were replaced as censors by professionals, and by 1989 the endorsement procedure in Harbin was as follows: The editorial committee of the *zhuanzhi* sent the draft to the Gazetteer Office. Then the editors of the volume and the office held an evaluation meeting (*pinglunhui*). Finally, the revised draft, now called a "draft for inspection" (*songshen'gao*) was sent to the gazetteer committee for final political approval. While this procedure still guaranteed the official status of the final product, it refocused the endorsement process more in the direction of professional quality.

The Harbin Service Trade Gazetteer: An Example

We received a vivid impression of the work at the basic level from Zhao Tian, a retired Commercial Bureau cadre who was editing the volume on service trades in Harbin. He was a model gazetteer worker who had been praised at city-level meetings. Concentrating on the pre-1949 period, he had built up a web of key informants who had worked in hotels and restaurants, including those owned by foreigners. Through the personal networks of these informants he was able to locate former workers from almost all the old restaurants in the city and interview them on themes like the ownership of the restaurant, what special dishes they had offered, and the wages of the workers. He had done more than a thousand interviews, which he combined with research in the city archives. In this way he was able to map out Harbin's restaurant life of the 1920s and 1930s in great detail. It is worth noting that his material was, to a large extent, collected in the field rather than in the archives. It is quite normal and strongly recommended from above that gazetteer writing groups engage in social investigation and survey research as well as in the compilation and analysis of documents.

In December 1991, the *Harbin Food, Drink and Service Trade Gazetteer* (Haerbin yin shi fuwu zhi) was published with Zhao Tian as the chief editor. This work covers exactly one hundred years, starting in 1890, when the first inn was set up by the Fu brothers, who thereby gave name to Fujiadian, which later became the most important Chinese section of Harbin. In over 600 pages the book tells the history of Harbin's restaurants, hotels, barbershops, beauty parlors, photographers, public baths, and laundries. It contains general chapters on economic management, wages, and training, as well as profiles of the most important establishments and personalities of the trades. A considerable number of documents and other data are rendered, from a 1923 set of public regulations about sanitary conditions in hotels, to investment, profit, and wage statistics from selected years, to menus from today's first-class restaurants. A final section is devoted to reportage literature on Harbin hotels and restaurants, together with lists of special phrases and idioms used inside the different trades.

The volume offers a great deal of information on social history, a field that generally receives little attention in China, with glimpses of restaurant life and work conditions particularly in pre-1949 Harbin. Another of the special gazetteers already published, the *Harbin Civil Administration Gazetteer* (Haerbin minzheng zhi), contains important data on, for example, the city's social welfare system, so taken as a whole the gazetteer project will doubtlessly be an important gateway to future studies of social history.

The Harbin History and Gazetteer

While the publication of the Harbin gazetteers is the most important event in local history writing in the early 1990s, the journal *Harbin History and*

Gazetteer (Haerbin shizhi) published by the Harbin City Gazetteer Editorial Office was the main channel for such work in the 1980s. It started publication in 1983 with first two and after 1986 four annual issues. Contributors came from all parts of the local history community, but many articles were obviously based on research carried out in connection with the gazetteer project. Whereas the style of the presentations found in the gazetteers is generally terse and impersonal, the journal allowed fuller and better argued expositions. Some of the articles have later appeared in shortened versions in provincial or regional-level academic journals. Like practically all other publications on local history, the *Harbin History and Gazetteer* is for "internal circulation" (*neibu faxing*, cf. note 4). Texts 1B, 2B, 2C, 2F, 2G, and 4A, 4B, 4C, and 4E have all been published in this journal.

As can be understood, the gazetteer project is really the juggernaut of the Harbin local history community. The other institutions dealing with local history have their distinct tasks and obligations, but the gazetteer project is so all-embracing that practically all the professional historians in Harbin have contributed to it in varying degrees. The gazetteer project, by definition, must produce a comprehensive account of modern and contemporary history, including periods and events that the cautious historian, if left to his own choice, might have wanted to evade. The gazetteer juggernaut moves head-on into some of the "forbidden zones" (*jinqu*) of modern and contemporary history, generating vast amounts of text as it moves along, and the ensuing work of sorting through and evaluating the material can exhaust the capacity of both the political supervisors and the local historians. In some ways the roles of political supervision and intellectual expertise merge in this process, but the local historians have the special role of providing normative examples of historical research, thus helping the cadres involved in basic-level gazetteer work find their way through the "forbidden zones." A large part of the texts in the journal *Harbin History and Gazetteer* is of this nature, and in a wider perspective much of the local historical writing in Harbin may be viewed as spin-off products from the gazetteer project. It also appears that in this process the authority of the professional historians has gradually increased during the 1980s.

The Historical Text Materials

The specific mission of *Historical Text Materials* (Wenshi ziliao) is the publication of memoirs, either written directly by the informants or edited by historians on the basis of interviews, diaries, letters, and autobiographical materials. As in the case of the gazetteers, this is a nationwide publication program involving several administrative levels. At the national level more than 120 volumes had come out by 1989. There is a provincial series for Heilongjiang, which has produced more than twenty volumes, and at the city level Harbin put out fourteen volumes up through the 1980s. Several counties publish their own *Materials*, among them Acheng County under Harbin's administration.

The compilation of *Historical Text Materials* takes place under the auspices of the Chinese People's Political Consultative Conference (CPPCC), a National Front organ reaching from the national down to the city, district, and county levels. As the CPPCC is designed to be a meeting point for the CCP and "democratic parties and personalities" loyal to the Communist Party, many of its delegates are leading veteran intellectuals, officials, and businessmen who were active in political and cultural life before 1949. When the program was initiated in 1959 on the initiative of Zhou Enlai, the period to be covered ran from the Hundred Days of Reform in 1898 up to the founding of the People's Republic, and the members of the CPPCC and their personal friends and associates therefore made up an excellent starting point. Until the Cultural Revolution more than 16,000 diaries, reports, and interviews were collected at the national level, and more than 38,000 at the provincial and city levels, but less than 10 percent of this material was ever published (*Guangming ribao* [Guangming Daily], December 8, 1980, p. 1). Still, all major political events, demonstrations, and strikes in the first half of the twentieth century were covered meticulously.

In 1978, at the Fifth Plenum of the National Committee of the CPPCC, it was decided to resume the project after a break during the Cultural Revolution decade. The upper limit for the time to be covered was now set at 1976, and special attention was to be paid to the post-1949 period, which had not been covered by the first wave of interviews. Neither Heilongjiang Province nor Harbin City, however, had published any *Materials* before 1978, and so they had to start from the beginning with the oldest informants. Maybe for this reason, or maybe because of the general tendency in the local history community to avert post-1949 issues, the *Materials* that we saw contained very little on the People's Republic.

In Harbin City, formal responsibility for the publication of the *Materials* rests with the Committee for Research into Historical Text Materials (Wenshi ziliao yanjiu weiyuanhui) under the Political Consultative Conference, and day-to-day work is carried out by a small unit with just five employees, the Office for Historical Text Materials (Wenshi ziliao bangongting). The unit started its work in 1982, and publishes one or two regular issues of the *Historical Text Materials* annually, together with a number of special issues. The series sometimes draws on guest editors from other corners of the local history community.

A detailed 1984 list of 274 topics to be covered by the Harbin *Materials* project shows a broad range of concern, with a preponderance of political and military history, but also with ample coverage of economic, cultural, and social affairs and even of the history of foreign nationals and the national minorities (*Haerbin wenshi ziliao*, no. 4, 1984, pp. 130–42). The individual issues of *Materials* are in some cases organized around a common theme, such as no. 8 from 1986, which was published in celebration of the fortieth anniversary of the CCP's power seizure in the city, and mainly contained reminiscences of the battles in 1945–46. Others are more loosely organized, like no. 4 from 1984, which contained a collection of profiles of steam mill owners in Harbin during the 1920s and 1930s, together with autobiographical accounts of prison life during the Japanese occupation.

Some volumes are for "internal circulation" only, while others in principle are freely available. The criteria for this classification are not obvious, and it is hard to see what sets the internal circulation volumes apart from the others.

The informants are mainly selected from among important persons, "personalities" (*renwu*), rather than among ordinary citizens, and many of them are members or friends of members of the city CPPCC. Some are veteran revolutionaries or even party members, but at least as many are former industrialists, merchants, professors, or other members of the upper echelons of pre-1949 China. For this reason, several had political difficulties during the antirightist campaign in 1957, and again during the Cultural Revolution decade, and it is therefore natural for them to watch their steps carefully when they tell the stories of their lives. Still, the unique quality of the *Materials* is exactly the personal angle and the unpolished view on periods and events, and many texts provide lively and interesting reading material. The task of the historians is explicitly to *collect* (*zhengji*) these materials, not to write them. In a few cases we found passages in different texts that were identical word for word, thereby revealing a more active role of the "collector," but only in the general descriptions of the political background. As for the accounts of personal experiences, the individuality of the narrator is often allowed to shine through.

The *Historical Text Materials* can be said to represent subjectivist history writing at the local level. The texts present themselves as unpolished memory, the quality and truthfulness of which are not questioned or checked against other sources. The political framework is visible in the selection of interviewees, and in the kind of topics they are asked to recollect, but the historian is allowed to disappear in the final product so that the subjectivity appears to be that of the historical witness, not of the historian. The "mass media historians" of the national scene apparently had no local counterparts in Harbin.

Texts 2E as well as 3A, 3B, and 3C have been taken from the provincial-level *Materials*, while Text 2D is from the city-level publication.

The Academy of Social Sciences

A third pyramidal research structure, represented in Harbin at both the provincial and the city levels, is the Chinese Academy of Social Sciences (CASS). The Heilongjiang Provincial Academy of Social Sciences had around 300 employees in 1989 and boasted no less than four specialized history departments, one for studies of the Bohai state, which ruled this part of China in the eighth and ninth centuries, one for the Liao (937–1125) and Jin (1115–1234) dynasties, one for Sino-Russian relations, and one for the history of Northeast China. These departments explored the history of Hei-longjiang or even Northeast China in general, and seemed to be only marginally engaged in research on Harbin in a narrow sense.

The history of the city was left to a small research unit with four full-time professional historians at the Harbin Institute of Social Sciences, which altogether had around seventy employees. The director of the institute was concurrently in charge of the local history unit, which dealt exclusively with the 1896–1949 period. He was a specialist on the Russian-dominated period, while another researcher worked on economic history, a third on migration to Harbin, and the fourth on the 1946–49 period. The freedom and flexibility in the daily work of the institute staff was striking. Researchers could work at home, in libraries, or in other places as they pleased, and they were required to show up at the local history unit only twice weekly: Tuesday morning for discussions of current research projects and Saturday morning for political studies. It is difficult to know whether the degree of academic freedom was correspondingly high, but work at the academy and the institute was clearly under less bureaucratic control than the gazetteer project and the collection of *Historical Text Materials*.

The Harbin Institute of Social Sciences publishes the prestigious *Harbin Yearbook* (Haerbin nianjian), which carries statistical information, reports on the work of the various local government agencies, introductions to Harbin institutions, and soon. It is a high-quality publication of more than a thousand pages, also containing a section on local history edited by the local history unit. Another publication by the Harbin Institute of Social Sciences was the quarterly *Harbin Research* (Haerbin yanjiu), which, among many other topics, also had regular sections on party history and local history, but which has now stopped publication. Texts 1A and 2A are taken from this journal.

The Party History Committee

At the national level, research on the history of the CCP developed quickly after 1978, and several important events have been re-evaluated. In Harbin, party history is the object of research for ten people belonging to the Party History Committee (dangshiwei) directly under the Municipal Party Committee. They work in two research offices devoted to the pre-1946 and post-1946 periods respectively, of which the latter was established as late as 1988. Party history is among the oldest branches of local historical research in Harbin; work had started by 1960 at the party school in Harbin. In 1981 the study of party history was resumed after the Cultural Revolution, first at the Harbin Institute of Social Sciences, and later, in 1985, in the present independent unit in a building adjacent to the Gazetteer Editorial Office. Some of the researchers were former party cadres or party school graduates, while others were university graduates in philosophy or Chinese, or had received special training in party history at the People's University in Beijing.

The Party History Committee published a *Party History Newsletter* (Dangshi tongxun), which was for internal circulation only, and which we never saw. The researchers also contributed to the publicly circulated *Heilongjiang Party History* (Longjiang dangshi), from which Text 4D is taken, and to most of the other Harbin publications on local history, from popular presentations to academic journals. Control from above was reportedly mainly quantitative: an associate researcher (*fu yanjiuyuan*) was expected to write a minimum of 25,000 characters a year, while an assistant researcher (*zhuli yanjiuyuan*) could get away with only 15,000. As for the choice of topics, the committee received some assignments from the Municipal Party Committee, but in general the staff said that they were free to design their own research. The articles from their hands that we saw were all quite uncontroversial, but we cannot exclude the possibility that the internal newsletter brought more daring interpretations.

Universities, Museums, and Archives

At the universities local historical research was found only at the Harbin Normal College (Haerbin shifan daxue), where one professor and one lecturer in the history department worked on the Harbin angle of Sino-Russian/ Soviet relations. They had a certain degree of contact with the local history community and contributed to local history publications. During the Cultural Revolution decade five professors from this department were sent to the Harbin Rolling Stock Factory (Haerbin cheliangchang) to help produce a revolutionary enterprise history. Because of its Cultural Revolution flavor, the resulting book, titled *The Thirty-Six Barracks* (Haerbin cheliangchang, Haerbin shifan Xueyuan Lishixi Bianxuezu 1980) after the slums where the factory's Chinese workers lived, is not an object of pride among local historians in Harbin today, and though the book is not totally negated either, this experience may have contributed to a distaste for local history among the university faculty.

The Heilongjiang Provincial Museum (Heilongjiang sheng bowuguan), established in 1922, has its strong points in archeology and natural history and contains little of interest for research on modern history. The Northeast China Martyrs' Memorial Hall (Dongbei lieshi jinianguan) houses exhibitions on the Anti-Japanese and Liberation wars, but its staff did not seem to be actively involved in research. The museum most active in research on modern history appeared to be the Exhibition Hall for Evidence of the Crimes of the 731st Unit of the Japanese Invasion Army in China (Qin-Hua Rijun di qisanyao budui zuizheng chenlieguan), which has played a major role in keeping alive the memory of the Japanese war crimes in the Harbin area. Text 3C was written by the director of this institution.

The Harbin City Archives (Haerbin shi dang'anguan), established in 1969, are an important part of the infrastructure of local history research. Historians can here find documents from earlier Chinese, Russian, and Japanese city administrations, as well as from that of the People's Republic. Publications from the archives take the form of collections of historical documents.

Work Units and Mass Organizations

The Rolling Stock Factory mentioned above has strong traditions in writing factory history. It was the dominant industrial workplace in early Harbin, and one of the first places where Chinese workers were introduced to Bolshevism through their Russian colleagues. The strikes against the factory management during the first decade of this century were therefore also among the first manifestations of the growing Chinese working class and as such of obvious interest to historians during the Cultural Revolution decade. In 1976 a study group from the factory published an article in the most prestigious national magazine, *Historical Research* (Lishi yanjiu) on strikes at the Rolling Stock Factory with Chinese participation during the 1905–19 period. In 1989 there were still a few people at the factory who worked on its history, but the major results had already been presented in *The Thirty-Six Barracks*. Text 2E, which is set in the same factory, has retained much of the Maoist tenor with a dramatic writing style and many explicit political and moral judgments.

The Harbin Labor Union, Women's Federation, and Youth League each had some people working on the history of these mass organizations and compiling materials for their gazetteers.

History Writing and Bureaucratic Control

This outline of the history community in Harbin shows that almost all research in this field is in one way or another part of larger projects with their own national significance, and that topics, research methods, and channels of publication are largely defined from the higher levels. The degree of individual choice depends on institutional affiliation: the gazetteer writers and the collectors of *Historical Text Materials* have clearly defined tasks, while researchers from the Academy of Social Sciences and the universities are on longer leashes. Little research originates from local initiative or interests. The writing of history, also at the local level, is a task for the state.

While the subordination of historical writing to bureaucratic planning and control constrains academic quality, the fact that the central bureaucracies treat all places in a uniform way and demand the same historical materials from everywhere has, perhaps, been a necessary precondition for getting off the ground in Harbin. As mentioned above, historical research in Harbin started late compared to other places in China, and historians seemed to believe that the city was too modern and even too foreign to be of any historical interest. Up through the 1980s, however, an impressive network was built up as part of the national efforts, and the results of this work are now beginning to show.

Bureaucratic control may also help to explain why the empiricist trend found at the national level is so prevalent in Harbin local historical work. When asked about their theoretical framework most local historians hurried to answer that they were just concerned with the "collection of facts." Only in the institutions furthest away from direct bureaucratic control, that is, at universities, and to a lesser extent at the Academy of Social Sciences, did the historians accept the suggestion that interpretation also played a role. In fact interpretation permeated all levels of local historical research, but with a marked difference between these levels. Among the grass-roots history workers, in mass organizations and work units, the traditional propagandistic superstructure of the 1970s appeared intact. The professional historians working in the local bureaucracies had largely discarded ideology, while it was only among the researchers at the university and Academy level that conflicting interpretations could be explicitly discussed. As the presentation of the debates on economic imperialism in Chapter 2 shows, Marxism is alive at the highest academic echelons but is not the undisputed authority; it is to some extent a matter of choice and personal conviction. Yet even at the highest local level the changing evaluations of other important issues were not openly discussed. It was noted in Chapter 2 that the attitude to Soviet policies in Manchuria in the 1920s and 1930s is changing from an across-the-board acceptance to a more critical view, and indeed it is possible to find manifestations of differences of opinion in the pages of Harbin local history. The actual process of reinterpretation, however, and the arguments that must accompany it remain invisible.

In the light of the Chinese bureaucratic tradition for strong sectoral divisions, one might expect to find water-tight shutters between the different organs engaged in local historical research. It was our impression, however, that the local history community in Harbin collaborates rather freely across sectoral borderlines. Most of the researchers seem to know one another personally, and they often publish articles in one another's journals. Since most branches of local historical research, including the gazetteer project, have at some stage been affiliated with the Harbin Institute of Social Sciences, many local historians have a common institutional background, and the personal links appear to have remained intact even when the institutional setting was changed. They also meet at the Harbin Learned Society for Local History and Gazetteers (Haerbin shi difang shizhi xuehui), established in 1980, which even accepts members who are not professionally involved in historical research.

Local History and Local Identity

History writing in China, even at the local level, is part of a national project not only in the bureaucratic sense but also in the ideological. The most significant dividing line in the writings on Harbin's history is drawn between Chinese and foreigners, and competing affiliations to ethnic groups, religious societies, or native places are systematically downplayed. The decisive factor as to whether a historical agent is described as moving into or invading the Harbin area, plundering its natural resources or developing its economy, creating new jobs or exploiting the workers, bringing in law and order or suppressing the population, is whether he belongs to one of the ethnic groups that are now considered part of the Chinese people (*Zhonghua minzu*). Particularly with respect to the early history of the Harbin area, it would be possible to write an alternate history of a region that was once habituated by Manchu tribes but later invaded by Han, Russians, and Japanese, of which the Han in the long run turned out to be the most successful. Such a history would be detrimental to the very gist of the Harbin local history project, however, which is to demonstrate the city's Chineseness in the nonethnic, state nationalist sense of the word.

The difficulties of assigning a meaningful historical role to the non-Han ethnic groups so evident in national-level history debates (e.g., Wang and Yao 1989, pp. 80–93) appears no smaller at the local level. Manchus never played any large role in Harbin, which was from the outset primarily populated by Han Chinese immigrants, but there is a fairly large Korean population as well as Mongols, Hui, Olunchun, and several other minority peoples. Even a few Russians are left, as well as "half" and "quarter" Russians (in popular language called *ermaozi* ["second hairy"] and *sanmaozi* ["third hairy"] in contrast to the full-blooded Russians known as *laomaozi* ["old hairy"]). But the ethnic diversity of Harbin has attracted little attention from the local historians.

Conspicuously absent in the coverage of local distinctness is also a treatment of "native place" (*guxiang*) identity among people in Harbin. In individual conversations it is noticeable—and no surprise in a city of immigrants —that some Harbin people tend to mention their family home place first when asked about their background, and well into the 1950s native place networks were of crucial importance for many Harbin citizens in terms of employment, business cooperation, and so on. Such features are definitely not high on the agenda of local historiography, reminding us that "local identity," at least in this part of China, is as much a contemporary construct as is its national-level counterpart.

Manifestations of local pride consist mostly in demanding that the concept of a Chinese people defined by the borders of the present-day national state is actually taken seriously by the historians from the Chinese heartland south of the Great Wall, and that the history of the Northeast is consequently accepted as an integral part of Chinese history. Particular emphasis is therefore put on those cases where Harbin has played a pioneering role in what eventually became part of the national heritage, such as the 1907 May Day celebration. Local identity is also strengthened by stressing Harbin's historical role as the economic and cultural center of the North Manchurian region, and the city's importance compared to its rivals in the Northeast, primarily Shenyang and Changchun.

These localist trends, however, are clearly subordinate to the key task: the writing of Harbin's history as a Chinese city.

Notes

1. Several valuable studies of recent trends in Chinese historiography have been put together by Jonathan Unger (1993). A useful survey of Chinese historiography in the 1980s is found in an unpublished dissertation by Hans-Günther Herrmann (1989).

2. The debates on *shi* and *lun* have been well covered in a dissertation by Susanne Weigelin-Schwiedrzik (1984).

3. For a more detailed description of the new *difangzhi*, see Thøgersen and Clausen 1992.

4. In the beginning the name of this journal was *Zhongguo difang shizhi tongxun* (Chinese Local History and Gazetteers Newsletter), and it was only for internal circulation. In January, 1982, it changed its name to *Zhongguo difang shizhi* (Chinese Local History and Gazetteers) and was freely distributed. The name was changed again in January 1983 to *Zhongguo difangzhi tongxun* (Chinese Local Gazetteers Newsletter) (again internal) and finally to *Zhongguo difangzhi* (Chinese Local Gazetteers) in 1986. Most materials on local history do, in fact, appear in internal (*neibu*) publications. This means that they cannot be bought openly in bookstores or subscribed to through the post offices, but are distributed only to people and institutions expected to have a professional interest in them. The official explanation for this classification is that they may contain incorrect data and interpretations and so can lead to erroneous views among unstable souls. In the 1980s it was normally not a problem for foreigners to gain access to such publications locally, but the customs authorities take the classification more seriously than most academics, making it difficult to send *neibu* publications out of the country by mail.

Glossary

baoxiao, jiagong, dinghuo
包销，加工，定货
daimao 戴帽
daiye 待业
dangdaishi 当代史
dangshiwei 党史委
difangzhi 地方誌
ding 鼎
Dongbei 东北
Dongbei liutongjuan 东北
流通卷
Dongliqu 动力区
Dongsheng 东省
ermaozi 二毛子
fangzhi 方志
fanshen 翻身
feixing jihui 飞行集会
fengkuang 疯狂
fu yanjiuyuan 副研究员
geming weiyuanhui 革命
委员会
geti jiuye 个体就业
gongye weichihui 工业维持
会
guxiang 故乡
Haerbin tebie shi 哈尔滨
特别市
Haerbin baoan zongdui
哈尔滨保安总队
hao 号
hong huzi 红胡子
jiegongsuo 街公所

jihua danlie 计划单列
jin 斤
jinqu 禁区
ju 局
kang 炕
kanwa yundong 砍挖运动
laojin 劳金
laomaozi 老毛子
li 里
li4 畾
lianhui 练会
lishi jishi 历史记事
lüeduo 掠夺
lun 论
minsheng gongsi 民生公司
neibu faxing 内部发行
paijiu 牌九
pianmu 篇目
pinglunhui 评论会
qitu 企图
quzhi 区誌
renwu 人物
san dong sheng 三东省
sanmaozi 三毛子
sanwen 散文
shang 坰
shi 史
shixue weiji 史学危机
shizhi 市誌
songshen'gao 送审稿
suku dahui 诉苦大会
tewu 特务

tiaotiao-kuaikuai   条条块块
wei   伪
wo shi   我市
wufan yundong   五反运动
xiang bei fazhan, xiang nan
    fangyu   向北发展，向
    南防御
xiangtuan   乡团
xiehehui   谐和会
yi min shi bian   移民实边
yi cu, bu yi xi   宜粗不
    宜细
yiku   忆苦
yingshe shixue   映射史学

you gai gongsi yishou jingli
    由该公司一手经理
Youyilu   友谊路
zhengji   征集
zhengtong   正统
zhengtong guandian   正统
    观点
zhidao xiaozu   指导小组
Zhonghua minzu   中华民族
zhuanzhi   专志
zhuli yanjiuyuan   助理研究
    员
ziweidui   自卫队
ziyihui   谘议会

Bibliography

Barmé, Geremie. 1991. "Using the Past to Save the Present: Dai Qing's Historiographical Dissent," *East Asian History*, no. 1: 141–81.

———. 1993. "History for the Masses." In Unger 1993, pp. 260–86.

Beasley, W. G. 1987. *Japanese Imperialism 1894–1945*. Oxford: Oxford University Press. 1987.

Borisov, O. 1977. *The Soviet Union and the Manchurian Revolutionary Base (1945–1949)*. Moscow: Progress Publishers.

Bu Ping, Guo Yunshen, Zhang Zonghai, and Huang Dingting (eds.). 1987. *Dongbei guoji yuezhang huishi* [A collection of international treaties relating to the Northeast with commentaries]. Harbin: Heilongjiang renmin chubanshe.

Chao, Kang. 1982. *The Economic Development of Manchuria: The Rise of a Frontier Economy*. Michigan Papers in Chinese Studies no. 43. Ann Arbor: Center for Chinese Studies, University of Michigan.

Cihai. 1989. Shanghai: Cishu chubanshe.

Coble, Parks M. 1991. *Facing Japan: Chinese Politics and Japanese Imperialism, 1931–1937*. Cambridge, Mass., and London: Harvard East Asian Monographs, 135, Harvard University Press.

Cordes, Ernst. 1936. *Das jüngste Kaiserreich* [The youngest empire]. Frankfurt A.M.: Societäts-Verlag.

Crossley, Pamela Kyle. 1990a. *Orphan Warriors: Three Manchu Generations and the End of the Qing World*. Princeton: Princeton University Press.

———. 1990b. "Thinking about Ethnicity in Early Modern China," *Late Imperial China*, 11, no. 1 (June): 1–35.

Du Que. 1985. "Zaonian juliu Haerbin de Ou-Meiren jiankuang" [European and American residents in Harbin in the early years], *Haerbin shizhi* [Harbin History and Gazetteer], no. 1: 39–42.

Elvin, Mark, and G. William Skinner (eds.). 1974. *The Chinese City Between Two Worlds*. Stanford, Calif.: Stanford University Press.

Fan Wenlan. 1980/1962. "Problems of Conflict and Fusion of Nationalities in Chinese History," *Social Sciences in China*, no. 1: 71–82.

Fang Shijun (ed.). 1989a. *Haerbin lishi biannian (1950–1965)* [Annals of Harbin history 1950–1965]. Haerbinshi renmin zhengfu difangzhi bianzuan bangongshi.

———. (ed.). 1989b. *Haerbin renwu* [Harbin biographies], vol. 1. Harbin: Haerbinshi renmin zhengfu difangzhi bianzuan bangongshi.

Fifth Report on Progress in Manchuria to 1936. 1936. Dairen: South Manchuria Railway Company.

Fochler-Hauke, Gustav. 1941. *Die Mandschurei. Eine geographisch-geopolitische Landeskunde* [Manchuria: A geographical and geopolitical introduction]. Heidelberg, Berlin, Magdeburg: Kurt Vowinckel Verlag.

Fourth Report on Progress in Manchuria to 1934. 1934. Dairen: South Manchuria Railway Company.

Gillin, Donald G., and Ramon H. Myers (eds.). 1989. *Last Chance in Manchuria: The Diary of Chang Kia-Ngau.* Stanford, Calif.: Hoover Institution Press.

Gladeck, Frederick R. 1972. *The Peking Government and the Chinese Eastern Railway, 1917–1919.* Ann Arbor: University Microfilms.

Gottschang, Thomas R. 1987. "Economic Change, Disasters, and Migration: The Historical Case of Manchuria," *Economic Development and Social Change,* 35, no. 3: 461–90.

Guan Chenghe. 1985. *Haerbin kao* [Examining Harbin]. Harbin: Haerbin shi shehui kexue yanjiusuo.

Guo Jiyun. 1986. "Zai Zhong–Su Youxiehui gongzuo de rizili" [The times of working in the Sino-Soviet Friendship Society], *Haerbin yanjiu* [Harbin Research], no. 2: 17–18.

Guo Lin. 1980. *Zaoqi de Haerbin jianzhu yu Haerbin difang jianzhu fengge* [Buildings from Harbin's early period and the local architectural style of Harbin]. Harbin: Zhongguo tiedao xuehui Heilongjiang fenhui.

Guo Linjun. 1986. "Zai Zilaishuichang gongzuo pianduan de huigu" [Some reminiscences from working at the Waterworks]. In Zhang and Li 1986, 182–89.

Haerbin minzheng zhi [Public administration gazetteer]. 1991. Harbin: Heilongjiang renmin chubanshe.

Haerbin cheliang gongchang lishi bianxiezu [The history writing group of Harbin Rolling Stock Factory] and Haerbin shifan xueyuan lishixi xiezuozu [Writing group of the history department of Harbin Normal College]. 1976. "Sanshiliu peng gongren de kang-E zhengdou" [The anti-Russian struggle of the workers in the "36 Barracks"], *Lishi yanjiu* [Historical Research], no. 3: 84–89.

Haerbin cheliangchang, Haerbin shifan xueyuan lishixi bianxiezu [The writing group of Harbin Railway Car Factory and the history department of Harbin Normal College]. 1980. Sanshiliu peng—Harbin cheliang gongchang shi [36 Barracks—The History of Harbin Rolling Stock Factory]. Harbin: Heilongjiang renmin chubanshe.

Haerbin nianjian bianjibu. 1987. *Haerbin nianjian 1987* [Harbin yearbook 1987]. Harbin: Heilongjiang renmin chubanshe.

Haerbin yin shi fuwu zhi. 1991. [Harbin food, drink and service trade gazetteer]. Harbin: Heilongjiang renmin chubanshe.

Haerbinshi dang'anguan [Harbin city archives]. 1985. " 'Wenhua da geming' qian Haerbinshi jihua danlie jiankuang" [A brief account of Harbin as an independent planning unit before the "great cultural revolution"], *Haerbin shizhi,* no. 2: 29–31.

Han Jing. 1983. "Haerbin jiefang yihou shi difang caizheng tizhi jianshu" [Brief account of the Harbin city administration's financial structure before and after Liberation], Haerbin shizhi, no. 2: 29–33.

Han Tiesheng. 1980. "Haerbin renmin zaoqi jiuguo fandi douzheng de pianduan" [Fragments from the early period of the patriotic, anti-imperialist struggles of the people in Harbin], *Heilongjiang wenshi ziliao,* no. 1: 30–41.

Han Xiao. 1985. "Ri-jun qisanyao budui faxisi baoxing jilu" [A compilation of the fascist atrocities committed by Unit 731 of the Japanese army], in *Heilongjiang wenshi ziliao,* no. 19: *Bu neng wangji de lishi* [A history we cannot forget]. Harbin: Heilongjiang renmin chubanshe, 1–35.

Han Xiao and Zou Deli. 1983. "Riben Guandongjun Pingfang xijun gongchang jishi" [A record of the Japanese Guandong Army's bacteriological factory in Pingfang], *Heilongjiang wenshi ziliao* [Heilongjiang Historical Text Materials], no. 9: 135–60.

Harris, Sheldon. 1991. "Japanese Biological Warfare Experiments and Other Atrocities in Manchuria, 1932–1945, and the Subsequent United States Coverup: A Preliminary Assessment," in *Crime, Law and Social Change*, 15, no. 3: 171–99.

Herrmann, Hans-Günther. 1989. "Les Historiens chinois après Mao. Entre société et pouvoir" [The Chinese historians after Mao. Between society and power]. Paris: Institut National des Langues et Civilisations Orientales.

Hinrichs, J. P. 1987. *Russian Poetry and Literary Life in Harbin and Shanghai, 1930–1950*. Amsterdam: Rodopi.

Huenemann, R. W. 1984. *The Dragon and the Iron Horse: The Economics of Railroads in China, 1876–1937*. Cambridge, Mass., and London: Harvard University Press.

Hunt, Michael H. 1973. *Frontier Defense and the Open Door: Manchuria in Chinese-American Relations, 1895–1911*. New Haven and London: Yale University Press.

Ibsen, Kai. 1981. *Den kinesiske traad. En dansk familiekroenike* [The Chinese thread: A Danish family saga]. Copenhagen: Woeldike.

Jiang Niandong et al. (eds.). 1991. *Wei Manzhouguo shi* [A history of puppet Manzhouguo]. Dalian: Dalian chubanshe (first published by the Jilin renmin chubanshe), 1980.

Jing Nan. 1985. "Haerbin kang-Ri baoweizhan" [The Harbin anti-Japanese defense war], *Haerbin shizhi*, no. 2: 32–42.

Jones, F. C. 1949. *Manchuria since 1931*. London: Royal Institute of International Affairs.

Kong Jingwei and Zhu Xianping. 1986. *Di-E dui Haerbin yidai de jingji lüeduo* [The tsarist Russian economic plunder of the Harbin area]. Harbin: Heilongjiang renmin chubanshe.

Lattimore, Owen. 1975 [1935]. *Manchuria: Cradle of Conflict*. New York: AMS Press.

Lee, Chong-Sik. 1983. *Revolutionary Struggle in Manchuria: Chinese Communism and Soviet Interest, 1922–1945*. Berkeley and Los Angeles: University of California Press.

Lee, Robert H. G. 1970. *The Manchurian Frontier in Ch'ing History*. Cambridge: Harvard University Press.

Lensen, G. A. 1967. *The Russo-Chinese War*. Tokyo: Sophia University, in cooperation with Tallahassee: The Diplomatic Press.

———. 1974. *The Damned Inheritance: The Soviet Union and the Manchurian Crises, 1924–1935*. Tallahassee: The Diplomatic Press.

Levine, Steven I. 1987. *Anvil of Victory: The Communist Revolution in Manchuria, 1945–1948*. New York: Columbia University Press.

Li Debin and Shi Fang. 1987. *Heilongjiang yimin gaiyao* [A survey of migration to Heilongjiang]. Harbin: Heilongjian renmin chubanshe.

Li Jitang. 1987. "Guanyu Zhongdong tielu de jige wenti" [On certain questions relating to the CER], *Haerbin shizhi*, no. 1: 53–66.

Li Jiyang. 1980. "Harbin—Metropolis of the Far North," *China Reconstructs* (March): 61–62.

Li Shuxiao (ed.). 1986. *Haerbin lishi biannian (1896–1949)* [Annals of Harbin history 1896–1949]. Harbin: Haerbin shi renmin zhengfu difangzhi bianzuan bangongshi.

Lin Huanwen. 1986. "Haerbin zai Jiefang Zhanzhengzhong de diwei he zuoyong" [The position and functions of Harbin in the War of Liberation], *Haerbin yanjiu*, no. 2: 8–11.

Liu Chengdong. 1986. "Wo zai Haerbin gongzuo de qianqian houhou" [An account of my work in Harbin]. In Zhang and Li 1986, 42–75.

Liu Dazhi. 1986. "Haerbin jiefang chuqi qiansong Riqiao gongzuo" [The evacuation of Japanese nationals in the early period after the Liberation of Harbin], *Haerbin yanjiu*, no. 4: 59.

Liu Hua'nan. 1987. "Jilin Ziweijun zai Haerbin ji qi waiwei de kang-Ri huodong" [The anti-Japanese activities of the Jilin Self-Defense Army in and around Harbin], *Haerbin wenshi ziliao* [Harbin Historical Text Materials], no. 11: 33–49.

Liu Shaotang. 1989. "Shilun Dongbei diyige dang zuzhi chuangjian de keguan tiaojian yu lishi yiyi" [Preliminary analysis of the objective conditions and historical significance of the establishment of the first party committee in the Northeast], *Xuexi yu tansuo* [Study and exploration], no. 2: 148–51.

Liu Yizhong. 1986. "Ji Minsheng gongsi" [Recollections concerning the People's Livelihood Company]. In Zhang and Li 1986, 194–98.

Loboda, I. 1990. "History of the Sino-Soviet Friendship Society in Harbin," *Far Eastern Affairs*, no. 1: 215–20.

Lü Lingui. 1985. "Zhongdong shijian fasheng qianhou de lishi qingkuang jiqi genyuan" [On the historical circumstances and causes of the CER Incident], *Haerbin shizhi*, no. 2: 44–53.

McCormack, Gavan. 1991. "Manchukuo: Constructing the Past," in *East Asian History*, no. 2: 105–24.

MacMurray, John V. A. (ed.). 1921. *Treaties and Agreements with and concerning China, 1894–1919*. Vols. 1–2. New York: Oxford University Press.

Madsen, C. 1926. "Beretning om Harbin" [Report on Harbin], *Det Danske Missionsselskabs Aarsberetning, 1925* [Annual Report of the Danish Missionary Society, 1925]. Copenhagen: O. Lohse.

Malozemoff, Andrew. 1958. *Russian Far Eastern Policy, 1881–1904*. Berkeley and Los Angeles: University of California Press.

Manchoukuo: Handbook of Information. 1933. Hsinking: Bureau of Information and Publicity Department of Foreign Affairs, Manchoukuo Government.

Manchuria Year Book 1931. 1931. Tokyo: Toa-keizai Chosakyoku (East-Asiatic Economic Investigation Bureau).

Melikhov, Georgi. 1990a. "Glimpses of Old Harbin," *Far Eastern Affairs*, no. 4: 158–79.

———. 1990b. "Glimpses of Old Harbin (Part II)," *Far Eastern Affairs*, no. 5: 165–74.

Melnikov, Yu. 1991. "Russian Fascists in Manchuria," *Far Eastern Affairs*, no. 4: 178–209.

Morimura Sei'ichi. 1983a. *Akuma no hoshoku* [The devil's gluttony]. Tokyo: Kadokawa Shoten.

——— [Lincun Chengyi (Chin. pron. of Morimura)]. 1983b. *Mogui de leyuan* [The devil's paradise], trans. by Guan Chenghe and Xu Mingxun. Harbin: Heilongjiang renmin chubanshe.

——— [Lincun Chengyi]. 1984a. *Mogui de leyuan, xubian* [The devil's paradise, volume 2], trans. by Guan Chenghe and Xu Mingxun. Harbin: Heilongjiang renmin chubanshe.

——— [Lincun Chengyi]. 1984b. *Mogui de leyuan, di san bu* [The devil's paradise, volume 3], trans. by Guan Chenghe and Xu Mingxun. Harbin: Heilongjiang renmin chubanshe.

——— [Lincun Chengyi]. 1987. *Emo baoshi (xiudingben)* [The devil's gluttony, revised version], trans. by Guan Chenghe and Xu Mingxun. In *Haerbin shizhi*, vol. 1.

Pepper, Suzanne. 1978. *Civil War in China. The Political Struggle, 1945–1949*. Berkeley and Los Angeles: University of California Press.

Quested, R. K. I. 1982. *Matey Imperialists? The Tsarist Russians in Manchuria, 1895–1917*. Hong Kong: University of Hong Kong.

————. 1984. *Sino-Russian Relations: A Short History*. Sydney, London, and Boston: George Allen & Unwin.

Ren Tingxi. 1988. "Haerbin Heli jixiechang de bianqian" [Changes in the Heli Machine Factory], *Heilongjiang wenshi ziliao*, no. 24: 19–29.

Romanov, B. A. 1974/1928. *Russia in Manchuria (1892–1906)*. New York: Octagon Books.

Sargent, Margie. 1971. "The Cultural Revolution in Heilungkiang." In *The Cultural Revolution in the Provinces*. Harvard East Asian Monographs no. 42. Cambridge, Mass.: East Asian Research Center, Harvard University.

Sixth Report on Progress in Manchuria to 1939. 1939. Dairen: South Manchuria Railway Company.

Stephan, John J. 1978. *The Russian Fascists: Tragedy and Farce in Exile, 1925–1945*. New York, Hagerstown, San Francisco, London: Harper and Row.

Sun, Kungtu C. (assisted by Ralph W. Huenemann). 1969. *The Economic Development of Manchuria in the First Half of the Twentieth Century*. Harvard East Asian Monographs no. 28. Cambridge, Mass.: Harvard University Press.

Tang, Peter S. H. 1959. *Russian and Soviet Policy in Manchuria and Outer Mongolia, 1911–1931*. Durham, N.C.: Duke University Press.

Taeuber, Irene B. 1974. "Migrants and Cities in Japan, Taiwan, and Northeast China." In Elvin and Skinner 1974, 359–84.

Teiwes, Frederick C. 1990. *Politics at Mao's Court. Gao Gang and Party Factionalism in the Early 1950s*. Armonk, N.Y.: M. E. Sharpe.

Teng Yingwu. 1986. "Diguozhuyi jingji ruqin dui Haerbin shi minzu shangye xingshuai zhi yingxiang" [The effects of imperialist economic penetration on the ups and downs of Harbin national-capitalist commerce], *Haerbin shizhi*, no. 4: 38–46.

Thøgersen, Stig, and Søren Clausen. 1992. "New Reflections in the Mirror: Local Chinese Gazetteers (*difangzhi*) in the 1980s," *Australian Journal of Chinese Affairs*, no. 27 (January): 161–84.

Tian Deshen. 1988. "Jiu shehui yanku haisi ren, xin zhengfu jiedu min huanxin" [In the old society the opium dens killed people, the new government banned drugs and the people rejoiced], *Haerbin shizhi*, no. 1: 25–26.

Tokayer, Marvin, and Mary Swartz. 1979. *The Fugu Plan: The Untold Story of the Japanese and the Jews during World War II*. New York and London: Paddington Press Ltd.

Unger, Jonathan (ed.). 1993. *Using the Past to Serve the Present: Historiography and Politics in Contemporary China*. Armonk, N.Y., and London: M. E. Sharpe.

Wang Chengli (ed.). 1988. *Dongbei lunxian shisi nian shi yanjiu 1931–1945* [Research in the history of the Northeast during the fourteen years of occupation]. Vol. 1. Changchun: Jilin renmin chubanshe.

————. (ed.). 1991. *Zhongguo Dongbei lunxian shisi nian shi gangyao* [An outline history of Northeast China during the fourteen years of occupation]. Beijing: Zhongguo dabaikequanshu chubanshe.

Wang Jiangfu. 1988. "Yi Haerbin shi Guangfu chuqi qingnian gongzuo" [Reminiscences of youth work in Harbin after the Japanese surrender], *Haerbin shizhi*, no. 1: 43–44.

Wang Shuqing. 1986. "Zhonggong Beiman linshi shengwei" [The temporary North Manchuria CCP committee]. In Zhang and Li 1986, 205–16.

Wang Xiliang. 1987. "Haerbin kang-Ri baoweizhan shulüe" [A brief account of the Harbin anti-Japanese defense war], *Haerbin wenshi ziliao*, no. 11: 1–20.

————. 1988. "Ri-wei tongzhi shiqi Dongbei zhimindi jingji xingtai de xingcheng, shenhua jiqi tezheng" [The formation, deepening and characteristics of the colonial economic status of the Northeast during the period of Japanese puppet rule]. In Wang Chengli 1983, 91–103.

Wang Yude and Yao Weijun. 1989. *Xin shiqi Zhongguo shixue yanjiu zhengming ji* [A record of Chinese historiographical debates in the new period]. Wuhan: Huazhong shifan daxue chubanshe.

Wang Yulang. 1986. "Haerbin yinggai chengwei 'Jin-shi' yanjiu zhongxin" [Harbin ought to be the center for Jin history research], *Haerbin yanjiu*, no. 3: 35–37.

Wei Zhenshan, Yang Mingde, and Wang Jianping. 1986. "Shilun Haerbin guoji maoyicheng de xingshuai" [Preliminary analysis concerning the rise and decline of Harbin as an international commercial city], *Haerbin shizhi*, no. 3: 20–24.

Weigelin-Schwiedrzik, Susanne. 1984. *Parteigeschichtsschreibung in der Volksrepublik China: Typen, Methoden, Themen und Funktionen* [The writing of party history in the People's Republic of China: Types, methods, topics, and functions]. Weisbaden: Otto Harrassowitz.

———. 1987. "Party Historiography in the People's Republic of China," *The Australian Journal of Chinese Affairs*, no. 17: 77–94.

Whiting, Allen S. 1953. *Soviet Policies in China, 1917–1924*. Stanford, Calif.: Stanford University Press.

Wieczynski, J. L. (ed.). 1976. *The Modern Encyclopedia of Russian and Soviet History*. Gulf Breeze: Academic International Press.

Williams, Peter, and David Wallace. 1989. *Unit 731: The Japanese Army's Secret of Secrets*. London: Hodder & Stoughton.

Wright, Tim. 1993. " 'The Spiritual Heritage of Chinese Capitalism': Recent Trends in the Historiography of Chinese Enterprise Management." In Unger 1993, 205–38.

Xiao Feng (ed.). 1982. *Xiao Hong sanwen xuanji* [Selected essays by Xiao Hong]. Tianjin: Baihua wenyi chubanshe.

Xiao Hong. 1979. *The Field of Life and Death and Tales of Hulan River*, trans. by Howard Goldblatt and Ellen Yeung. Bloomington and London: Indiana University Press.

———. 1986. *Market Street: A Chinese Woman in Harbin*, trans. by Howard Goldblatt. Seattle and London: University of Washington Press.

———. 1991. *Xiao Hong quanji* [Collected works of Xiao Hong]. 2 vols. Harbin: Haerbin chubanshe.

Ying Wu and Jing Shi. 1986. "Jiefang chuqi Haerbin de funü fangsha yundong" [The housewife spinning campaign in the early period after the liberation of Harbin], *Haerbin shizhi*, no. 2: 91–94.

Zhang Benzheng, Ma Guoyan, and Li Lixin. 1981. "Xinhai geming zai Dongbei" [The 1911 revolution in the Northeast], *Shehui kexue zhanxian* [Social Science Front], no. 4: 79–88.

Zhang Chunlin. 1986. "Haerbin tebieshi jianzhi yange" [The establishment and evolution of the special municipality of Harbin], *Haerbin shizhi*, no. 3: 113–24.

———. 1987. "Ri wei Haerbin shi zhengquan jianzhi yange" [An outline of the political power structure in puppet Harbin City under Japan], *Haerbin shizhi*, no. 2: 60–65.

Zhang Fushan. 1984. "Haerbin lishishang zui zao de gonghui" [The first trade union in Harbin], *Haerbin shizhi*, no. 2: 15–18.

Zhang Mei and Li Shuxiao (eds.). 1986. *Jinian Haerbin jiefang sishi zhounian zhuanji* [Special issue commemorating the fortieth anniversary of the liberation of Harbin], *Haerbin wenshi ziliao*, no. 8.

Zhang Ruilin. 1981. "Zai manman chang ye zhong—ji Haerbin dixia douzheng de jianku suiye" [In the endless night—Remembering the cruel years of underground struggle in Harbin]. *Heilongjiang wenshi ziliao* [Heilongjiang Historical Text Materials], vol. 2: 18–49.

Zhang Tong. 1984. "Ershi niandai shouhui Zhongdong tielu bufen liquan shi shulüe" [A brief historical account of the partial recovery of rights on the CER], *Haerbin shizhi*, no. 1: 23–32.

Zhao Dejiu. 1986. "1913 nianqian Haerbin minzu yu guanliao ziben gongye" [National-capitalistic and bureaucrat-capitalistic industry in Harbin before 1913], *Haerbin yanjiu*, no. 6: 44–46.

———. n.d. "Haerbin minzu ziben jindai gongye fazhan kaocha" [An investigation of the development of Harbin's national-capitalistic modern industry]. In *Dongbei diqu zibenzhuyi fazhanshi yanjiu* [Research concerning the development of capitalism in the Northeast], 193–204. Harbin: Heilongjiang renmin chubanshe.

Zheng Changchun. 1987. *Zhongdong tielu lishi biannian (1895–1952)* [A Chronology of the Chinese Eastern Railway (1895–1952)]. Harbin: Heilongjiang renmin chubanshe.

———. 1988. "Zhongdong tielu jianshe Haerbin shuniu de chenji" [Record of how Harbin was built as a railway hub of the CER], *Haerbin shizhi*, no. 2: 43–45.

Zheng Yingshuang. 1988. "1932 shuizai jishi" [Records of the 1932 flood], *Haerbin shizhi*, no. 1: 32–33, and no. 2: 47–49.

Zhong Ziyun. 1986. "Geming—zhandou—shengli. Yi wo zai Haerbin de suiyue" [Revolution, struggle, victory. Remembering my time in Harbin], *Haerbin wenshi ziliao*, no. 8: 1–23.

Zhongguo difangzhi zonglan 1949–1987 [A general view of Chinese Gazetteers 1949–1987]. 1988. Hefei: Huangshan shushe.

Zhu Xianping. 1985–86. "Di-E ziben dui Haerbin jingji de lüeduo" [The plunder of Harbin by tsarist Russian capital], *Haerbin shizhi*, no. 1: 63–74, and no. 2: 97–102.

———. 1986. "Di-E bazhan Haerbin shizheng de jige wenti" [On some questions relating to the tsarist Russian usurpation of Harbin municipal administration], *Haerbin shizhi*, no. 3: 74–90.

———. 1988. "Haerbin Zizhihui—Eguo bazhan difang shizhengquan de yizhong teshu xingshi" [The Harbin Self-Administration Council—A unique form of tsarist Russian usurpation of municipal political power], *Dongbei difangshi yanjiu* [Research on the local history of the Northeast], no. 4: 49–52.

Zhu Xuefan. 1986. "Wo canjia di liu ci quanguo laodong dahui he zhengzhi xieshang huiyi de jingguo" [My participation in the sixth all-China labor congress and the political consultative conference]. In Zhang and Li 1986, 24–41.

Zou Deli (ed.). 1985. "A Panorama of Harbin." Hong Kong: Red Flag Publishing Company.

Index

Søren Clausen graduated from the University of Aarhus, Denmark, in political science and Chinese. He is an associate professor of modern Chinese language, history and society at the department of East Asian Studies, University of Aarhus. He has published mainly in the fields of contemporary Chinese politics, Chinese Marxism and economic thought, and modern Chinese history. Professor Clausen's recent publications deal with Chinese political culture, Chinese historiography and issues related to Chinese identity.

Stig Thøgersen is an associate professor of modern Chinese language and society at the department of East Asian Studies, University of Aarhus. He is the author of *Secondary Education in China after Mao: Reform and Conflict* (1990), as well as of several articles on Chinese education and local history, and translations of Chinese prose and poetry. He is presently working on the modern history of education in a county in Shandong Province.